How Nations Choose Product Standards
and Standards Change Nations

Pitt Series in Policy and Institutional Studies

Bert A. Rockman, *Editor*

How Nations Choose Product Standards and Standards Change Nations

SAMUEL KRISLOV

■ *University of Pittsburgh Press*

Published by the University of Pittsburgh Press,
Pittsburgh, Pa. 15261
Copyright © 1997, University of Pittsburgh Press

Manufactured in the United States of America
Printed on acid-free paper

10 9 8 7 6 5 4 3 2 1

Krislov, Samuel.
    How nations choose product standards and standards change nations
    /   Samuel Krislov.
        p.   cm. — (Pitt series in policy and institutional studies)
    Includes bibliographical references (p.) and index.
        ISBN 0-8229-3969-X (cloth : acid-free paper). — ISBN
    0-8229-5622-5 (pbk. : acid-free paper)
        1. Standardization.   2. Commerical products—Standards.
    1. Title.   II. Series.
    T59.K75 1997
    338'.002'18—dc21   96-45919
                                                                                        CIP

A CIP catalog record for this book is available from the British Library.

Contents

Preface

To my amazement and chagrin, half a dozen years have passed since I set out to study product standards. This investigation is the first major fruit of my efforts. That pace was partly dictated by the intricacies of a new subject, partly by other obligations, and partly by my own failings.

The quest began with puzzled conversations at the European University Institute in Fiesole regarding the minutely overprecise nature of European Community legislation. My co-authors C. D. Ehlermann, Joseph Weiler, as well as Jacques Pelkmans, quickly educated me in the fact that the EC was faced with reconciling the standards of a dozen variously regulated societies. These discussions also confirmed de Tocqueville's observation that many functions in the United States were handled by voluntary participation that were handled by governments in Europe.

This insight led to the proposition of this volume—that "standards" are different phenomena in different cultures, sometimes formulated in sharply different ways. It led to the further insight that the resulting formulations and the processes chosen to implement them affects the nature of the individual society as well.

When I begin this inquiry, the subject of product standards was a truly exotic topic. When I organized a Law and Society panel on the issue, a leading writer in the field observed to me as we walked into in the meeting room, "Of course, only a dozen people in the world are interested in our topic." To our amazement, the room was chock full of participants, evidence of a growing awareness of the topic's significance. Since that time, the EC's new emphasis on product standards and a wider appreciation of Japan's efforts in this area has swelled the ranks of scholars and others who are interested in the subject.

The difficulty has become, therefore, not to demonstrate the importance of the topic but to define its dimensions. This is my first attempt to tackle the topic, but not the last. Everyone I discuss it with adds another aspect to my recognition of its importance and universality.

I have incurred many obligations in reaching this first level of understanding. Thanks to Ross Cheit, Liora Salter, David Fogel, and Bryant Garth for their comments on my written work as well as helpful discussions of the topic. Asher Arian, Carol Gordon, Daniel Krislov, and especially Judith Gillesspie have encouraged me in countless ways. The Graduate School of the University of Minnesota facilitated this study with several strategic grants, and the Department of Political Science kindly granted time for research. Work in Japan was made possible by a Fulbright "Japan Today" award. A goodly portion of the manuscript was written at the Rockefeller Foundation's incomparable Villa Serbollini in Bellagio, Italy. Fellow residents there and my colleagues at Minnesota and Hawaii were kind enough to listen to and critique full-scale presentations, as have colleagues at Law and Society Association meetings.

Finally I must give special thanks to Robert Connelly of Tokyo and the TÜV Rhineland group. Mr. Connelly not only provided office facilities in space-starved Tokyo, but also offered me access to his collection of fugitive documents on standards issues gathered during his years of service in the Japanese American Chamber of Commerce. One of the world's premier for-profit developers and testers of standards, TÜV provided me with access beyond interviews and their valuable bulletin over many years. I am also indebted to the openness of the National Institute of Standards and Technology and other standards organizations described in my study.

Part I

A Standards Primer

1

An Introduction to Standards

What They Do and Do Not Do

*Standards are everywhere, but
not always the same ones.*

IN THOSE HALCYON DAYS WHEN THE AMERICAN
dream still centered on trading cars in biennially, when McDonald's hamburger stands were multiplying in Malthusian fashion, and the ultimate mystery of how to tame business cycles was believed to be the property
of any competently trained Ph.D. in economics, product standards were not
a lively topic, even in sophisticated economic circles. We lived in a world in
which there was an inevitability, a cloak of universality about American products, the biggest and the best, made the right way, maybe even God's way. In
a sense, all Americans were like the automobile executives who accompanied
President Bush to Japan to complain about lack of sales there, and who
seemed surprised and puzzled to learn that the Japanese drive on the other side
of the road and regard the driver's seat on the right as an impediment to purchasing American cars.

The beginning of awareness comes with travel, as tourist, soldier, or business person. The American tourist's discovery of the range of electric cycles,
plugs, and types of current is often the first acquaintance with cultural difference, though variations in toilet paper may cause the first alert. A traveler soon
learns that, far from being in the natural order of things, many of our American products are different from those in the vast majority of countries. Indeed,

"American exceptionalism," the extent to which foreign countries are more like one another than like us, is well known.

The American traveler, however, tends to find this a basis of complaint and is likely to consider deviations abnormal. Like the famed British tourists who were sure that if they talked loud enough the natives would understand them, American tourists spend so much money that hotels abroad have adjusted to permit them to travel without a kit of eight or nine convertible plugs and an AC-DC adapter. Even the toilet paper can be naturalized to suit American tastes.

Of course, what attracted permanent attention to product standards was the change in the relative economic situation of the United States. The integration of Europe has promoted "harmonization" of standards. A centerpiece of EC 1992, the advanced European Union's plan for a more integrated common market, was its emphasis on more coordinated standards. Now, whenever a regime of common standards is not agreed upon, all products legally produced in a European Union country are exportable everywhere in the community.[1]

At virtually the same time, American awareness was becoming increasingly focused on the significant role played by legal and administratively manipulated standards in Japanese economic policy. The growth of the European Union has led most major legal firms dealing with business in Brussels to open branches there. It has put the issue of standards in Europe on the business page—even occasionally the news pages—of daily papers in the United States. But the Japanese problem makes Americans grit their teeth, unable to cope or respond. It, too, has brought to our consciousness the ubiquitousness and importance of product standards and the centrality of standards for daily life and even cultural identity. Standards affect our lives in many ways, large and trivial, overt or subtle.

Electric and electronic equipment present obvious and complex problems. Generally speaking, you should not take a personal computer when you travel worldwide, unless you can operate it on batteries and find a way to recharge it. Differently cycled current can create interesting results. I experienced this when I bought a clock radio for a European country that was supposed to adjust automatically to that current. In fact, electric current in that country was a shade erratic. The finely tuned Sony gained a few minutes each day and readjustment would have cost more than it was worth. It worked perfectly in the United States and Japan.

For over a century, governments, private companies, and international organizations have worked to achieve uniform rail gauges and standard railroad cars. Yet narrow and broad gauges persist and create physical and fiscal problems. Passengers between Spain and France must change trains (which involves a small walk) or pay a premium to ride trains with adjustable wheels. The long-delayed opening of the "Chunnel" to traffic still does not permit through trains from the continent into the English countryside because of Great Britain's narrower rails and cars.[2] Similarly, East-West European inter-action is limited by gauge differences. Multiple gauges are found even within a single country, making total integration of systems difficult.

Standardization may emerge from circumstances and may control future outcomes in undesirable ways. The VCR format of videotape virtually eliminated the technically superior Beta format because the public, responding to wide promotions, bought the VCR in droves. Stores making a living preferred to stock one type of taped films rather than two. The greater availability and variety of tapes in turn induced a new generation of consumers to buy VCRs! A *conscious* manipulation of standards by some manufacturers can be best identified as the "Gillette strategy": razors are distributed cheaply, requiring the purchase of compatible blades.

One remarkable triumph of social mores is the dominance of upright bikes over recumbent bikes. The latter are much more efficient; they achieve speeds of 65 mph, but have been regarded as improper in daily use, and have been prohibited as racing vehicles, presumably as a relic of the old Victorian reaction that they were sexually suggestive.

Lack of standards can have surprising repercussions. Screws, nuts, and bolts have standard sizes but not generally specified compositions and strengths, presumably because it was assumed that strength and durability were fixed by their other physical attributes. An overseas manufacturer created an inferior product that could be sold at a low price. To the embarrassment of the United States government, it was ascertained that at least some of the inferior product was sold to the military and used in highly strategic weapons and vehicles. Multimillion dollar war machines might well fail because manufacturers saved a few pennies. This led to the Fastener Quality Act of 1990, and federal regulation, a first for this product.

The most criticized aspect of standardization is its use as an instrument of economic advantage. This is called "protectionism" when enforced against foreign competition on a legal basis, and "monopolization" or "restraint of competition" when used internally. Nations often pass restrictions that entrench advantages for domestic industry. For example, the traditional German prohibition on "unadulterated" beer (i.e., beer not produced by the time-honored methods that the great German brewmasters have historically preferred) excludes extra ingredients that other people actually value for taste. Americans have generally found beef from other countries (especially cheaper Argentinian products) suspect of hoof-and-mouth disease.

Quaint requirements may cause surprising complications; reexamination of standards may yield unexpected problems or improvements. A Europewide set of computer standards drafted to facilitate a communitywide market aroused ire in Spain when it became apparent that it invalidated Spanish laws requiring a tilde on machines with typefaces. The Spaniards objected to "culturicide," arguing the measure would lead to the gradual elimination of its distinctive marking. After a flurry, they became convinced it would not be onerous or expensive for manufacturers to provide an *optional* additional tilde (and other linguistic alternatives for other societies) and that its interests were better served by the free flow of computers, where the tilde was preserved by other means than requiring it on *all* computers.[3] Similarly, the development of European condom standards resulted in problems for the Italian condom industry. Experts agreed that the most popular Italian brands were either inadequate in size (and therefore less protective against disease) or lacking in strength (and therefore less than optimal in preventing leakage and conception).[4]

Rapidly developing industries may find that the pace of progress thwarts standard setting. Classically, the computer industry found that its intense creativity outstripped even the fastest possible application of the processes prescribed by the American National Standards Institute (ANSI), or by any reasonable, orderly standard-setting process. A tacit agreement to avoid needless complexity emerged, with IBM serving as an informal industry standard setter. As the alternatives proliferated and IBM became less dominant, however, users began to be less tolerant of incompatible systems and of the need to start afresh again and again as a result of the industry's obsessive uniqueness. (This was analogous to the Houston experiment of placing no zoning restrictions on realty development. At early stages, it was immensely encouraging for developers in that city to be free from restraints. But at later stages, expensive and dangerous complications developed: for example, sewage disposal incompatibility and lack of adequate records of pipes and conduits did not permit the diagnosis and correction of problems.) Computer users were increasingly unhappy with the idea of redoing their office and relearning a system every time they added or upgraded a part of it. The computer industry has the additional problem that new developments continue at such a rapid pace that arrangements in other industries cannot serve as a model for standards or training.

Essentially, the computer industry has created its own nonbinding standard system. Two clearinghouses have developed based upon two different systems of computer "thinking." Knowledge about potential incompatibility and an inventory of new products permit design engineers to plan and minimize "unique" products that customers would not be able to link to other hard- and software products. Buyer resistance has been the key to developing this loose "familial" standard setting, but there are also technical reasons—e.g., the need for systems to be able to speak to one another—that reinforce the commercial motivation to loosely integrate, to find a minimal level of standardization.[5]

Definition and Background

There are numerous definitions of the word "standard." It is in fact a term of art, part of a century-old international movement of considerable gravity that has its roots and branches in the consumer movement and in the "industrial sociology" efficiency approaches of the first quarter of the century. Yet the recognition and effectiveness of standards have been stunted by the amorphousness and innocuousness of the label. There are "standards" of all kinds, after all—of decency and conduct, of physical measurement. There are standard characteristics for persons and things. Indeed, there is no standard way of defining standards.

Since the turn of the century, the term has been used prescriptively to define physical qualities required for sale and use of industrial or commercial products, sometimes for regulatory social protection purposes, whether set by government or by other commercial powers. Such standards have been the concern almost exclusively of surprisingly specialized groups—reformers, trade organizers, negotiators, corporation experts who deal exclusively with domestic and international standards, independent experts, and laboratory staffs.

Standards, whether basic (weights and measures) or complex and specialized (What is an acceptable flush toilet? What types of paper and what margins meet the official standards of the American Textbook Publishers Association?), are significant features of modern living. Some standards (for sanitation devices, for instance) are enacted into local law; others are loosely enforced by consumers through recognizable symbols (Underwriters Laboratory), by producers in concert with each other, or by trade associations, in literally hundreds of arrangements and variations (What sizes and shapes of plywood are to be manufactured and available in inventory? What is "blue" in tiles or other standard household ceramics? What sizes and speeds are to be manufactured in film cassette machines and the cassettes used in them?).

Standards of these kinds are invisibly at work throughout our lives, usually with little awareness on our part. Most are or have been contested or arrived at painfully and by overt or covert bargaining. Often products *must* meet established criteria, whether they are legally required to do so or not. Standards of quality or of safety have particular force even when adopted by private organizations, no matter how weak. Even self-serving standard-setting groups favoring a specific interest are likely to have inordinate weight if no other standard is set forth in the society. That is because, as the old saying has it, "you can't beat somebody with nobody." When disputes occur, a decision maker—judge, arbitrator, what have you—will lean heavily on the crutch of preexisting published standards. That is human nature. The decision maker will find it easier to follow a beaten path than to create a new standard. Since resolvers of conflict generally have legal expertise rather than technical know-how, they are more likely to accept established standards, even those not formally approved. There is also an assumption by judges, arbitrators, or insurance agents that when there are established standards, the party not following them has a positive duty to inform the other of the intent to "opt out" of even a "voluntary" standard.

Many insurance companies will insist on compliance with known standards. Even if they do not, the company may cite nonadherence to standards as a basis for nonpayment of a claim. The insurance company's temptation to refuse the claim may become irresistible with very small sums or very large ones, where discounts for quick settlement may be a considerable factor.

When "voluntary" standards have been enacted into law in some localities, they reinforce the legal and insurance leverage even in nominally uncontrolled locales. Most U.S. plumbing, electric, and other household standards are promulgated as "voluntary" by producer-controlled organizations, usually with considerable elements of self-aggrandizement. Large municipalities adopt them, perhaps with small changes, because it would be too expensive or risky to develop independent standards (sometimes there is considerable local political pressure as well). In rural areas the nonexistence of codes is less liberating than it seems. The law's "rational man" would be hard put to defend using nonstandard products should there be a legal dispute. Potential house buyers will be leery, particularly if they are inexperienced with anything nonstandard. And the likely problem in finding replacement parts years later will raise the specter that subsequent costs may dwarf present savings.

In short, many "voluntary" standards are highly coercive. In fact, only a small portion are created by law, but complex social factors determine the degree to which they prevail. Those same factors may operate to create informal standards that coerce the citizen to much the same degree as formally enacted standards. Indeed, some standards create law by force of their usage, by the mere fact that every society favors uniform rules and firm expectations. Voluntary behavior may ultimately force legislation itself.

Most striking is the fact that many government units incorporate construction standards by reference to standards set by expert or industry committees, which usually means that changes in the "voluntary" standard automatically become law when adopted by the standardizing group, without even passing through the formality of review by government authorities. To be sure, the "voluntary" standards (or the ordinances establishing them) often permit the administering authorities to allow exceptions based upon demonstrated equivalency, but the fact remains that such private action creates legal norms in semiprivate circumstances.

How and Why Standards Emerge

Not surprisingly, because of the sparseness of descriptive literature on standards there is a pronounced dearth of theoretical literature. Only with the new generation of business and technological historians, who are no longer preoccupied with writing the biography (verging on hagiography) of entrepreneurs, has there been an account of the interactive history of invention and convention. The past decade has taught us more about our technological past than has any previous period.

It is relatively easy to account for the emergence of basic weights and measures. The medium of money, itself a sophisticated type of standard, and the need for easily verifiable exchange calculations, led to standard weights and measures. Money in standard units generally replaced a set of competing conventionalized media of exchange. Such arrangements can develop simply as a result of voluntaristic advantage without legal enforcement (though they are enhanced by certification of a specific quantity and quality of gold, for example) because such standardization facilitates trade. Inevitably, however, the power to punish counterfeiters establishes itself as a useful tool. This gives governments great advantages. Nongovernment and government money standardizers have always found easy rewards for their services. A coinage charge or equivalent is easy to assess for money, but an enforcement process increases the value of the coining process. This and other standards become vehicles of authority and prestige, a route to power.

Standardization of language is also a basic process, where motivation and desirability literally speak for themselves. The elementary processes that allow languages to be formulated and small groups to reach a common language have not been established empirically or formally. Nor are they likely to be, since these elementary stages are inherently preliterate and cannot be replicated among human groups with established linguistic conventions.

On the other hand, linguists have studied and mapped the process by which related localized dialects become a single official language, often as an adjunct to the emerging consciousness of a national, or at any rate widespread, ethnic identity.[6] That process consists of asserting ethnic transcendence over merely local claims and of bringing forth a "high culture" dialect, which is seen as unifying the ethos. That "high culture" dialect is never just the adoption of an existing dialect; usually it is both a "refinement" of the language of the dominant unifying elite and an amalgam that contains elements of others. Literary Arabic, "pure" Castilian, and literary English emerged as standard languages through the incorporation and amalgamation into a major dialect of some elements of "lesser" dialects.

Ernest Gellner has generalized the work of the linguists, suggesting that this is the process by which national identity is formed.[7] A core elite sells to a general and more diverse group a contrived and modified "high culture" version of the elite's own culture. Usually the core group, the vehicle for asserting shared identity, is in the group's geographic center, which becomes the ethnic capital. The degree of fit between the core group culture and the standardized artificial "high culture" is partly a reflection of power politics and partly a matter of strategic salesmanship. The elements of such "high culture" are often symbolic and eclectic. Gellner writes sardonically of the wives of the elite in Central Europe who attended opening night at the symphony or opera in peasant costumes, usually at a performance of the masterpiece of the recognized "national composer." Today, such "peasant costumes" may be accepted as the equivalent of formal wear at restaurants, which otherwise exclude males not wearing a necktie and jacket.

Standardization is not confined to culture, however, and the fruits of standardization are not limited to symbolic or organizational elements. The material benefits of standardization have long been understood and studied, even in the context of emerging communities, regimes, and rulership.

From a materialistic point of view, the bedrock of standard setting is fundamental standards that encourage trade and barter and that facilitate specialization and interdependency. These obviously include a medium of exchange (money) and weights and measures that help define the units involved in an exchange (value). Economists rightly emphasize the inherently personal and subjective nature of value. Diamonds, like old comic books and baseball cards, are worth what people will exchange for them rather than some "objective price" based on function. But even subjective worth is affected by quantity and quality, and objectification facilitates exchange. It is easy enough to barter fifteen or sixteen cows for a bride, and whatever is in the pot right in front of you for a birthright, but when exchanging cloth for raw lentils, a concept of what a bolt of cloth or a certain volume of lentils is helps to make haggling meaningful and, it is hoped, leads to a meeting of minds.

Standardization of quantities is helpful but also goes hand in hand with some degree of uniformity in quality. Gold of a certain weight has greater value, and that value can be more easily estimated, if its level of purity is also known.

Both logic and history suggest that standardization can be imposed by noncoercive groups, even in an anarchic society. The advantages of such processes are obvious and appreciated. Robert Nozick has demonstrated that a "protective association," totally voluntary at the beginning, could logically emerge as the sole definer of law, especially the law of life and death, the kernel of sovereignty by any definition.[8] Yet, he argues, this can occur without force or conquest, the means usually assumed to be the bedrock of any legal order. He envisions a process similar to that by which a county waterworks ends up servicing a nearby town. Once some arrangements for water have been arrived at, both the county and the townspeople see great economic advantage to being part of a united watershed. A "protective association" with a need to protect its clientele in the larger vicinity will offer to exchange its services beyond its original group, so that its rules will be guaranteed to its members—all its members. The people in the neighborhood see that they gain by the exchange and join.

Much the same process can lead to standardization, but, for the standard to be useful, a body of rules or the authority of a standard setter does not necessarily have to be accepted. Accepting the measure alone is enough. History supports this more inclusive, less expensive possibility especially well in the powerful and comparatively recent example of the Hansa. This mercantile group operated as its own multinational trading organization with its own rules and enforcement. The Hansa used military and legal power, though it chose to remain a confederation of traders and never assumed the full trappings of government. Nevertheless, its coins and measures were used by others—even though they resisted its rules—simply because it was convenient to use the established quantities.

While standards *can* exist outside a forcibly enforced domain, there is a strong dynamic that makes standards and legal-political institutions go hand in hand. Standards cry out for enforcement, particularly against fraud. Most conspicuously, the counterfeiting of an exchange medium has devastating effects of social unrest in any society.

Ambitious rulers quickly recognize that they can perform a service that is virtually uncontroversial and can reap fiscal benefit from it. The first "royalty" was the king's skim, the minting of standard units of precious metals with less than the nominal value of the coinage. Users were generally willing to pay for the advantage of uniformity, but kings were often greedy, and quickly learned they could exact a huge profit from mintage when they had sufficient power to enforce their highly trimmed products as legal tender. The process is the same as today's even more overt and profitable issuance of unlimited paper money. The real check on this practice is the possibility of rejecting the preferred standard and the availability of other media of exchange. The international exchange rate is useful, but making money nonconvertible may mask some consequences.

Standardization is usually fastest when it fills a need and is coercively enforced. No one seems to have studied how those two dimensions interact, but punishing counterfeiting, for example, clearly makes a unit's coinage more valuable. A sovereign gains in authority as well as wealth by extending the domain of coinage. Historically, standardization has therefore almost always gone hand in hand with the creation of government units. Developing standards has important utilitarian advantages. It also has the less obvious, but equally important, consequence of helping establish a community by differentiating those who have distinctive standardized dress, speech, customs, weights, measures, foods, weapons, community dances, or material products, as well as a distinctive standardized religion and set of gods.

"Modernity" can be viewed as a process of emphasizing technological standardization and eliminating other established or culture-based standards. Both aspects of the process of "modernization" emphasize universalism and utilitarianism. Both technological and cultural standards tend toward homogenization and fungibility of all aspects of life, but they proceed from opposite directions, driven by their inner logics.

Standards and the Definition of Culture

Culture-defining norms usually reduce the free flow of resources, material, and personnel. It is therefore "rational" to relax unique standards of dress or rigid norms of behavior, such as Sunday rest, or strict laws regarding the form of permissible loans. Those culture-defining standards all create internal friction and inhibit the growth of social mores around adaptive and creative new social patterns. If computer printouts had been seen as prohibited "graven images," modern science, business, and even the arts would have been thwarted, channelized, and limited, much as the visual arts were restricted for centuries.

Conversely, if Levi's become the dress of choice for the young in major parts of the world, and if their unisex nature makes them less objectionable for wear by young women even in Islamic countries (since their principal rival might be short skirts that exhibit bare skin), young people may move more comfortably within and between cultures. An international costume facilitates both international and local movement of individuals.

The original use of jeans was utilitarian and, loosely speaking, "technological"; that was part of their appeal. They are an especially fine product. The dominant maker still sets the standard. But wearing them can have other connotations—youth, westernization, some degree of unisex equality. When other cultures accept Levi's for young women, they are gambling that their own cultural values will be better served by the compromise than the values of other cultures. In Iran or Saudi Arabia, of course, little or no quarter is given to dress. Even so, electricity and motor cars are not questioned, since they are viewed as even more detached from the original value system that was their crucible, and hence as usable by those rejecting Western values.

Early on, a prescribed religion was often considered socially disruptive: it was clear that the boundaries of citizenship and belief were not identical in Europe and that to insist that one implied the other was unacceptable. The breakdown of atheism as the prescribed religion of Eastern Europe may leave only Islamic countries to demand a fully standardized religion from their citizenry. The former Soviet empire, however, may revert to small nations, reviving established religion states that generally existed prior to the nineteenth century. "Ethnic cleansing" in the former Yugoslavia is a manifestation of atavistic irrational purity, and, though it was originally promoted by political aggrandizers, it follows a drive of its own.

In other cultural matters, we seem to have largely settled on a "thin international" culture,[9] shared primarily by a small elite and the restless young in various countries, and based loosely on American tastes and media appeals. Among these are cultural standards that are not only followed by those groups but also pursued by them, even when proscribed by their governments. These include Western music—"cultured" music for the upper business class, jazz and rock for the young, and both for the true elites. Food and clothing are now part of the world scene—McDonald's hamburgers and Coca-Cola are the most conspicuous examples. These artifacts coexist with their predecessors, seldom replacing them entirely. English as a lingua franca, and elements of physical grooming (lipstick, Western haircuts) are all part of this "thin layer" of universalized culture, which has other concomitants that are not yet dominant but even more consequential: central heating, air conditioning, birth control, even standards of human rights.

This thin layer of Western standards facilitates communication and trade and the more efficient movement of persons and resources, but the accommodation is much more precarious and delicate than it appears on the surface. Even in core Western (not Westernized) societies, older, more parochial and primitive standards still persist, or are revived in tough economic times: consider Jean-Marie Le Pen in France, Pat Buchanan in the United States, or "little Englanders" in Britain.

Can Standards Be "Only" Efficient?

Technological standardization, on the other hand, seems to have no hidden costs. Safe electric devices are sought or at least countenanced by virtually all religions. Most groups use and appreciate better and safer insulation, cheaper production of goods, fungibility of related products, and better and more available repair parts. All the major advantages and by-products of standardization seem in principle inoffensive and unobjectionable. Indeed, ultra-fundamentalists in many societies flock to engineering and computer programming, perhaps out of a desire to "average out" modernity, accepting Western values in the "purely technological" areas, while clinging to unadapted standards in life and social relations.

Even that accommodation, however, is now (correctly) seen as having more profound implications. Technology is not always the simple, neutral gift it seems to be. Innovations are also harbingers of, and potent sales arguments for, different patterns of living. They imply different standards of life. The degree to which technological intrusion can be kept separate from other cultural standards lies at the root of resurgent Islam's quarrel with "modernization," and of fears of fundamentalist groups such as the Amish or various movements of national resurgence throughout the world. These profound theological and ideological issues transcend the concerns of this monograph. At the same time, however, they are decisively related to it.

In many areas, it is clear that the wider the agreement on standards the better. Railroad gauges are an obvious example. Yet the high cost of total replacement of infrastructure and equipment sometimes retards universality, dwarfing in importance the occasional physical restrictions (e.g., narrow mountain ledges) that require deviations. No doubt savings would accrue from replacing narrow or wide railroads, but immediate capital costs overwhelm the decision makers.

Comprehensive standards offer potential economies of scale, compatibility of units, and, perhaps most important, a supply of spare parts. (The ultimate supply method is cannibalization.) In the 1920s the "simplification" movement, dominated by Herbert Hoover, claimed that totally standardized factories would be 30 percent cheaper than existing facilities; in some instances, they claimed, 50 percent savings would be realized.[10] A positive example of such a program is nuclear production of electricity in France. The French standardized all atomic energy plants, thereby reducing design costs, facilitating changes indicated by experience, and permitting effective safety programs.

Universal standards, however, can discourage innovation, perpetuate inadequacies, and, by compelling excessive investment in a design, make introduction of even clearly advantageous new technology an elephantine process. The level of capital investment involved may encourage some to suppress evidence of design inadequacies. Indeed, superstandardization and stagnation were characteristic of the defunct Soviet economic system in the Eastern bloc. In the United States, economists were ultimately dismissive of strident standardization, pointing out that full and rigid implementation would be stultifying. This criticism had to be impressive, inasmuch as the power behind the original report, Hoover, had used all his authority as secretary of commerce and as president, *and* his vaunted reputation for efficiency and planning, to sell the simplification program.

Universalized standards may also be compromised arrangements that thwart efficiency. In the infancy of color television, the Federal Communications Commission chose a less than optimal color TV system, which permitted existing black-and-whites to share the signal. European Union standards necessarily mediate between many preexisting national prescriptions, and, like the General Agreement on Tariffs and Trade (GATT) and other worldwide standards, have been accused of being hybrid monstrosities. The initial economic gains may over time be dwarfed by the less than optimal arrangements chosen for political, not economic or utilitarian, reasons.

Product standards, then, are not efficient or inefficient per se; indeed, they can change from one to the other as environments change. They can also promote or discourage progress, can promote openness or guarantee autarky, anarchy, or stagnation.

"Purely technological" safety standards can be used for multiple purposes and from real or sham motives. The fact that some standards are genuinely determined by technology allows many contrived arrangements that benefit the formulators to be justified in the name of safety or efficiency. As Alfred Kahn has noted:

The efforts of trade associations to standardize products, impose quality standards, and prevent fraud all in a sense make markets more nearly perfect. Standardization enables buyers to make intelligent price comparisons; it may also reduce costs of production and distribution. Quality standards may protect buyers from their own ignorance, as well as scrupulous firms from losing business to the unscrupulous. But standardization is also essential if collusively fixed prices are to be truly uniform and may also suppress socially desirable quality competition. Particularly if they are enforced, as they sometimes are, by concerted refusals to handle the products of transgressors, quality standards may be employed to deny price cutters or product innovators access to the market. All too often trade association "codes of ethics" or of "fair competition" have really tried to suppress all effective rivalry.[11]

The Use and Misuse of Standards

Once a community has mechanisms for setting standards, the machinery is available for complex and compound usage. There is no evidence of a simple or progressive pattern whereby "basic" standards precede others. It is not impossible, however, that in prehistoric times, elementary standards preceded state formation and that complex standards came into being at a later stage. But in recorded history, "night watchman" standards—weights, measures, purity—seem to be immediately accompanied by efforts to regulate other matters of social importance and to redistribute wealth, grant monopolies or control, and even present a social self. "Modern" standard setting is characterized not by a change of *type* of standards, but rather by the specificity of the processes created to prescribe them, and by the multiplicity of standards, their ubiquity, and their formality.

It is difficult to distinguish conceptually between standards of purity designed to prevent fraud and, for example, standards designed for health. Moldy food products constitute both an improper representation of goods and a danger to the community. Historically, meat and fish products have often been closely regulated and prescribed because of their perishability, but other products present a form of the same problem. Both products and buildings that involve potential danger of fire have been the occasion for historical protection through preventive standards.

Other regulatory purposes can also be served through standard setting. Religious interests can be promoted through prohibition of symbols repugnant to a faith, or of symbols or goods necessary (or believed to be necessary) for worship of rival groups.

Internal social differentiation is carried out by all known communities, and in "primitive" societies usually includes very severe differentiation by gender of clothing and day-to-day duties. It is also not unusual for communities to reinforce complex stratification through required dress, body ornamentation, etc., based on rank.

These "simple" social regulatory standards illustrate the broad range of possibilities available to any community with the capacity to set standards. These include a broad range of possibilities. Sumptuary laws designed to set a proper social tone, health-promoting standards, use-of-resources regulations, and prohibitions against certain raw materials are common, as are disguised regulations affecting the social division of labor and conditions of work. In short, standard setting can lead to leveraged regulation and legislation.

The potential advantages of standard setting within a group are readily apparent. Indeed, an extrapolation of Mancur Olson's basic proposition suggests that the introduction of standards would also normally come with a price or bonus for the promulgating elites.[12] As noted earlier, coinage went hand in hand with a mintage bonus for those inaugurating it. Standards can also serve the purpose of establishing monopoly or rent advantages. Limiting "chianti classico" or French wines to prescribed growing areas is of considerable economic advantage. But knowledgeable locals can buy wines grown a few feet away from the protected name, often at half the price of those products granted a premium through prestige labeling. The prohibition of some products can boost the value of those that are permitted. Those with heavy investment in an old-fashioned plant can require new producers to duplicate that cost, and hence will have no worry that new processes that are simpler or cheaper will make their obsolete plant an albatross.

Ruling circles may assign themselves monopolies or assign rights to secure support. Alternatively, they may require a return or "royalty" for such rights. Other groups may make claims to their own advantage. Usually, they will claim a social or altruistic purpose. The "chianti classico" label is claimed to be for the advantage of the consumer, who might be misled into paying for an inferior product, though any wine region in fact yields quite diverse quality. Health and safety claims (including negative claims about competitors) may well be valid, but they may also be dubious, exaggerated, or outmoded. Italy still bans bismuth-based remedies, even though the policy was formed on the basis of a turn-of-the-century problem that all other countries believe was resolved decades ago. The problems of flexible-cable water pipes are real, but are largely exaggerated by many local U.S. codes, under the influence of plumbers who know that flexible cable can be easily handled by do-it-your-selfers and that fixed piping cannot. Flexible cable's advantages—easy installation and the use of the water flow head as both a spigot and a flexible shower—are much valued by groups other than plumbers and apartment house owners (who must pay for some small increase in water damage). Of course, in general, those two groups exercise far more power over local ordinances than other groups.

Much the same analysis can be made of the effects of standards on international trade. Whether they take the form of local use standards or actual import barriers, they can, for example, prevent importation of dangerous goods (by prohibiting seafood from infected waters or arms), develop a social policy (by banning furs from endangered species), or protect the consumer from fraud (by eliminating mislabeled goods).

At the same time, protectionism may be enforced to protect infant or endangered industries (Hamilton's *Report on Manufacturers* or the traditional emphasis on U.S. bicycle standards serve this purpose), to entrench union or other desired factory and wage conditions, or simply to aid local companies in preference to others. The diligent protection of the United States consumer from "hoof-and-mouth" disease in Argentinian beef has not found a parallel in other countries, which (like Argentina itself) have found its cattle as healthy and as carefully inspected as those in the United States. Our domestic meat and poultry slaughtering standards are not excessively admired abroad, and most countries do at least as well as we do. Even the Canadian trade agreement in 1991 produced angry charges in the *New York Times* and other national media that Canada aided and abetted, or at least permitted, export of poorly inspected and inferior meat, charges that were devastatingly refuted almost instantly.[13] Local producers make such claims quickly and apologize slowly. If they get tougher standards for imports enacted, they do not apologize at all.

At the heart of the American conflict with Japan is the claim that we are genuine free traders and that they cheat. A decade or so ago, the Japanese rewrote their statutes, and most observers agree that Japan's importation laws are, if anything, less restrictive than ours. But written law is only partially determinative of formal policy. It is agreed by most observers that the Japanese bureaucracy, far more powerful than ours, with a tradition of discretion and a more overt differentially administered practice than its American counterpart, uses such devices as week-long delays in food inspection to discourage non-Japanese products from entering their markets. How much these ad hoc administrative practices tilt the balance is difficult to assess, but we can concede that they have some unknown influence and are seen by some as the main obstacle to the entry of American agricultural products in particular. However, most keen observers of Japanese practice believe the labyrinthine and highly personalized Japanese distribution system, reinforced by the failure of American companies to master and cope with its complexities, is even more significant in discouraging imports. In any event, like EC 1992, the Japanese enforcement of standards and its consequences for our prosperity have drawn American attention to the significance of standards in the modern world.

Performance Standards and Design Standards: A Gresham's Law of Standards

Weights, measures, and patents all involve design standards and, for most simple products (like the three-prong versus the two-pronged plug), specification of the design or product standard accomplishes all that is desired. It is simply a word picture or a drawing of the permitted product.

Even in the case of the electric plug, however, the true purpose of the regulation is to enhance safety through proper electric grounding. If the regulation were phrased in terms of achieving that result, we would have a performance standard. Any plug achieving that result, however bizarre-looking or misshapen, would be up to code or lawful.

There are many areas where directly required performance standards are clearly all that is desired. Environmental regulations have sensitized us to this topic. It is pollution rates and totals, defined in performance terms, that are regulated; that is the target, goal, and purpose of the regulations.[14]

While performance measures almost invariably have clear advantages, they have the conspicuous disadvantage of being difficult to enforce, because of the problems of measurement and of variation due to circumstances. Effluent rates are affected by the environment into which the effluent is released. Thus, air pollution measurement under extreme situations of atmospheric inversion might result in every smokestack being technically in violation of the law at some moment of its operation. Requiring a rate of efficiency in automobiles might well involve continual legal challenges claiming that different traffic and driver characteristics make the original standard irrelevant or distorted. Holding manufacturers responsible for subsequent failure of performance, even when the driver had altered the motor or other major equipment, would be counterproductive and unfair. Thus, while performance standards are superior for achieving what we desire, they are usually much more difficult to enforce.

Design criteria, though often a poor surrogate for performance standards, have significant legal and recriminatory advantages. When a product meets original requirements, the producer is liable only for concealed production flaws or hidden design irregularities. Exact conditions of use—especially extreme ones—the weather, air flow, stop-and-go traffic—are not generally at issue between the regulator and regulatee. Designs are correct or improper, not conditionally in compliance and at times improper.

Anything that creates conditions of greater ease for both regulator and regulatee and also works for easier accommodation between them has great staying power. Whether by law or in practice, design standards drive out performance standards because of the day-to-day comfort and long-range planning afforded the primary participants in the regulatory process. Third-party arbitrators generally settle for a reasonably effective design standard as sufficiently accomplishing their goals.

Design standards have a socially undesirable effect that is of great hidden advantage to those regulated, a form of hidden compensation to them. By fixing technology (or at least retarding innovation) design standards help underwrite existing capital investment and discourage entry of new participants and new advances.

Performance standards, in contrast, encourage new and different forms of participation, another reason why entrenched regulated industries are not enthusiastic about them. "User fees," which tax the extent of violation at a specific rate, are therefore attractive to both advocates and opponents of regulation because they are basically a performance standard presented in a way more palatable to producers. By flexibly focusing on social compensation rather than assessing penalties or labeling violators, user fees operate to diminish defensive claims rooted in the intractability of measurement problems. Regulatory disputes still color the relationship, but the issue becomes, "how much do you pay?" rather than, "you are a polluter and social miscreant."

Economic and regulatory ingenuity may overcome the historical tendency to enshrine design standards, just as it has usually eliminated dual monetary systems. But the historical evidence points to the prevalence of acceptable design standards (usually preferred ab ovo, often supplanting legalized performance standards). The costs of social interaction and the power of interest groups mean that regulatory convenience is served as "bureaucratic rationality" drives out "substantive rationality."

While "standardization" refers to a protean and ubiquitous process, "product standards" or "physical standards" have been viewed as precise terms of art. Sometimes they overlap in meaning, and those who use the terms may tend to equate product or physical standards with the totality of all "standards," and to employ the words in that comprehensive sense.

The Standards Movement, Its Progenitors and Its Progeny

There is a historical parallel to this linguistic displacement. At the turn of the century, the "standards" movement was seen as a large-scale social reform movement. With the test of time, it became obvious that the aspirations of the "standards" people were diverse and that many people had quite different interpretations of the movement. Those who were essentially consumerists wished to enlighten and enable purchasers, and discovered that "standards" were just one means to that end. Moralists aimed to reduce costs by creating fewer "irrelevant" choices—like Henry Ford, they favored the mass distribution of identical cars, all painted black—and emphasized uniformity. They were to lose out in Western society, though ironically, they triumphed in Eastern Europe, assuming the form of Communists of the drab, anthill variety.

The technicians who remained true to the standards slogan after World War I believed they were advocating engineering truths, translating into physical products the forces and facts of nature. "Standards" were physical embodiments of metes and measures: weights and lengths in their primary physical form, models or blueprints translatable into finished products in their more complex, industrial form. Prescribing such measured physical and natural facts was a careful and precise engineering enterprise, which ensured efficiency and low cost to those faithful to nature.

The simplicity of the definition and the nominal diffidence of engineering standardizers concealed the strong Uriah Heep aspect to the approach. "Standard setting" implies an ultimate knowledge, a reductionism as sweeping in engineering as any in science. Indeed, it reemerges as "total quality control," a sweeping claim for the primacy of "quality" over the human beings involved, primacy of the enterprise on its own terms. Standardization is just the ultimate form that a Veblenian deification of the "engineer" can take, a belief in the product for its own sake. In contradistinction, the profit motive has room for consumerist preferences, and for production for use, not design. The argument is analogous to that between the architect and the tenant, which raged so strongly in the first half of this century.

Another simplification of the claims of product standardizers is the suggestion of an inevitability of form emerging from the product, of its virtual self-definition. In fact, standards are usually exceptionally malleable and protean. Vice President Al Gore's 1993 Commission on Reinventing Government dwelt on the irrationality of the government standard for chocolate syrup, which lovingly runs on for five single-spaced pages, or for ashtrays (eight pages), which specifies the number of pieces an ashtray should break into when dropped from a specified height. In short, standards can be elaborated beyond reason; certainly, prescribed standards are determined at least as much in the mind of the prescriber as in any inherent limits imposed by nature.

Interestingly, in the arena of "basic" measures, length and time—seemingly the most artificial and arbitrary—have evolved in the direction suggested by "pure" engineering interpreters of standards. Thus, a "foot" was originally defined as the length of the then-reigning monarch's foot. The need for greater uniformity and constancy resulted, first, in an enduring measure that outlived the king, and subsequently, for most countries, in a decimalized measure, the meter, which was arbitrarily chosen. This length was first defined by a bar constructed to specifications. Such measures are now eclipsed by definitions involving naturally occurring physical phenomena, which can be measured anywhere with the proper equipment. Intervals of space, time, and temperature are no longer measured against artificial prototypes, but by phenomena chosen to be more precise, less variable, and more easily referenced than a bar held in a vault at a specified temperature.[15]

Does this vindicate the "purist" approach? Not really. In fact, these arbitrary criterion standards are constantly found to be inadequate for newer and more exacting measurements required by ongoing human activity. When nature provides the opportunity for greater exactitude, people seize it with gratitude. But those measures in nature have no ultimate meaning. The naturally occurring distances between waves emitted by a heated substance permit us to replace an arbitrary metal bar, but those wavelengths are themselves simply more useful and more steady artificial criteria. Although found in a natural process, these criterion standards must still be extracted. Furthermore, they have nothing to do with product standards, which establish both defining characteristics and qualitative assets (silkiness, durability, etc.).[16]

The Internationalization of Formal Standards

The growth of international trade has, not surprisingly, resulted in an emphasis on international standards. The focus is on a set of products of industrial complexity and technical advancement in which the value added by the producer is considerable.

Industrial newcomers have a particular reason to conform to the highest international standards, and to urge adherence to them. These standards are influenced by major industrial powers, and those same countries are often the customers being courted. In any event, newcomers are following the Japanese strategy of assuring potential purchasers that they are world market competitors producing world-class products.

Defining International Organization for Standardization (ISO) standards is a laborious process that is largely natural and technocratic. The larger and more established industrial powers have no reason to fight their advance. They are derived from standards already used in their production processes and they facilitate their access to new markets. Industrial powers also benefit from guarantees regarding the quality of the purchases they make, even though this might diminish their sales.

Virtually all players operate from the principle that they gain from growing internationalization of standards, and, perhaps more important, that such interinvolvement is inevitable. Helping design the international system is an advantage, even though it entails commitment and a loss of autonomy. It is easy enough to cheat at the fringes when vital interests are at stake, just as it is easy to argue that standards have been infringed upon if imports exceed expectations. But the main thrust is toward the growing use of recognized standards as a core definition that is helpful on all sides.

It is also easy enough for large companies to maintain international standards while retaining local ones. Where these standards differ, small adjustments may be the most economical solution. While the effort to reeducate U.S. consumers to the metric system has been largely a failure, large companies have had little difficulty and minimal cost in redesigning products or producing parallel goods to meet both markets. They can maintain a department of technologists proficient in the problems of meeting requirements in even more complex ways. Small companies encounter more difficulties, especially since American products of many varieties are often subtly differentiated from those of other countries.

The most organized and comprehensive manifestation of the drive to international standards is to be found in GATT and its successor, the World Trade Organization (WTO). While the requirements for such standards are—like most GATT regulations—phrased in general terms with less than Draconian precision, their general applicability has wielded and will continue to wield vast influence. Nations have acted to move in the direction indicated by GATT and the WTO. Diplomatic representations and protests have often been effective, particularly in the most blatant cases where nations have ignored clear principles. Finally, there are procedures for ultimate judicialization of disputes, though the ultimate recourse remains voluntary compliance.

The most basic and probably the most important GATT requirement is the emphasis on "transparency." This coined term has come to embrace the ideals of a known and open process in adopting standards, so that foreign business people and importers, not just bureaucrats and exporters, have a say. "Transparency" also entails open interpretation of regulations and a rejection of hidden memoranda or directives concealed within the administration, which can nullify or even reverse the otherwise open process. In short, the bureaucracy is to be knowable, the rules of the game clear, and the process of defining those rules open and observed.

Two decades ago, the antithesis of "transparency" could have been indicated simply by observing Japanese processes. Regulations were incomplete and fragmentary; decisions often hinged on secret directives, the text of which was not always provided to challengers, especially non-Japanese. Administrative behavior was unpredictable, not uniformly applied to those in the same legal category, or even to the same entity on different occasions. It was a world of mystery and arbitrariness, engendering deep, all too justified suspicions.

The most dramatic effect of GATT, therefore, can be seen in Japan's embracing of the call to transparency. While there is dispute about GATT's economic impact, Japanese regulation formation and standard setting, and a good deal of its bureaucratic behavior, have already moved toward GATT-like transparency.

Of course, Japan has the greatest stake in an international system that makes it the big winner. It should and largely does comply with formal GATT requirements—at least on the surface. It may well be the largest group in the world to comply with international standards, may even use ANSI standards more than Americans do. In any event, that is not an excessive price to pay for maintaining an open world system that especially benefits the world's most effective exporter. As to specific high cost issues, the Japanese have been quite willing to persist at the litigation stage. Even for domestic purposes, the Japanese have called for a less arbitrary bureaucracy.

Other societies have responded to GATT and the World Trade Organization (WTO) in much the same way, making the small and inexpensive changes easily, resisting where national self-interest makes the stakes higher. Most nations have fewer hidden agendas, so less structural change is involved. On the whole, GATT and WTO have been a wholesome and continual, though not a dramatic, force for a more open international order.

A good example is the stated GATT preference for performance over design standards. As a result, shipyard hoists of safe design, for example, now move efficiently, whereas once countries were able to exclude designs not manufactured domestically. The ability to hoist specified weights without snapping is easy to establish from an engineering standpoint and in practice.

The factors that encourage use and permit abuse of design standards also make those standards defensible. Unique characteristics of the population or the environment have always been invoked to suggest that products used safely in many environments over long periods would wreak havoc in the country at hand. GATT can therefore be invoked as an argument for universal, performance-based standards. That is not always a winning argument, however.

In short, the current international system comes close to allowing nations to have their cake and eat it too. There is some bite to the regulations and an educational element as well. No one has to sacrifice too much on the altar of freer trade, and the pace of that sacrifice is largely, though not completely, determined by domestic rather than international pressures. In the long run, it seems that international standards do prevail, but the pace is often agonizingly slow.

2 The Diverse Strands of Standardization

Some Historical Trends and Events

STANDARDIZATION OCCURS IN MANY WAYS and for many reasons. In a few instances, nature and necessity impel uniformity, but in most instances there are mixtures of the necessary, the useful, and the accidental in final design. Where multiple possibilities abound, the formal decision—whether by government, by expert body, or by collusion—may be a choice from among options. Finally, there is the influence of mass opinion, whether of buyers or of citizens, in creating standardization.

In one sense, as George Soule suggested in 1934,[1] all machinery represents a move toward standardization. And yet, that is not the primary purpose of mechanization, and simpler machines like the potter's wheel still permit considerable craftsmanship and individual variation. A conscious effort to produce uniform products is a later stage of development, and the standardization of machine parts yet another. The reasons for standards are manifold: the desire for a consistent product, assured qualities, more rapid production, less required skill and training, easier and cheaper repair of the machinery, and more predictable inventory of both supplies and machinery. In short, standardization helps to minimize surprises and emergencies.

Much of the history of technology, largely unwritten, consists of a slow but inexorable movement in the direction of standardization. Two key moments in history are almost universally cited as landmarks in establishing the desirability of such processes. The first was in the late seventeenth century, when the Dutch (themselves following a medieval Venetian tradition) created "fishing buses" from modular parts, which limited the number of replacement parts and facilitated quick production. Legend has it that the Venetians, in order to impress Henry III of France, constructed a galley while he was having dinner. The Dutch were systematic, their works well known; there remains a strong Dutch school in the study of standardization to this day. The second landmark was the innovations of Eli Whitney, called the father of standardization for his work with rifles and guns, but who also applied the approach to textile manufacture.[2]

The manufacture of railroads and ancillary equipment promoted standardization, since the advantages were apparent. In addition, steamboats dramatized the need in a way sailboats had not, since makeshift arrangements created quandaries for subsequent users, who could no longer safely rely on such adjustments.

Dramatic events also created landmarks in the drive for standardization. The great Baltimore fire in 1842 is often cited as a stimulus. Fire departments from the general area rushed to help and had to stand helplessly by since the couplings for their water hoses were incompatible with local designs.[3]

Early landmarks are something less than a full historical account, since the process was continuous and often unconscious. The demonstrated and felt need was reinforced by the crystallization of European nationalism and the emergence of an American national market in the later half of the nineteenth century.

The European tradition of minute, precise regulation of commerce continued and expanded. Usually, prescribed standards were national in scope, though, as in Germany, considerable local control, particularly of foodstuffs, was sometimes permitted.

The United States was writing on a clean slate, and government intervention was frowned upon, particularly in the nineteenth century. Most claims by guilds for monopolies were rejected during the colonial period as unnecessary and wasteful. Indeed, there was even a reluctance to grant patents, except for labor-saving devices.[4] As the nascent national industries grew, they relied on self-regulation, usually imitating a dominant firm at first, but gradually adopting industry association measures. National regulation of commerce was strongly resisted and largely avoided. Local interests were kept in check by the Supreme Court's use of "substantive due process," primarily invoked in the period between 1890 and 1937 to prevent state standards, in order especially to guard against local advantage over national enterprise. A pale shadow of this power is exercised to this day by the courts over state regulation of interstate commerce, though even that aspect is largely subordinated to the Supreme

Court's deference to congressional plenary authority under the commerce clause.

A recent popular economics book suggests that voluntary standards and mass production were a key element in the American "take-off" during the nineteenth century, together with cheap land and growing transportation.[5] Following the arguments of Nathan Rosenberg,[6] Jeffrey Madrick suggests that the American willingness to accept crude products geared to machine needs rather than consumer requirements gave an extra advantage over a fussier Europe. This allowed rapid growth of mass manufacture and gave an added bonus to the affluence of Americans. He also argues that the move to systems of "flexible," less than mass production, which permit diversification of product lines at close to mass production prices, has diminished American affluence (see below, chapter 10). In any event, in the nineteenth century, Americans took to standardization with little government involvement.[7] Nonetheless, a surprising degree of uniformity in standards was achieved through a maze of increasingly uniform state laws, the clout of insurance companies, the growing leverage of government purchasing, and (by the time of the Hoover administration) growing national responsibility for the economy.[8]

Thus, by different routes, national systems of standardization were established. The American system developed in considerable isolation from the European, and its machinery and other infrastructure—nonmetric system, alternating current—was not easily utilized or even understood abroad. More important, other nations were discouraged from entering the American market.

European countries developed their own patterns, depending on the strength and style of government regulation and the degree of autonomy of the industrial system. These balkanized regulatory systems were sometimes deliberately, sometimes haphazardly, created.

The Four Strands in Modern Standardization

The impetus to standardization has four major and diverse sources. It is important (and difficult) to disentangle them, especially since they sometimes move at cross-purposes and sometimes coincide. These involve, first, the creation, maintenance, and regulation of national economies; second, international efforts aimed at scientific cooperation and the facilitation of international trade and communication; third, technical and scientific expertise interested in the aesthetics of technology and simple efficiency; and fourth, the promise of scientism, a popular concern especially strong at the turn of the twentieth century, which understood standardization in terms of various ideological commitments and possibilities (experience has demonstrated that these commitments and possibilities are related, but seldom live up to ideological expectations). The most important spin-off of standardization has been the emergence of the American consumerist movement with its emphasis on testing and ratings.

The national regulation of standards blossomed with industrialization and the growth of science and technology. The need was created by technological elaboration, and the means for control testing, tracking, and budgets were enhanced by that growth. The ends of national standardization are multifaceted, but may be regulatory, allocatory, or nation-building in purpose, depending on the particular standard. The seekers of such standardization have usually been producers, but may be traders or consumers, and the state often has much to say about the form and universality or restrictiveness of the standard sought.

Facilitating International Communication Through Uniformity

Originally, the international effort at standardization was in large part an attempt to avoid confusion and permit exchange of science and information, but it also involved the infrastructure of transportation and communication. Early formal international bodies, called unions, dealt with railroads, post offices, and telephones, and with the metric system and time zones.

Internationalists of various kinds have always had a fondness for historic old meetings on international standards, harbingers of the hope depicted in *Locksley Hall,* where "the war drum throbbed no longer, and the battle flags were furled in the parliament of man, the federation of the world." In their dream, this new "international order" was and is being created from the ground up in little cooperative steps.

Perhaps the clearest statement of such an approach is to be found in David Mitrany's formulation of neofunctionalism.[9] In his view, UNESCO, with its on-the-ground projects in developing countries, constitutes a more significant building block for the future than an artificial, legalized, but empty debating structure like the United Nations itself.

The ultimate incarnation of this approach is the European Union (first called the European Coal and Steel Community and then the European Economic Community), which intentionally evolved from a simple cartel trying to cope with the decline of specific key European commodities to a comprehensive economic system of cooperation that is striving to become a protogovernment. According to the dreams of those who believe in small steps, this will lead to the ultimate grand design of a truly unified Europe.

The first baby steps in international standard setting dealt with such issues as metricization; agreed-upon time zones, railroad gauges, and postal letter sizes; and classification of available services. The last quarter of the nineteenth century and the first years of the twentieth were high points in such ad hoc efforts.

Those beginnings generally reflected an international faith in expertise and the objective, scientific resolution of problems, both characteristic of the turn of the century. Furthermore, this movement coalesced into internationalization of trade and travel, to the point that it was urgent to resolve some basic issues—e.g., consistent time zones—and at least minimize variations in others.

The wider the agreement and the more far-flung the community accepting the rule, the easier it is for individuals to move about in a broad region without learning new skills. Because of conventional presumptions, we in the United States, like people in most countries, have automatically adopted right-handed vehicles. Transportation engineers agree that left-handedness would have been a better design, because cars out of control would veer away from, rather than toward, the center of traffic. But since the danger of retraining drivers far outweighs the slight advantage that would accrue from redesigning to deal with a relatively small number of occurrences, the international scene sees more countries converting to right-hand drive, preferring economy of scale and ease of driving for visitors to theoretical safety advantages. (A similar anomaly exists in public transportation seating. We would be safer facing away from the direction of movement, but many persons experience feelings of nausea or dislocation "traveling backwards," so marginal safety during accidents— rare occurrences—is sacrificed to the day-to-day preferences of riders.) The need for a single rule on the road is overwhelming, but there are other issues where the advantage of uniformity is almost as evident.

Rational standards were also a feature of the Enlightenment. Imitating French institutions was the vogue in the eighteenth century, though it was subject to the vagaries of emerging national identities and bureaucratic structures. The city of Bucharest, a Balkan version of Paris, is a physical monument to this role of French models. So, too, is Washington, D.C.

Problems of a technical nature transcend individual national boundaries. Cooperation in measuring the earth is economical, for example, and helps us to understand gravitational and meteorological forces more quickly. Standardization of weights and measures facilitates trade. Study of weather conditions is both a safety measure and a business and agricultural boon. Sanitation and health problems profoundly affect neighboring countries downwind and downstream from them.

In the middle of the nineteenth century, these obvious truths began to be recognized, not in bilateral agreements that could only partially, or very cumbrously, deal with the problem, but in government-sponsored international unions, with some minimalist permanent machinery and narrow mandates. Historically, Europe had considerable experience with political conferences and entities and with waterways and customs unions. These same principles were now to be applied to continuing practical and theoretical problems that were shared across the continent. Postage, transportation, health programs, and safety and sanitation issues could be dealt with in a regularly recurring congress that had a clearinghouse office with at least some initiative power. A joint definition of time, geographical markers, and even more technical matters could also be attempted. Indeed, one of the earliest such conferences held in Brussels dealt with the subliminally nonpolitical, universal problem of statistics. It drew representatives of twenty-six nations, established a permanent bureau, and led to biennial conferences to facilitate growth in that study. Other early meetings dealt with sanitation (beginning with Mediterranean concerns), established a postal union, and standardized marine signaling.[10]

The rate of growth and decay of such efforts was rapid, occasionally because problems were resolved, more often because political or economic issues interfered. In 1900 only 11 public international unions were operative. In the interwar period, some 20 such organizations were created. But the post–World War II years were the period of real efflorescence for such structures. Between 1941 and 1966, 170 such organizations saw the light of day. By 1986 there were 378 IGOs (International Governmental Organizations), according to the Union of International Associations Yearbook, which predicts 450 by the year 2000. The UN charter facilitates formation of such entities as loose affiliates. Article 71 allows the Economic and Social Council to consult with such unions and with nongovernment international or even national units. Its main vehicle is the Committee on Non-Governmental Organizations, inevitably known as CONGO.

The growth of nongovernment international organizations (INGOs) "has been even more spectacular. There were nearly 5,000 in 1986 leading to a projection of nearly 11,000 by the year 2000."[11]

The post–World War II proliferation of nations and of international structures facilitating mutual involvement has undoubtedly contributed to the multiplication of such structures. The increasing number of nations makes bilateralism even more inefficient, while the UN, the EC, and regional structures facilitate the creation of more and more specialized bodies. But growth has far outstripped even the rate of new states, as we proceed "from empire to nation"[12] and multiply the number of units. It seems self-evident that technical and practical problems also present themselves in urgent ways in a world of such technical complexity.

The late nineteenth and early twentieth century saw the forging of cooperation in transnational standards, with a surge of optimism and faith in expertise that was belied by the underlying and more deep-rooted efflorescence of nationalism, even tribalism. In the short run, these latter influences clearly dominated the century, but international agreements have also been remarkably enduring.

Primarily, such agreements involved mapping the world in both a figurative and literal sense. Various problems were dealt with in similar ways. Experts met in conferences on their own, with philanthropic financing or at government expense; or a conclave was conducted with teams of formal rep-

TABLE 2.1
Some International Standardizing Efforts, 1850–1900

1853	General Conference as to Statistics, held at Brussels.
1853	Maritime Conference for the Adoption of a Uniform System of Meteorological Observations at Sea. Held at Brussels.
1863	Conference of Paris on a Postal Union. Led to that of Berne in 1978.
1864	First International Conference on Weights and Measure, held at Berlin.
1865	Conference of Paris on Telegraphic Correspondence.
1870	International Commission on the Metric System first met at Paris. Thirty powers represented. At a subsequent meeting in 1875, a convention agreed to, May 20, setting up at Paris an International Bureau of Weights and Measures (Le Bureau Mètre).
1872	Conference of the International Telegraphic Commission.
1874	Conference of Berne, September 15, on a Postal Union. Resulted in a convention forming a permanent international bureau maintained at Berne since 1875.
1975	Congress of International Telegraphy, at St. Petersburg.
1881	Conference of Berne to regulate railroad transportation. Convention agreed on at a later conference at Berne in 1890.
1884	Conference of Washington on a Prime Meridian. Adopted that of Greenwich.
1890	Conference at Berne as to Railroad Transportation. Nine powers represented. Convention agreed to, October 14, establishing a permanent bureau at Berne.
1896	The International Maritime Committee formed.
1897	Conference of Paris as to Ocean Telegraphy.

Source: Adopted from *American Journal of International Law* (808–829) as printed in Mangone, *A Short History,* 92–96.

resentatives of national organizations or governments. Diplomatic or other political representation was sometimes included and the relative influence of experts versus politicians varied with the issue. Proposed solutions (seldom novel, except perhaps when two or more plans that had previously been bruited about were combined) emerged and were approved (or rejected) by a large number of countries. "Nongovernment organizations" to enforce or continue to improve the designated rules were established (often, these were in fact government sponsored and subsidized.)[13]

Some Cooperative International Ventures

Agreements on geographic terminology and time zones, metric weights and measures, and postal arrangements are classic examples. The need obviously antedated the turn of the century, but even in a venture such as the international postal services—where the enterprise was generally a government monopoly and the need for mutual rules obvious—progress was slow. This example serves as a good (though relatively early) heuristic of the process of standardization.

Bilateral agreements, occasionally involving multiple parties, were numerous from 1802 onward.[14] In 1862, the U.S. postal department called for a conference, which was held in Paris the following year; there, principles were discussed and agreed upon. Dissatisfaction with implementation by each country on its own led to the establishment of an organization in 1874–1875. Subsequent meetings of the Universal Postal Union laid down additional principles regarding newspaper exchange, rules of required delivery, and the like.

The International Union of Railway Freight Transportation—actually a European structure—emerged in 1845 and held conferences in 1878 and 1882. It truly began to function after an 1890 conference, the results of which were finally implemented in January 1893. It provided for a crucial single bill of lading for international transportation, which permitted the free flow of goods; it also fixed ancillary regulations. Precisely a century later, a similar single bill of lading was a major accomplishment of EC 1992.[15]

The growth of the metric system is said to have begun with the discovery of the statue of King Goudea, a Chaldean figure from the first millennium B.C. The statue included figures that were interpreted as indicating basic measures used by Babylonian carpenters and sculptors. The word "metric" may have originated from such functions, though the physical definitions evolved from "rational" measures that were products of the French Revolution.

The linkage between a building-block unit and a decimal system is generally attributed to the advocacy of a Dutch mathematician and of numerous writers (including Sir Christopher Wren), who urged a link to a physical phenomenon. The French Constituent Assembly, at the urging of Talleyrand, in 1791 adopted length and weight standards constructed on such principles.[16] An international meter and kilogram were finally agreed to in 1872. Actual bars and weights were defined physically and the conditions (length at zero degrees Celsius, weight in a vacuum) were also specified. The physical standards were to be stored at a French site, and a secretariat to coordinate future cooperation on such issues was located in Paris, with an admonition that conferences take place at least every six years. A treaty confirming these arrangements was signed by nineteen nations; Great Britain acceded to the treaty a decade later. A metric union has facilitated meetings and consultation. Successive improvements in precision have culminated in the replacement of the metal meter bar by a definition based on the wavelength of light emitted by krypton 86.[17]

These are accounts of fairly typical international unions representing the first wave of functional unions. Generally, they made important contributions to world safety, comfort, or knowledge at the time of creation, but offered much less thereafter. By and large, they became commonplaces of international trade or intercommunication, performing indispensable but mundane and limited tasks. Tightly circumscribed by their terms of reference, they were dominated by proficient but nonadventurous bureaucrats. Seldom did the organization undertake new ventures, and it remained a gray shadow in the service of an order dominated by the nation-states.

A parallel nongovernment organization, the Association of Railway Congresses, was established in 1885 to deal with technical standardization of such things as gauges and techniques. It was nonlegislative (more typical of nineteenth-century structures, therefore) but tried to reduce the wide diversity of trains and their infrastructure in the interest of cutting costs and permitting interchangeability of equipment.

Similar organizations were developed in the areas of maritime and automobile regulation. The development of the latter was facilitated by an agreement on universal road symbols, as a result of a 1909 conference. Many of these organizations were absorbed into the League of Nations and later into the United Nations.[18] Others, like the primordial postal and railway unions, remain independent intergovernment structures.

Congresses with more limited agendas were not uncommon, and included meetings to define electric units, held in 1882 and 1908, and an 1884 conference on fixing a prime meridian. One-shot meetings were more prevalent in the nineteenth century. Experience taught there would be problems in follow-through; therefore, continuing organizations (which may meet every four years or even every ten) are now much more favored. These structures often have permanent, often part-time secretariats, sometimes formally housed in a national government or academic setting. They may be affiliated with the prevailing international authorities.

With the establishment of the League of Nations, it became easier to deal with specific problems or sectors through one of the congeries of League or UN affiliates. Generally, there have been fewer efforts simply to define or frame standards, and more to establish a standard-setting structure. While, in general, exploratory meetings are initially set through the UN or some other existing international structure, resulting organizations may go their own way and may well emerge as INGOs in their own right.[19]

Certainly, there is little conscious thought that such congeries represent a seedbed for international growth or development. Whether these organizations are incorporated into the international governance structures or are technically or really "nongovernment," they are exceptionally sterile and artificial, limited in scope, aspiration, and imagination. They are indeed well described as "functional," but their aim is to fulfill their assignment and run; they are not building blocks toward anything.

Their failure is perhaps less pronounced than the purely juridical approach of Woodrow Wilson, or the Kellogg-Briand Pact, which "prohibited" war. That type of thinking is still visible in the United Nations and was even more evident in the League. But insofar as the League and the UN absorbed the old, highly limited, single-task organizations of the turn of the century, they also represent a failure of yet another sort: single-purpose structures of an international sort seldom expand in aspiration or achievement. International bureaucracies follow a "Gresham's law" in driving out creative or truly internationalist bureaucrats.[20] Such functionaries are trained to respond to national programs and demands. They would have to be foolhardy, not merely courageous, to maintain the integrity of their assigned functions, let alone transcend or build upon them. The "support" of an invisible community of the future, unborn and undefined, is hardly a basis for conformists to defy existing, tough-minded, and entrenched nationalist forces that often maximize petty but clear and understandable goals, including national patronage in the bureaucracy or an upper hand in international trade. Technocratic needs or the claims of expertise are clearer rallying points, but they seldom show the way to international authority. Even in such areas as health, pollution, and crime, where contagion physically transcends borders, nation-states are loath to grant extraterritorial power and usually require use of conventional channels of procedure, even though such means slow down or dilute effective response to the problem.[21]

Standardization at the National Level

Standard setting is obviously part of nation building, and standards are the specific objects of much, and perhaps most, of a nation's early legislation. But systematic and conscious national standards bearing that name come subsequent to, and as a by-product of, the success of international standardization.

The aleatory nature of the borders of the national state was quickly demonstrated by the success of efforts at the supranational level. Geographic conventions on issues such as latitude and longitude were supplemented by meetings on time zones, railroad gauges, agreements about mail, and regulation of the seas, air, and airways. This tradition of international standard setting also permitted efforts to eliminate piracy, slavery, inhumane warfare, and ultimately (though with a glaring lack of success) war itself. Not all these efforts were even minimally effective, but the tradition of international standards, arrived at in interminable conferences, was firmly fixed.

Within the nation-states, a laissez-faire approach to standards seemed more and more a luxury. Negative information on effects of products, for example, was not a priority among manufacturers. Monitoring deleterious consequences of new products was a social good, but was also found to facilitate technological innovation. Standards units could also, using their initial and experiential expertise, channel and promote such efforts.

Prior to World War I, there was only one official standard-setting unit, Great Britain.[22] The desirability of such organizations was underscored during the war, when testing and development of weapons brought expertise dramatically to the fore. Standardizing units were seen and sold as scientific research units, leading to new and profitable products. But the standardizing and standard-developing organizations also proved their worth in testing routine products—foodstuffs, uniforms, communication devices—and in minimizing the promotion of shoddy goods by profiteers, one of the many sad phenomena that accompanies war.

By the end of the 1920s, more than a dozen national offices for standardization were officially established.[23] They had in fact been present in most countries, including the United States, though without full recognition, credit, or financing appropriate to their function and task. Even after gaining full recognition, they were seldom amply funded, especially since they were ambiguously entrusted with regulation, inspection, and technological development, with little or no instructions as to what mix of these tangentially related functions they were expected to pursue.

While such organizations were touted as scientific product innovators or even superlaboratories, they are best understood as offering testing and certifying services and as coordinating and systematizing the development of standards by others. In this scheme of things, the U.S. organizations ANSI and ASTM (the American Society for Testing Materials) are even more important to American standards than is the National Institute of Standards and Technology (NIST). The latter is the legal scientific developer of basic or scientific norms only, a coordinator at the margins of the complex voluntary system. ASTM develops definitions of performance norms or basic designs for industrial processes, and ANSI sponsors a network of designers. NIST was expected to sponsor a network of certifiers who would test conformity to these developed norms, but has disappointed congressional expectations in this regard, probably because of its history, structure, and financing.

Other countries combine those functions in different ways, depending on the degree of centralization sought. There are different models of the standards organization itself, which control the recognition of industrial and scientific standards, the degree of autonomy in such organizations, and the degree to which they share the field with professional societies or trade associations. Again, certification and testing may be tightly controlled, but are usually the most decentralized functions of all.[24]

Standardization, Rationalization, and "Scientific Management"

One of the key elements in standardization has been its alliance with statistical theory. Because of the admixture of scientific principles, engineering efforts, and sampling theory, there has been an irresistible attempt to scientize human behavior in the process. The most conspicuous example is the American phenomenon of "Taylorism," boosted by its adherents as "scientific management." William Edwards Deming's "total quality control" is a related modern offshoot.[25]

Sampling enters the picture most prominently as a check on the operating system involved in production. It is one thing to develop a prototype; it is another to assure successful duplication of the product and consistent quality in production. While continuous testing of every product for every expected quality is theoretically possible, mass production makes it impractical. Some qualities (how well the product burns, for example) may even make total testing impossible. Often, too, total testing trivializes the pursuit, numbs vigilance, and results in poor quality control, as Deming vociferously claimed. A perfect example is U.S. poultry inspection, where the examiner has seconds per fowl to look for defects or disease. By selecting a sample of products, inspectors can pinpoint the extent and cause of failures. By limiting inspection, they can intensify it.

Sample theory is also useful in more basic ways, for example, in the construction of a standard by testing supposedly required features or the efficacy of alternatives. In its application, it is useful in determining effectiveness of specific products or goods. As was illustrated dramatically in a recent case of Canada's failure to follow the protocols in breast cancer research, small deviations from correct sampling can threaten the validity of conclusions.[26] In that instance, the conclusion was subsequently reverified, to the immense relief of the medical community.

The standards movement has used the skills of many applied statisticians and engineers, some of considerable stature, and has been rewarded with their attention. In this century, there has been particular attention paid to the concerns of standardization by schools of Dutch, English, and American statisticians, industrial sociologists, and engineers.[27] While the proclamation of standardization as a "new discipline" seems a bit overblown, the fact remains that there are hard-core achievements and day-to-day contributions attributable to such practitioners, in theoretical as well as practical areas.

The most famous form of standardization is Taylorism, and that effort continues to fascinate commentators and critics. It did a disservice to standards, because its exaggerations of the approach led to a rejection of standards, while what was most fascinating to evaluators lay largely outside standardization. Taylorism detracted attention from standardization and diminished it in a devastating way.

Taylorism was avowedly an offshoot of standardization, and represents well the protean nature the approach had at its inception.[28] Frederick Taylor and his followers believed they had taken a technical concept—standardization—and built around it a broader social program for each enterprise they studied, including its human aspects.[29] Half a century later, Deming made similar claims.

Essentially, Taylorism emphasized not standardization of the *product* but standardization of the *task*. This shift in focus was accompanied by an assurance that the scientific nature of the Taylor approach adequately protected the worker: thus, unions were unnecessary. Taylor and followers believed they would create a human spirit that went beyond mere materialism, and that management would be constrained by spiritual imperatives. In fact, Taylor and followers became what they proclaimed standardization to be: a tool of management.[30]

It was not only Taylorism that became a management instrument by emphasizing standardization. The veneration of science and the vagueness of the concept led to broader hopes that standardization would resolve management-labor conflicts, end business cycles, and provide the ultimate answer in the search for the good life.[31]

The indebtedness of Taylorism, that is, of "scientific management," to the standards movement is clear and up-front. The two-volume authorized biography of Taylor published by the Taylor Institute has an interesting item in the index. Under "standards and standardization," we are directed to see "scientific management."[32] F. B. Gilbreth quite explicitly states that the Taylor school saw "standardization" as key to its purpose,[33] but Taylorism seems to emphasize standardization of the human element more than technological and product-centered norm setting. Essentially, product standardization was a vehicle for endowing the "industrial engineer" with the authority to find the "one right way" to do everything and to set norms for the human activity involved. Taylor and his following were almost certainly sincere in their desire to transcend labor-management conflict. But "scientific management," "quality control," and other related approaches were essentially available on hire to management only. In the hands of such consultants, they proved pliable and useful to employers. The unions opposed Taylorism at first on principle, later from experience. The altruism in scientific Taylorism that attracted Louis Brandeis and led him to write a laudatory preface to Taylor's *Principles of Scientific Management* proved illusory in practice. The "one right way" of time and motion effort was hardly "scientific." It proved to be premature robotics practiced on humans.

Deming's "total quality management" (TQM) school arose more precisely from the tradition of sampling and statistics. While direct influence of the standards movement on him personally was slight, the basic thinking came from a common source. It is more akin to the aims of turn-of-the-century standardization than Taylorism's time and motion approach, especially since the latter was consistently applied for managerial purposes. Deming (like Taylor personally, though not necessarily his epigones) emphasized that his is a transformational system, and that the important thing is a change in attitude, not specific devices.

TQM is total, both in the sense that it is aimed at "zero defects" rather than a cure through a quality control unit, and in the sense that it is comprehensive in its search for quality.[34] Its attempt to revitalize social purpose and to eliminate authoritarian, "one right way" approaches set from the top derives primarily from Deming's response to his Japanese industrial experience, but is also a reaction to what has been in practice a caricature of the early idealistic claims of standardization and "scientific management." A major difference is his acceptance of the Japanese model of a single supplier and of supplier continuity in order to build quality, in contrast to the American model of specifying standards to control price. Deming's fanatic devotion to "quality" is also a dominating vision of society as a whole, while the original standardization movement included those who saw the consumers' demands and personal preferences as more interactive, and their aims more legitimate, than pure efficiency and production.[35]

Historically, the "rationalization" approach that developed from standardization was a more explicit "total integration" vision than even TQM has yet advanced. During the years of the Weimar Republic (1917–1933) the Germans, both in official policy and academic discussions, embraced an economic approach they labeled *Rationalismus*. While explicitly drawing on standardization and scientific management notions, they also proposed to transcend them. They distinguished between "technical rationalization"—largely intraplant operations—and "economic rationalization," which largely took the form of regulated cartelization.[36] In essence, this was an advanced capitalist effort to combat claims by Communists and Nazis that they were uniquely able to meet the economic needs of the people, and to coordinate industry to avoid irrational duplication and the peaks and valleys of economic cycles. This was to be accomplished by government-supervised cooperation among giant cartels, whose predatory impulses were to be reined in by government and strong unions. Somewhat analogous to Japan's political-economic structure of today, "rationalization" involved strong elements of what political scientists call "corporatism," a system of interaction among major industrial players similar to Italian Fascism, though without any political dictatorship. The building-block social forces were encouraged to be as economically strong as they could get and were then coordinated by government ministries, interacting through consensus-building committees and official and semiofficial bodies.

In the six decades since Weimar, society has placed a different emphasis on the motive for coordination, a shift particularly evident throughout the second half of the twentieth century. The early efforts were "technical" in the standards sense and spuriously "scientific" in nature, dictated by technology. "Scientific management" emphasized the human and psychological aspects but sought to find an objective basis for them. "Economic rationalization" explicitly recognized that technology was only a context for social decisions that far transcended technological imperatives. Economic decisions allocate resources, and technological imperatives are merely one of the many factors involved.[37]

The Soviets apparently regarded "rationalization" as a vindication of their own planning processes.[38] They used the terms "standardization" and "rationalization" during the New Economic Policy (NEP) and subsequent periods.[39]

Taylorites directly embraced rationalization, not as a transcendence of their work but as an exemplification and clarification of it. Lyndall Urwick wrote a monograph on rationalization (which influenced H. G. Wells among others), and included architects of the approach in the hagiographic sketches of *The Golden Book of Management*.[40] The martyred Walter Rathenau was of course included as the principal architect of rationalization.

The leading American interpreter of "rationalization" was the economist Robert Brady, who played an important role in developing the popular understanding and scholarly interpretation of standards. His *The Rationalization Movement in German Industry* is a fascinating account of the interweaving of "scientific" claims and the growing cartelization of German industry, and a prelude to his classic *Business as a System of Power*,[41] which alone among his works does not confine its attention to the scientific-technological issues of modern industry. Still later, Brady coined a term of his own, "unitization," which was meant to convey the integrative nature of the economy.[42] The successive use of different terms to encompass roughly the same idea is always a good indication that the previous term has not swept the field or captured many hearts and minds. "Standardization" was to ebb sharply with the eclipse of Taylorism. "Scientific management" had its fling, but seems now to be a cult concept and a dwindling one at that. "Rationalization" never got much play outside Europe, and "simplification" is by its nature a very limited term. "Unitization" does not appear to have had any play beyond Brady's book, dying at birth.[43]

Looking back on his work in the 1950s, Brady seemed to want to assimilate under his own heading all approaches to economic integration. For example, he included the early stages of the EEC as an example of "unitization." Clearly, the EU owes a considerable debt to standardization (or especially, rationalization), but only at a very low level of applied functions. It is the dream of a transcontinental European system, more than the scientific forces immanent in product quality, that drives EU policy. Brady was almost alone in the middle decades in continuing to emphasize the turn-of-the-century impulses deriving from hyperscientism. Like Deming, he linked technological imperatives to a broader purpose, much as the Weimar theorists had attempted to do.

One person who was much influenced by all those rationalist approaches was Herbert Hoover. He played a key role not only as an engineering authority sponsoring standards but also as a moralist impressed with "simplification" and minimal duplication.[44] He brought a strong commitment to standards to the Department of Commerce, but also a commitment to nongovernment—if not wholly private—enterprise. Deming states flatly that Hoover founded the American voluntary standard system in 1921.[45] While this claim is more definitive than history would suggest, Hoover did set in play machinery for standards only loosely coordinated by government. And in many measures, most prominently the establishment of the Reconstruction Finance Corporation, he showed a commitment to a weak form of "rationalization," a desire for a government unification and simplification of the economy and its products. In this, he was the true predecessor of Roosevelt's first New Deal and its corporativist National Industrial Recovery Administration. Hoover sought freedom for trade associations and sided with their efforts to exchange information on business. He disagreed with the Department of Justice's antitrust suit against flooring manufacturers and cement producers, who had used their association to exchange such information, and applauded a 1925 Supreme Court decision holding that exchange of information was not in itself a violation. Hoover would have relaxed antitrust legislation even further, relying on loose supervision through his Department of Commerce to control abuses.[46]

His drive against waste reflected his sense of simplicity and order. That drive was resisted and was largely ineffectual. Still, in 1964, when Walter Heller asked Thomas Balogh, chief science advisor to the British prime minister of the time, to name the greatest American of the century, he named Hoover, because he standardized electric fittings, something Britain will not achieve at all this century.[47]

During his time in the Department of Commerce, Hoover fostered the formation of four hundred trade associations. Not only did he push for exchange of information and standardization, he also encouraged the drawing up of codes of behavior. Fully two hundred codes were in operation at the end of his presidency and at least four were accepted by National Recovery Administration (NRA) as written.[48]

All this rationalism aroused skepticism. Inevitably, Ruskinlike questions about the evils and drabness of industrial society seemed magnified in a "rationalized," "unitized," or standardized society. Would standard products all be stark, uniform, unadorned, functional, and unaesthetic? To some puritans, "standardization" efforts were attractive for precisely that reason: They envisioned simple wants without frills, everyone in overalls, perhaps, consuming food capsules three times a day, living in prestressed concrete module apartments. An anti-industrialist, procraftsman critique was therefore neither irrelevant nor unprovoked.

Hoover recognized this critique and its appeal. He endorsed a program of "simplification" to get industry to avoid duplication in machinery and to enjoy the efficiency benefit of uniformity under war conditions.[49] As secretary of commerce, he added an Office of Simplification and a simplification project to the National Bureau of Standards. Oddly, this effort to avoid the connotations of drab uniformity actually called attention to the fact that his program was one of heavy-handed sameness at the cost of creativity. While that emphasis was not necessarily inherent in the rich multipurpose origins and use of standardization, "simplification" tended to give standardization a bad name among economists, who saw it as an effort to hold back progress.[50]

Utopian Thinking and Consumerism in the Standards Movement

The standards movement seemed to provide a societal focus when it first emerged in the late 1890s. It invoked science (and scientism) and suggested that expertise was the wave of the future; the vagueness of its applications meant that many embraced its approach, for wildly diverse reasons. Some simply wanted to upgrade the goods of modern society. Some saw it as a step toward a drastic restructuring of society.

The standards movement of the 1890s attracted such thinkers in part because its very scientism was congruent with the times. Socialist Fourierists and followers of Saint-Simon thought standards would lead to a restructuring of society. H. G. Wells and other Fabians attended standards conferences and hailed the movement. Puritan simplifiers like Herbert Hoover and the Galbraiths were enthusiastic because it promised an efficient, disciplined society. Others saw consumerism and truth in selling as the purpose of standardization.

The veneration of science made the concept of standards seem a godsend for society, a tool of efficient management, a weapon for the consumer, or indeed all three, depending on one's point of view. Thus, alongside international conferences of experts on specific narrow subjects, there were popular sessions, small rallies for standards in a vaguer and broader sense, improbable as that might seem.

The nontechnological, more intellectual concern with standardization attracted many with a broad view of industrial statesmanship, people as diverse as Lenin, Hoover, and Walter Rathenau, H. G. Wells and Stuart Chase. Not surprisingly, they found they were not talking about the same thing. Reversing the familiar adage of the blind men and the elephant, each had conjured up different images of societies and embodied them in the term "standardization." Nonetheless, that confused period, from the end of the nineteenth century to almost the middle of the twentieth, saw many different and largely constrictive efforts to employ ideas of standardization. While the popular and idealistic strand of standardization seemed vague and utopian, many of its ideas and ideals have reemerged in a more hard-headed form a century later.

A number of Fabians, including Sidney and Beatrice Webb and George Bernard Shaw, attended turn-of-the-century sessions on standards. Among latter-day Fabians, H. G. Wells and William Robson were clearly influenced by the approach. There is, however, little in the early program or history of the Fabians to indicate any real influence of the standardization movement on them, or vice versa. Rather, it was the similarity of thought that made it logical for them to spend a moment scrutinizing it, then deciding it had no special message or appeal, before going on to other things. Standardization was not rejected so much as bypassed or subsumed under other concerns.

As Fabian socialists, the Webbs rejected violence, with their famous phrase, "the inevitability of gradualness." As Wells put it:

Socialism ceased to be an open revolution and became a plot. Functions were to be shifted, quietly, unostentatiously from the representative to the official he appointed . . . and these officials constitute a scientific bureaucracy as distinguished from haphazard government . . . a pretty distinctly undemocratic socialism.[51]

Therefore, to the Webbs, who saw government as, socially speaking, "an association of consumers," standards were logically part of the arsenal of the experts acting on behalf of society. Technological imperatives would drive definitions of what was productive, and experts would manage for the benefit of all, for the citizen as consumer and for the citizen as citizen. All this was already in motion in municipal government and special projects. One had only to recognize and accelerate it.[52]

With his zeal for simplification and standardization, Shaw was naturally also attracted. His moralizing puritanical opposition to luxury led him to condemn most forms of variety as the needless and pointless vanity of the rich. Seeing himself in the tradition of Ruskin and Morris, he believed in simple craftsmanship and traditional design, condemning most variations as waste and "illth," the antithesis of wealth.[53]

Even Wells, the great fictionalizer of science, who recognized the scientific necessity of creativity and freedom and who incurred the Webbs' scorn for predicting that repression in the Soviet Union would retard science, was willing to sacrifice new inventions to secure sure and uninterrupted employment.[54] In relation to those of other Fabians, his writings nonetheless show a more direct influence of the concepts of certification, brands, standards, and quality, and less of the notion of one traditional stylized product. In his fullest economic discussion, *The Wealth, Work and Happiness of Mankind* (1931), Wells devotes a section of his discussion to the "rationalization" effort, including standardization, and he reiterates the need to contain technology and control innovation in order to control business cycles.[55]

Oddly, the lone Fabian tract on the issue of standardization was written during a period long after the initial contact with the standardization movement, by William Robson, who was not of the founding group. The book suggests there was some continuing interest in standards and some carryover from growing American consumerism that was unlike the puritanical Luddite simplification stand of earlier Fabian writings.

Robson's *Socialism and the Standardized Life*[56] attempted to deal with the relationship between standardization of goods and freedom of thought, efficiency, variety, and choice of life. Robson was particularly interested in defending socialism from the charge of drabness and enforced preferences: "Comes the revolution, you'll *like* strawberries and cream."

Robson argues that standardization is not uniquely associated with any specific political order; in his view, the two countries where it had been most emphasized were the United States and the USSR, at opposite poles of the political spectrum. There were dangers in restricting product choice by any means: the habit could carry over from the consumer domain to the intellectual and artistic domain. Again, in his view, Leninist Russia and the United States—suffering from the Red Scare of the 1920s—exemplified those dangers. There was also little to be gained by prescribing what type of necktie should be manufactured or how to decorate cakes. Life and color should be favored, unless they clearly impeded economic efficiency. But, he suggests, Socialist states could put that principle to work as well as capitalist ones. In the political situation of a neophyte, with Bernard Shaw and the Webbs the grand old leaders, Robson needed courage to argue that many socialists had enunciated a too restrictive view of what choice of goods would be like under socialism.

At the same time, his commitment to standardization emerged as evangelical.

Standardization in matters industrial seems, indeed, to be not only an accomplished fact, but a process which must be pushed to its logical extreme....The standardization of certain kinds of thought, behavior, organization and material, [sic] goods and services, is in many respects essential for the maintenance of Western civilization.[57]

The contradictory attitudes embodied in the multifaceted intellectual position are remarkably illustrated in F. R. Leavis and Denys Thompson's *Culture and Environment: The Training of Critical Awareness*,[58] which is largely an attack on the muddling of thought by the bane of advertising. Drawing heavily on Stuart Chase, who combined consumerism with resistance to faulty logic, the authors parallel his concern with the testing of claims, the evils of conformity, and scientific standards as a solution to purchasing and good citizenship. They acknowledge certain areas—like fire hose couplings—where standardization is highly desirable. Yet, in the main, the work is an attack on modernism in the tradition of William Morris and John Ruskin, seeing it as limiting real choice and substituting machine ugliness for the simple bucolic and (on the whole) prosperous Middle Ages. A link is explicitly made between "product simplification," with its elimination of choice, and "intellectual simplification," e.g., book clubs that amass members and all but dictate their reading choices. Leavis and Thompson's book reflects standardization "stood on its head," used to attack what its main espousers revered.

The popularized standards movement was fated to lose its reformist zeal. The stated purpose of the movement was too general, too contentless, to move society very much in any particular direction. From its inception, the widely diverse goals of its devotees exacerbated the problem, and their various enthusiasms tended to limit one another's visions.

Every social movement has its diverse elements and its power struggles. The history of Marxist parties is notoriously a chronicle of left and right wing "deviations," "infantile disorders," and changing troikas, each of which purged its predecessor. Even the Nazis had a Strasser-led "left" faction and groupings close to pre-Weimar elites.

The diversity of the popular standards movement was even greater and its goals more ambiguous; as a social movement, it all but vanished, leaving behind only national and international standards offices (which had usually originated in the early or middle nineteenth century) and some industrial or trade association interests. While a few people understood that the method of standardization promised real but small-scale accomplishments, the most fervent had believed they had found a largely cost-free method for social transformation. They became disillusioned and sought a new and more precise focus—Socialism, Taylorism, or consumerism.

This trend was clearest with respect to consumer organization, where a clear trail led from standardization to testing to independent organizations with the avowed purpose of product evaluation. The 1930s and 1940s saw the consumerist element in standardization separate out and become a force in its own right, with a focus on testing and ratings. When the effort to use government information as an important consumer educator was thwarted, former standardizers in the United States formed consumer research organizations and established successful forms of information testing and dissemination outside the government. They could then also act as an interest group in the formation of consumer-oriented standards. With good leadership and effective publications, these organizations have become established icons of public libraries, but they can also claim considerable social effectiveness. They are vaguely part of the materialistic culture, however, promoting consumption as much as (or more than) improving production. They have been diverted from their original purposes and attract a quite different membership than they set out to do. This is not unusual for successful organizations: the original impulse is reflected in periodic attempts to return to social reform (e.g. health concerns or critiques of the insurance system), yet the desire to inform pulls them in other directions (the Consumer Reports Travel Newsletter, for instance).

The standards movement exemplifies the vagueness and ultimate disillusion of the technocratic dream, of which it was part. Thorstein Veblen, for example, analyzes it as the shift of industrial control from owners to managers to engineers. Experts replace the price system with a rational engineering set of values. Miraculously, society is transformed. An even more naive form of the same approach was Lenin's belief that all that was needed to run an industrial system was training in engineering and knowledge of elementary accounting. Not too surprisingly, Lenin was also a firm "standardizer" and rationalizer. A more sophisticated form was Arthur Pigou's "welfare economics," which assumed one could price the social utility of scrubbers to prevent smoke pollution by comparing their cost to the amount saved for cleaning bills and other negative costs. The "wreck of welfare economics" comes when those "negative costs" include, for example, cases of lung cancer: while an implicit monetary figure for medical bills, loss of earnings, and "pain and suffering," can be concocted, societies cannot readily agree on the weight to be accorded the avoidance of disease or death. The dollar figure does not generally match society's actual attitude toward death risk or toward its other basic commitments.

Values are not reducible to simple facts. Social priorities are often deeply hidden in the choice of policies, and only the most superficial unraveling of those hidden values occurs through more careful specification of costs and needs. Whose lives we protect through regulation and whose we put at risk are seldom well thought out and sometimes seem quite accidental. Risk is seldom clearly defined and societies do not seem to welcome information about it, since those put at risk are likely to object strenuously.

Choice of standards exemplifies this well. Some choices involve concealed trade-offs. A marginal increase in cost of electric products to prevent fires and death is easily accepted, but to specify the utility of atomic energy over other forms of energy production one must make decisions about acceptable risk rates for dangerous accidents. How does one balance low but significant death rates against one highly unlikely eradication of a whole neighborhood or city? Statisticians can calculate expected death rates, but society may prefer a higher death rate spread over time and thus socially absorbable, to more difficult catastrophic events. The resolution of such issues is technical or empirical only in its smallest part.

Some advantages that standardization offers are real and cumulative, however. Having a good supply of repair parts or eliminating obviously poor products may not restructure institutions or save souls or lives, but may ease costs and physical pressures. That type of advantage is independent of ideology or social reform. It can be simple, routine, or bureaucratic, but it is undramatic and even boring. Thus, technicians have taken over and perpetuated the standards movement as a limited and uninteresting effort, while the zealots have left because the big issues remained unresolved.

Those who strove for social justice and those who were interested in standards as consumerists went their different ways. Originally, the standards movement was in part a program of technocratic dreamers. It became the domain of the narrow specialist, the engineer with highly limited goals, bound to elaborate minute specifications.

For a shining decade or so, the standards movement was all things to all people. The reformist left saw in standards a scientific road to legislation that would break away from parochialism and would tame capitalism. Some even believed the substitution of international standards would lead to broader, principled, universal governance. Others were certain scientific production would eliminate shoddy products and limit the quest for selfish profit. Moralistic engineers embraced planned interchangeable machinery as a further extension of the logic of the assembly line, expecting parallel savings for society. Extravagant and unnecessary features like style or expensive competition would be eliminated.

In a sense, then, the standards movement has had its right and left deviations. The left included those who believed one could transcend nationalism with scientific standards. They became internationalists, became (or were) technocratic socialists like the Fabians. Another group on the left was interested merely in curbing the excesses of capitalism by flexing the muscle of consumerism. The deviationists on the right were profit-oriented capitalists who thought Henry Ford's "Hobson's choice" production—any color as long as it was black—would benefit efficiency and profits. That position was largely demonstrated as economically untenable. But some of that viewpoint was absorbed by Salazer and Franco's Fascism and by other authoritarian regimes. They demonstrated (with historical precision) that the approach leads to stagnant and soulless societies.

The Resurgence of Standards

The period following World War II, however, saw a new interest in the functional approach and the recapture of standards from the technicians. The Marshall Plan proved that multinational purposes could be implemented successfully, and the newly prestigious American influence was exercised on behalf of pan-European efforts.

The economic effort was mounted by the EEC, but its barely disguised military auxiliary—NATO—was headquartered across town in Brussels and reinforced these efforts. The EEC was seen as a snowballing operation, gaining momentum from its limited economic efforts in the European coal and steel community to its emergence as the European Economic Community and now the European Union. Even the Coal and Steel Community had structures associated with government, as opposed to strictly economic arrangements. The EEC's Parliament and court, and especially its far-reaching legal authority, stamped the EU as something more than the older forms of single-function international operations. Even on its face, the Treaty of Rome involves a protogovernment struggling to assert itself over parochial nationalism, but anxious to avoid any head-on confrontation with it. It is difficult to accept

Margaret Thatcher's argument that she was seduced into increasing European arrangements and was unaware that the wicked continentals expected more later.

Even more pointed than the document of the Treaty of Rome were the voiced aspirations of the Eurocrats and their true believers. Walter Hallstein, the active implementer of the EEC, had no doubt the community would eventually absorb defense functions, and articulated that view throughout the 1960s.[59] The argument of the neofunctionalist Hallstein was precisely that progress in one domain would create an imbalance between function and structure and would lead to changes in structure in other domains. Scholars such as Ernst Haas, Stuart Scheingold, and Leon Lindberg in political science, and Bela Belassa in economics, furthered this theme and influenced not only the bureaucrats but also the judges of the European Court.[60]

Denied much expansion of functions, the EEC technocracy paralleled the history of most continental bureaucracies. Technocrats concentrated on the powers they had, especially those deemed least controversial. In so doing, they stumbled on the importance of standards and helped revive large-scale policy interest in what had seemed a trivial industrial pursuit.

Parallel to that development in the EEC was the renewed international commitment to standards. In both instances, economic and equitable concerns dominated interest in standards in the latter half of the twentieth century, much as scientific and technical concerns underlay fin de siècle concerns.

The EEC came upon the issue of standards originally in its effort to stamp out parochial favoritism. The first major topic, discriminatory taxation, was to prove a secondary force, outweighed by "nontariff barriers." It was believed that, to eliminate local preference disguised as innocent, neutral regulation, local regulations on exports, imports, and actual use required "harmonization." When the smoke cleared, uniform regulations for a host of discriminatory products were in place, and it became clear that the community had benefited in numerous ways. The internal market was wider and more open, making many products available and profitable. Consumers benefited from greater competitiveness, compatibility of products, and the availability of replacement parts. In its effort to use performance and other genuine standards to ensure free competition, the Community did not so much concentrate on standardization as stumble upon it, backing into an emphasis on it step by step.

Much the same thing happened internationally. GATT principles were also designed to facilitate exchange by minimizing protectionism. The procedure was vastly enhanced by standards that permitted assessment of what was a relatively uncontaminated standard. Much of GATT was process oriented, calling for "transparency"; thus, unfair processes were prohibited. The substantive rules were even more vague. As a result, GATT established what are for the most part the principles under which nations spar, wrangle, and negotiate. There was also a slow and cumbersome GATT juridical process, but it was a last resort, and was seldom used. The cumulative effect is that discriminatory standards and processes have become the focus of controversy, and are generally fostered by governments only for politically and economically crucial industries, or at crucial times such as recessions and elections.

Paralleling all this was the establishment and emergence as a major player of the International Organization for Standardization (ISO).[61] The earliest international general-purpose standardizing organization was established in 1926 by some twenty different bodies as the International Federation of Standardizing Associations, or ISA. Given the times, it is not surprising to find that the strength of the organization was in the field of mechanical engineering. Several countries withdrew from membership in the late 1930s, and in 1942 the organization officially ended its efforts.

A temporary wartime organizing effort by the UN drew together eighteen countries. Later, in 1946, the ISO was established; it went into operation when the fifteenth nation ratified it on February 23, 1947. The organization had only modest results in its early years but began to move more rapidly and play a bigger role in the 1960s. Dramatically, it more than doubled its publication of standards between 1968 and 1971. By that time, its national membership had grown to seventy countries and its council represented twenty-eight nations. It also encouraged and cooperated with half a dozen or so regional associations. ISO has avoided most political power divisions by emphasizing technological fidelity, but its existence is particularly helpful to newcomer countries who wish to meet world product standards. It is not particularly controversial or creative but does much quantitatively and qualitatively to symbolize the internationalization of the market. It helped bring Japan and other Asiatic countries to a common awareness of standards under conditions that maximized considerations of science and quality rather than trade shares and competitiveness.[62]

The ISO, GATT (and its successor, the World Trade Organization), and EU constitute a relatively advanced institutionalization of both standards and principles about standards. They demonstrate the significance for international trade and symbolize the growing respect for the importance of standards, bringing them back to respectability and public attention.

The reemergence of standards as a popular focus in recent years is largely a product of a global economy. If goods and services are to be freely exchanged across boundaries, given the complexities of multiple legal systems, the nature of the transaction must be precisely identified. The complexities of legal issues are a strong argument for the desirability of up-front understanding. Worldwide ISO standards are difficult to negotiate, so other sources of definition also become more significant. In the wake of growing world trade, even self-definitions and avowals are useful for some purposes. Self-certification by a nation that it is meeting others' standards is at least an avowal and a warranty of sorts. ISO-9000, a form of such self-certification currently in the field of international requirements, is thriving and expanding.[63] Any regime of standards fosters communication and trust. High national standards and standards compatible with the purchasers' requirements are valuable, useful, and salable attributes. The claims of the standardization movement of the 1890s no longer seem so utopian and vague; in the 1990s they are hard-headed and are worth cash on the barrelhead.

3 The Many Faces of Standards

STANDARDS CAN BE USEFULLY REGARDED AS BUNDLES of information with different messages for different recipients. For producers, they represent blueprints, requirements, aspirations. For the consumer, they convey assurances, description, lists of ingredients, minimum levels of skill and attention. These are conveniently conveyed in summary form. The consumer need have only a minimal knowledge to read and understand them, but they tap into a broader range of information from producers. They are shorthand for precise blueprints, substitutes for experience and intuition; they are intended to bypass the need for testing.

Standards have many rivals and substitutes—subspecies, if you like. In the contemporary world, these include government regulation, brand names and labeling, and specified information. All these have distinct advantages and disadvantages for those involved, and have proven over time to have staying power in their own right.

The distinct advantages and disadvantages, the multiple purposes of each type of standard, shed light on why, historically, the standards movement fell apart. Different groups began to realize that their goals were not intrinsically the same. Such goals could best be pursued independently, rather than in tandem with those seeking other ends.

Government Regulation as Standards

Government regulations represent a rich source—historically, the richest source—of standards. Anything can be regulated and the most obvious source of enforcement is usually the preexisting police machinery, the long arm of the law. Groups that wish to establish their priorities and transfer costs, while at the same time exercising considerable coercive power, turn to government for regulation. This includes those who, for whatever reason, wish to formalize standards.

Turning to government is not without cost. This is true in the trivial sense that the initiating group will end up paying some share of the marginal cost generated by those regulatory schemes that do not recoup their costs through fees. Government regulation can also involve purposes quite remote from quality or information giving, and such broader goals will often be tacked onto standard setting. The coercive power of government and its multigroup, multipurpose nature mean that of all potential standard setters government is likely to have both the greatest means available for transstandard regulation and the greatest motivation for pursuing it.

A good example is meat regulation in medieval Europe. Generally, a town established a monopoly over slaughter in a meat market centered in town. This permitted a maximum of inspection at low cost, ensuring relatively high health standards. A tax based on purchase levels not only covered the costs of inspection and facilities but also raised revenue. It was often viewed as a sumptuary tax since meat was seen as a luxury, much as we now see it as unhealthy. Tax rates remained relatively low out of a fear that people would butcher their own meat in the country or that sale of such pirated meat in town would defeat the basic health and sanitation goals of the regulations.

But the regulatory scheme permitted much more than that. There were a finite number of stalls, so the number of butchers was limited. Licensure and assessment of fees were government prerogatives; established local families were usually favored and allowed to pass on the privilege as an inheritance, sometimes with a town tax exacted.

Other regulations followed: regulation of the days of the week or the season when meat could not be sold at all facilitated prohibition of consumption during prescribed holidays. Amounts or types of meat purchasable may have helped reinforce class lines. Work times could be enforced better in a visible, central place. The power to de-license was a weapon in the battle for public conformity.

"Who rides on a tiger cannot dismount." Government machinery has intrusive powers which by and large it defines. Fiscal costs may well begin to mount; government regulation can be a "buy now, pay later" arrangement of considerable size. More important, since policy formulation is in many hands and often anonymous, regulation can be unpredictable. Resorting to regulation for consumerist purposes entails regular monitoring, which consumer groups may not have the capacity to provide. Producers' purposes, on the other hand, are usually well defined and more or less continuous. Producers risk less, since they are likely to have well-understood demands and their expertise also makes it likely they will be consulted on most issues as a matter of course.

Much of this is summed up in the old populist slogan that opposes the creation of regulatory agencies on the grounds they risk "capture by the interests." The populists argue that regulatory agencies inevitably become arms of the group being regulated, since that group is invariably the major power base for that regulatory power. This suggests that standards would tend to be buttresses of monopoly, or that they privilege existing technology enhancing its capacity to recoup its investment. At worst (as notoriously with poultry inspection) regulation may involve a nominal maintenance of standards that deludes consumers into believing in nonexistent protection, at minimal cost to the producer.

Studies by James Q. Wilson and his students (not all of whom share his idealogy),[1] suggest that capture by the interests is by no means the usual state of affairs in an agency. "Capture" was historically an a priori claim, made in opposition to the very first major regulatory agency, the Interstate Commerce Commission (ICC). The best-known formulation of the thesis—Marver Bernstein's cycle of agencies—was also an excogitated, nonempirical, and nonhistorical argument.[2]

What careful chroniclers find is a much more fluid situation in which the inner life of the agency becomes more important than anticipated. Since neither the evolution and power of an industry nor the attitudes of political leaders are constant, this claim is persuasive.[3] Nonetheless, there is also evidence, at least in the American and Japanese systems (and some literature suggests in the EU), of what are called "iron" or "cozy" triangles, by means of which the business, political, and bureaucratic elites form a mutually supporting system.[4]

All too often, producers oppose initial standard setting and indeed most regulation, preferring simple subsidies. Most of the time, they not only make their peace with regulation, but come to welcome it. Most airlines resisted deregulation, though most banks did not. It is not clear whether this is simply human nature ("I don't want anyone telling me how to run my business, even if I'll sell more and earn more if the customer knows it's a safe product. They ought to trust me anyway.") or whether there is an investment and economic advantage in every way of doing business, so that any change entails risk and may well entail cost, thus breeding reluctance.

Economists have divergent views on the desirability of government standard making. Since fraud prevention is a government function, even in a night watchman state virtually everyone concedes the necessity for societal definitions. Otherwise, misrepresentation would be limited to an inquiry about the exact words of the parties in a myriad of instances and in a context devoid of implied standard meaning. Conversely, the potential abuse of standard making is obvious even to those who embrace regulation. In many ways, the most interesting questions are what the process costs and what the risks of manipulation might be. These risks include the effect of the system's rigidity and of time lags, alleged to be the consequence of politicizing aspects of economic life.

Few today embrace the view that government should not involve itself directly or indirectly in the definition or regulation of physicians and should simply let the consumer determine the pedigree and training of potential healers, with the marketplace weeding out incompetents in the "long run." The market model does not appeal to many when the price to be paid for "long run" efforts is so clear.

Neoclassicists such as Alfred Marshall and Charles Kindleberger note the advantages of standards. Kindleberger remarks at length on the assurance that comes through packaged information and offers a theoretical defense of standards.[5] At the same time, even strong regulatory advocates such as Walter Adams, a fervent critic of predatory large industry, note that the essence of monopoly is not typically collusion in pricing or even production, but generally involves control over the type of goods legally producible or similar regulatory arrangements. By definition, cartels implicate government approbation; Walter Adams and James W. Brock persuasively argue that monopolies do so as well.[6] Furthermore, for the powerful people who define standards, standardization easily lends itself to subtle advantages that are often indiscernible to the naked eye and may fall far short of monopoly.

It is not difficult to find individual examples of standards manipulation that benefits an interest. Naturally, there are many cases of dispute and judgment, but there are also instances of overwhelmingly clear bias and favoritism. The difficulty is that these instances, however extensive, are potentially offset by many "just so" stories of successful, profitable, and desirable standardization efforts by government. A study of gain and loss is difficult, since in real life only what is implemented produces observable results; all other cases must be evaluated on the basis of assumptions.

A classic tale of standards reemerged in 1994 over the definition of "fresh" and "frozen" poultry.[7] "Fresh" commands a premium of about fifty cents a pound. Department of Agriculture "policy" (a category of enforcement well below a formal "regulation," but one that major producers obey) defines "frozen" as zero degrees Fahrenheit or below. In 1988, in the last year of the Reagan administration, agriculture officials issued a new policy, based upon studies showing physical deterioration and ice crystallization beginning at twenty-six degrees Fahrenheit. Before the policy could go into effect, leading producers (including southern and border state poultry giants) put enormous pressure on the administration, pointing out that shipping of their products at higher temperatures would increase the growth of bacteria and that labeling freeze-chilled poultry as frozen would devastate the industry, which had come to rely on the department's definitions. Efforts to find an intermediate term failed: "Fresh frozen" loomed as an oxymoron and "chill-packed" was discovered to be a proprietary term already in use. The Reagan administration reversed itself in a new policy and the Bush administration never touched the issue.

California poultry interests regard "Southern chicken" as an invader, and the competition, thawed "fresh" chicken, as a fraud. The absurdity of U.S. definitions is that poultry can be shipped rock-hard, at temperatures well below normal home and commercial freezer temperatures, then thawed and sold as "fresh," with consequence for both taste and health, particularly when an unwary purchaser refreezes what was thought to be a never frozen product. Joining forces with consumer interests, the California poultry industry helped pass a bill unanimously through both houses of the legislature, based upon the USDA's 1988 findings. The state law was declared void, based upon federal preemption of poultry and meat regulation.

Nonetheless, the suit focused attention on the oddity of the existing definition. In the light of the Clintons' close contacts with both Tyson Poultry (an Arkansas-based giant) and consumerist organizations, the media raised embarrassing questions about inconsistency between pious aspirations and practical immobility. Vice President Gore's commission on restructuring government raised even more fundamental issues. It recommended all regulatory functions on meat be transferred to the FDA to eliminate conflict between the Department of Agriculture as a promotional unit built to serve farm interests and the department as a regulator.[8] The transfer was recommended as an efficiency measure as well, but the suggestion that the department was too responsive to producers and not responsible enough to consumers was also stressed.

Hearings in the summer of 1994 before a government operations sub-committee revealed much more. "Red meat," it became evident, is "fresh" even if frozen below zero degrees and then thawed; the department opposes "fresh" to "cured," and has no policy definition of "frozen." A study by Research Triangle Associates in 1994 was commissioned by the department to evaluate the laws and regulations applying to meats; it concluded that fowl regulation is more detailed and stringent, largely due to the fact that the basic law was passed fifty years later than the early "red meat" law. Although both laws have been amended and reenacted many times, the more regulatory atmosphere prevailing at the time of enactment has left the poultry regulations more comprehensive and strict on paper. Department representatives, however, reluctantly (and rather confusingly) noted that implementing a recent "action program" had made red meat inspection more effective and stringent than inspection of the poultry industry, where such a program was in "the planning stages."

A number of aspects of this case study are worth noting. The "problem" is a product of discrepancy between established standards and physical realities. No dilemma arises in Europe because "frozen" is defined as zero degrees Celsius (or thirty-two degrees Fahrenheit). It is possible, but not likely, that the specialized and somewhat strange dichotomies (fresh vs. frozen and fresh vs. cured) were initially created to the advantage of influential processors. Probably the ambiguities permitted a growing practice to minimize spoilage in poultry, extending available market delivery. The extent of frozen red meat sales is unknown; the problem is less detectable by taste and the supply market is less segmented, lowering the possibility of complaints or even discovery.

It is clear that, when the department sought to act in 1988, the industry raised significant objections merely to "precipitate action," but it won a total victory for a considerable length of time. The problem was not put on the table but recurred only due to the vagaries of politics.

The 1988 abdication was not craven, but was rather an acceptance of political reality. This was demonstrated when the department did propose revising the regulations to require "previously frozen" labels, in 1994–1995. Through a rider on the appropriation bill for the Department of Agriculture, Congress struck down the regulation. Led by Southern and border state delegations, they called the proposed labeling anticompetitive, an effort by California poultry dealers to impede the flow of interstate commerce. In 1996, the department resolved the matter by prohibiting the use of "fresh" in labeling poultry cooled below twenty-six degrees. However, it did not require any special labeling to indicate that thawing had occurred.

Such characteristic tugging and lurching have been emphasized by a neoliberal economist turned activist, Alfred Kahn. As a professor, New York State utilities commissioner, architect, and, as chair of the Civil Aeronautics Board, implementor of federal airline deregulation, he emphasized the dangers of standards and regulation generally, particularly with respect to mechanical or routine regulation, and the persistence of inappropriate, or especially, no longer worthwhile regulation.[9]

Since government standards are often the result of a catastrophe or of worst-case publicity, which are sometimes needed to overcome political inertia, rigidity is often a reaction to previous laxity.[10] It is also alleged that this pattern of response to crises only accentuates the tendency, in Stephen Breyer's expression, to expend the bulk of the effort to deal with the last 1 percent of the problem.[11] By focusing on unrealistic goals of purity, government budgets often do not reflect cost-efficient standards.

Certainly, the phenomenon of gold-plating exists. Justice Breyer has made a reasonably persuasive case for its extensive existence in the environmental field, but that is a regulatory area characterized by little experience, less knowledge, and excessively quick judgments on all sides. The Delaney Amendment is a manifestation of the same phenomenon.[12] But Naderites and the "Greens" have equal horror stories about measures being rendered ineffectual through compromise on "reasonable" accommodations. They make the case for holding out for the "last 1 percent," which turns out to be where the policy bite occurs.

While rigidity and excessive purity—an "all or nothing" enforcement—is said to prevail in government, this is hardly the whole story. Eugene Bardach and Robert Kagin found a pervasive phenomenon of the "good inspector," who helped inspectees reach standards while turning a blind eye to immediate violations, so long as progress was being made. David Vogel argues that the English favor such a flexible practice as their national regulatory style. While he later came to view this as less dominant than he originally thought, he clearly demonstrates both its use and effectiveness in improving English water quality. In obvious contrast, the virtual elimination of smog in London involved zero tolerance, heavy fines, and immediate action.[13] And, as noted earlier, Ross Cheit's small sample of regulations found government regulation more rigid and more far-reaching than voluntary ones, but to a far lesser degree than he had anticipated.

In short, both the positive and negative aspects of standards have been documented. And yet, no one has attempted to create a balance sheet of standardization or find the proper mix of political and economic theory,[14] or even developed a theory of the optimal conditions for such standardization. Only anarchic thinkers exclude all political regulation, and every known society, past and present, has enacted and enforced standards. A weak theory about when government specification of standards is inappropriate has been developed, and some rather vague characteristic costs have been identified.

Trade Associations and Guilds as Certifiers

Historically, the main alternative to government standards has been the voluntary trade association or guild. It is often difficult to distinguish between guild action and government regulation since, historically, guild regulations were often enforced through the state or powers conferred upon the guild by the state. These sometimes included licensure fines or access to markets. Additionally, guilds achieved independent power of inspection and enforcement, including the legendary Northern European Hansa, which had its own complex legal system. In the modern world, the trade association is usually less intimately a partner, constituent, or agency of government, but nonetheless, the very concept of a trade association engenders not just suspicions, but presumptions of predatory collusion. Why should dealers cooperate except to gain advantage? And at whose expense, other than the customer's, the public's? If Adam Smith's suggestion is true, that when two businessmen play golf, a conspiracy against the public good is inevitable, what may one expect from regularized interaction by business rivals? If we view with suspicion government regulation as a tool easily leveraged by the nominally regulated, what cynicism is adequate to account for "self-regulation"?

There are, however, many positive contributions to the public good, that are generated by such associations, both theoretically and demonstrably. Not the least of these are standards beneficial to both the constituents of the association and to the general public.

With respect to creation of interchangeability, simplification, and other forms of reducing inventory complexity, voluntary associations offer another (perhaps the most natural) forum where rivals in industry can compare notes and reach agreements, explain their problems and share solutions. There are many interindustry issues that can be best agreed upon by universal rather than biparty negotiation. Many of these will involve economies of scale or economies through compatible practice. Some benefits may ultimately be passed on to the public in the form of lower prices or better service.

Like governments, associations may set quality standards for both internal and external dealings and may establish enforcement machinery and penalties. In both cases, there is efficiency in such standardizations and often advantages in salability or augmented value or profit, as a result of this warranty by a party external to the sale.

The system breaks down quickly when challenged from any source. The association generally tries to function as an independent third-party umpire, but it is ultimately an agent of one side or the other. This affects its credibility on the one hand and its freedom on the other. Like sports commissioners, trade associations are arbiters within very narrow limits, but are instruments or agents within rather broader boundaries. Like Better Business Bureaus, they tackle small, flagrant violations of minor enterprises but avoid basic or pervasive problems fundamental to transactions.

Voluntary associations are typically subject to "free rider" problems.[15] Nonparticipants may often enjoy the benefits of "public goods" without paying the freight. Standard-quality goods will often be available and identifiable even to those who do not pay for maintenance of the defining association or subscribe to its regulation. For example, an enterprise may be able to produce and sell not only standard but substandard or above-standard products without joining the association.

Because of "free rider" problems an association may be discouraged from making tough decisions; a major enterprise may withdraw in whole or in part. This poses a serious threat of damage to the organization, its finances, and the regulatory regime. This threat is always present and participants must be conscious of it. Voluntary associations resemble mediators more than adjudicators in terms of their ambiguous rights of office, weak law and minimal powers of enforcement. The threat of exit—in Hirschman's terms—is omnipresent.

If government is viewed by theorists as a priori inclined to rigid, over-punitive, overreactive attempts to deal with historic catastrophes, self-regulation is viewed as overly weak and often delusory. Some writers suggest it is essentially a sham; trade associations police violations that would cost their members dearly in lawsuits or government prosecution, but wink at infringement of other regulations.[16]

Others blandly accept voluntary regulations at face value. There are professional aspirations at stake and reputation is money, they argue. Consumers are sophisticated: they punish poor quality and violations of established standards.

Violations—even gross violations—are too common for us to have faith in the reality of self-regulation, but its theoretical justification is also too evident for us to dismiss it cavalierly. The consumer seems surprisingly protean:

he or she remembers some publicized transgressions and acts on them, but in most instances is easily manipulated by bland public assurances and public image games.

The best judgment is that voluntary regulation is less than draconian, but by no means irrelevant or ineffectual.[17] Self-regulation tends to err on the side of consensus and practicability, but certainly leads to reasonable standards of safety, since it is costly for the manufacturer to pay damages for defective products.

While prototype standards in voluntary regulation are only slightly less restrictive than government standards (though differences may be significant), enforcement is likely to be considerably more lax. Associations have little policing power and are less likely than government to discipline or coerce. The net effect, according to the prevailing literature, is that voluntary standards result in a weaker, though perhaps more generally obeyed, standard.[18] In times of stress, in weaker firms, or under pressure for profits, violations can easily occur with relative impunity. To be sure, the literature on the "free rider" problem suggests that other inducements can be added to secure adherence, ranging from insurance programs to prestigious honors and awards. Obviously, trade associations are skilled practitioners of ancillary inducement, but the bottom line is not likely to be altered. Major companies would balk at truly tough standards and would be likely to bridle and bolt.

The case for voluntarism must then be made in terms of process (greater flexibility of procedure, ease of participation by the truly expert, and a more scientific and less bureaucratic, legalistic, or political proceeding); content (increased probability of meaningful and achievable goals, phrased in terms understood by and acted upon by the regulated); cost and efficiency of developing and modifying standards; and increased adherence to standards at the nonpunitive and regulatory level.

Three studies have attempted to give a rough measure of these assessments. Cheit's study indicates that voluntary standards and government standards are more alike than had been theoretically predicted, but that the fundamental nature of the difference between them was correctly predicted.[19] The late Robert Dixon, distinguished scholar and former Department of Justice official, undertook an evaluation of the National Fire Protection Association (NFPA) as a result of antitrust troubles. He gained access to a critique of existing practice of the self-regulation system in an internal memo of the Department of Commerce by filing a Freedom of Information Act request. The departmental memo listed twenty-eight cases deemed failures of the voluntary system, one of which Dixon characterizes as at least as much a consequence of the Department of Housing and Development's actions as those of the standard setter. In three instances, the voluntary regulatory organization criticized by the memo granted previously denied approval when faced with a suit. For Dixon, this begs the question: did they merely retreat when they should have fought? Without attempting a technical assessment, Dixon concludes that only two, or perhaps three, allegations of favoritism through standards appeared justified. The provenance of the assessment (a study on behalf of a voluntary standardizer) and the casualness of Dixon's evaluation make this somewhat dismissive conclusion unconvincing. Even so, it seems clear that the commerce department's list was neither qualitatively nor quantitatively much of an indictment of the voluntary system even if taken at face value.[20]

The most extensive study of the system, by Dale Hemenway,[21] sets forth a rigorous theoretical argument in favor of limitations, and details the failings of voluntarism in a generic sense rather than in specific cases. While more extensive than Cheit's and more intensive than Dixon's, this study gives no sense of how common the problems may be and provides little guidance for measuring the magnitude of the achievements or transgressions of voluntary standard setters.

One can also glean some sense of the problems from recurring antitrust cases involving standards. About a dozen of these have reached the decision stage and are therefore reported as federal cases. It is hard to know how many of these are also reported in Hemenway and the Department of Commerce memo alluded to by Dixon. On the whole, those cases seem to involve a variety of specific complaints, many of them unusual. These cases do not suggest a pervasive or systemic weakness.

Dixon's theoretical discussions are much more impressive and convincing than his treatment of actual infringements, especially the seriousness with which he tackles the issue of representativeness and representation in standard-setting organizations. *Democratic Representation,* which won the Woodrow Wilson Foundation Book Award was no doubt one reason the NFPA (which was being sued for letting its "majoritarian" processes be abused), turned to him for guidance.[22]

In a modified *Federalist* analysis, Dixon suggests that the scope of interests embraced by a standard setter may test the legitimacy of its work. An organization representing a broad consensus combining both experts and practical-minded utilizers of standards may be a more valid formulator of durable policy than a group based on either political majoritarianism or internal democracy. Standard-setting organizations based on consensus may result in minimal regulation, but, if adroitly organized, may also minimize abuse and self-serving actions. (The NFPA created additional, less majoritarianist, veto mechanisms to respond to claims of industry manipulation of standards, as did ASTM. Eventually, ANSI imitated them by also creating an appeals mechanism within the organization.)[23]

The natural basis for such an approach exists in hybrid organizations such as NFPA, which has regulators, safety experts, and insurers watching each other with Madisonian awareness. This creates factional and countervailing powers. ASTM's problem is even knottier; it has "individual memberships," all nominally disinterested. By and large, such an organization is more easily captured. In practice, companies provide the bulk of the organization's income by advertising and by paying dues for many of its members. In addition, as amicus curiae briefs in the *Hydrolevel* case emphasize, committee members and other "volunteers" typically work at their posts on company time and have their expenses paid by their firms.[24] While standards activity is enriching and expands the expertise of participants, companies obviously view it as an investment in outcomes as well as in their employees.

It is paradoxical that nominally individualized "objective" membership groups are usually more open to exploitation and "capture" than "mixed" groups with organizations directly represented or with sectorial representation (e.g., government, research, industry, and consultants). Dixon's advice to build upon differentiation and create more than one forum with multiple vetoes may be less applicable to some organizations than to others, but it has been attractive to leading standard setters.

The message is clear. If your mission is similar to that of a government, you must be more like a polity.[25] Since the basis of the organizational authority is not really democratic, but rather grounded in expertise and experience, more diverse internal structures based on those qualities are called for. Like a polity, standard-setting organizations must be not simple but richly textured.

Interestingly enough, economists have found parallel theoretical and empirical evidence to support this proposition. Standards organizations with broad concerns are more likely to advance standards that encompass "public" concerns and are less likely to be challenged as protectionist.[26]

It is hard to imagine the U.S. government suddenly faced with the necessity of redefining fifty thousand standards, or at least, the fraction of that number that would be absolutely necessary for industrial and commercial life. The variety of organizations, methods, and justifications that exist should be a source of comfort and pride to all pluralists, who want life and norms to take place outside the sovereign state as much as possible. The high repute of ANSI and ASTM standards outside the United States and their use in many systems with government-defined standards suggests (though it does not prove) that a voluntary system does not necessarily develop standards that err on the side of protectionist exclusivity or lax anticonsumerism.

Brand Names and Self-Labeling

When a restaurateur proclaims a dish "specialty of the house," there are three standards issues involved. First, the dish may not be one you like; hence the label is irrelevant for you. Second, the assertion may not be true; the dish may be "the highest markup in the restaurant" or "yesterday's leftovers" aggressively marketed to strangers and one-time customers. Finally, the label may be true, but the chef may be bad or inconsistent. In essence, self-definition of standards rests on an estimation of the veracity, skill, and dedication of the producer, in other words, of "that priceless ingredient, the integrity of the maker."

The own-brand vendor such as Sears Roebuck (before it turned to outside brands) asserted it stood behind its products, which by and large it did. It gave few assurances of quality, however. Presumably, the price reflected the value. Some stores had "testing programs" and made assertions about value, but these were not consistently applied throughout a store and its methods were not familiar enough to customers to convince them they could buy with a specific knowledge of the qualities of the product. It was the store's name and assurance that customers relied on, rather than, say, assertions that the product was grade AA. A higher price might reflect durability or expensive materials or a premium paid for fashion; thus, apart from the store name, the information conveyed was not always reliable. Once the enterprise became larger than a Ma and Pa store, the unreliability of clerks and incomparability of individual outlets also created problems.

Brands seek to fill that gap. They reassure consumers that they can rely on continued assured quality even as they repeatedly announce the product is "new and improved." How the consumer adjusts psychologically to this paradox is not clear; presumably, they assume that only tiny changes occur and that they are truly "improvements." Most brand loyalists probably assume continuity and, if they notice "new and improved" claims, discount them. In the end, trust in a brand name revolves around confidence that the maker will be careful not to jeopardize his investment by destroying the brand name's image through lower quality. New products are assumed to be of comparable value.

This presupposes that the brand image rests on quality and that the consumer really can tell the difference. Even with a product line such as canned food, however, which is evaluated close to home, consumer taste seems to be affected more by product labeling and image than by the can's contents. Consumers Union's tests consistently showed the Ann Page line of canned goods, marketed by the declining food giant A&P, to be better than those it was priced to immediately undersell, and even better than supposedly premium products selling at several cents (and a hefty number of percentage points) more per can. The A&P product in a dowdy can, sold in small, dowdy stores, was a superior product sold at a bargain price, but was perceived universally by consumers as of average quality. The premium price product lines, average or slightly above average products that were highly advertised and sold in cans with colorful labels, were highly regarded.

When A&P was drastically downsized, moving from the leading food chain in America to a struggling localized enterprise, it found it an asset to sell off its high-quality plants. The overpriced, highly touted food lines of the 1930s also experienced difficulties, and are now much smaller enterprises with fewer products. But their brand names have remained an asset and are sold at a premium. The Ann Page and other A&P lines were not an asset and, with a few exceptions (coffee, for example), have disappeared.

Reliance on the manufacturer is usually, but not always, reciprocated. Small companies often sell out to big ones. Big companies may have a different concept of what a reasonable earnings ratio is, or to what extent quality contributes to the sale. Products may be upgraded or downgraded by decision of the new investor, who may have built up considerable debt and be anxious to dissolve it. Often a subtle, creative edge is lost when a company, distinguished for its innovation as an extended Ma and Pa store, a labor of love, is absorbed into a large, investment-oriented bookkeeping conglomerate. A chain of Bob's ice cream parlors may have Bob's recipes and patents, and Bob may be doing publicity for it, but it may not have the brilliance and consistency it had when Bob was mixer, taster, and dreamy-eyed dispenser. Purchasers of fashion labels and clothing lines are notorious for ruthlessly exploiting the reputation of an acquired name. They cash in quickly on shoddy or lower-quality merchandise before the consumers catch on.

Change of ownership is only one way products deteriorate or fail to keep step with rivals. Brand names insulate producers from the consequences of slippage in standards, but presumably the consumer detects departures over times. The information conveyed by the label is no longer fully valid and may continue to mislead, but not indefinitely. Most consumers are not one-brand fanatics, but exhibit brand preference or choose from a range of brands. Small changes in price, fashion, or quality can therefore lead to shifts that are much more rapid than a total loyalty model would suggest. When Coca-Cola found a majority of its own users preferred a lighter, Pepsilike flavor, it felt it had to move in that direction and announced "new Coke." The furor of the loyalists forced the restoration of Classic Coke, which remains the best seller to this day. Presumably, a significant number of Classic consumers like the taste of new Coke or Pepsi under blind testing, but prefer the "classic" experience over the choice their taste buds would make.

At the time, some cynics suggested Coca-Cola had deliberately maneuvered to create a great launching pad for dividing its brand, establishing two product lines, and successfully garnering free publicity. But the company's panic in coping with the problem seemed genuine, costs of quickly restoring Classic Coke were higher than they had to be, and the perceived threat that management might topple has convinced observers that this was, in fact, a classic case of miscalculating the delicate nature of brand identity and brand loyalty.

An extreme example of brand manipulation, albeit under monopoly conditions, was the Soviet labeling game. In many product lines, two brands were maintained: one standard, one premium. Since the Eastern bloc maintained that socialism immunized it against inflation, and that pricing was solely determined by social factors, increases typically came by "eliminating" the standard brand and introducing a new premium brand. The old premium price was now being paid for what was in fact the old standard brand, and the old premium product had a new name and higher still price. The sequence of this maneuver could vary, but Soviet consumers, having detected it in the ever sensitive vodka prices, garnered what enjoyment they could from detecting the onset of the ploy with other products.

There has been a proliferation of brand names amassed by successful companies and aimed at various levels of the quality market. Proctor & Gamble, for example, has half a dozen laundry detergents in addition to the giant bestseller, Tide. Such efforts, when successful, not only bring in profits but also discourage competition by blanketing the market. However, product diversification and products in competition with one another often require bureaucratic segmentation and increased staffing to coordinate rival advertising, distribution, and production, which a company may feel necessary to be competitive. Product line differentiation may result in more fixed "niche" patterns so as not to compete with other lines, freezing innovation, or, as in General Motors, multiple products may overlap (as with the highest priced Buick and lowest priced Cadillac). For many reasons, it is difficult to keep competing multiproduct enterprises lean and trim.

The 1990s have become notorious as a period for downsizing enterprises, and especially managerial bureaucracies. Just as robotics once permitted owners to eliminate workers who were performing routine repetitive tasks, the computer permitted them to eliminate middle managers making routine decisions.

Brand-centered enterprises have joined in that slimming of the workforce, as even profitable businesses such as Proctor & Gamble face the recessionary 1990s. Such companies have seen market share slip and the cost of brand recognition costs.[27] They are particularly affected by growth of chain and store-owned brands. Unlike the old A&P tradition, in today's market the store's label appears side by side with national brands, and generally boasts a "compare our value" sign. Often these store brands are manufactured by prominent companies willing to produce off-brands at prices that represent their marginal cost plus the usual profit, or less.

The question raised by lower market share is whether off-brand purchasing represents a short-term reaction to recurrent economic squeezes or something more enduring. Proctor & Gamble's downsizing in 1993 was motivated by studies indicating that even prosperous consumers increasingly regard name brands as quality products, but believe they are overpriced relative to equal or not decidedly inferior store brands.

Concluding that this was a long-range development not limited to immediate economic pessimism, Proctor & Gamble has cut down on name brands, consolidated marginal and struggling brands, and limited new products or brands.

In summary, we can draw three conclusions. First, brand names convey information that depends on consistent behavior from producers, but permits considerable market manipulation by them. Second and not surprisingly, producers tend to favor brand names over rival information systems. "Trust Me" is not the exclusive ploy of manufacturers and can sometimes be in the best interests of those addressed. Third, in the modern world, the quality of information, as well as the quality delivered by brand products, is probably increasing, but it is also probably overpriced. In short, brand names will survive, but the strategies behind them will have to be carefully reconsidered.

Special approval seals, usually letters of the alphabet in some distinctive but unobtrusive logo format, compete with brand names. These seals may be the registered mark of a self-chosen authority or group. The seal simply asserts that the product involved meets whatever criteria the group has established.

We may learn that a product is made of pure wool, is believed to be electrically safe, complies with kashruth laws (at least as interpreted by a group of rabbinic authorities of a known orientation), or is "guaranteed" to perform as specified in the advertising pages of *Good Housekeeping* magazine. The use of approval logos is flexible and any group may contract to give its approval to any products that potential consumers may desire.

Perhaps the oldest continuous use of such seals is the stamping of a K sign on eighteen-carat gold, though this is more an example of self-certification than of third-party approval. The first important use in the United States was the UL sign of Underwriters Laboratory, but that group does not claim to be the first of its kind. It is likely that the practice was obvious, having long been present, for example, in guild insignia, though wide awareness of it seems to be a product of this century.

The creation of Underwriters Laboratory by the insurance industry was motivated by a desire to lower fire rates.[28] Electric devices and insulation were its first specialty, though it will on contract test all kinds of equipment and award use of its logo. To assure a reputation for objectivity, it freed itself from underwriters and is now a nonprofit independent operation. Like most certifiers, it therefore depends on fees for financing. It has been criticized for unimaginative testing methods and occasionally for excessively minimalist standards, but since many products that fall below its requirements can still meet government requirements, this criticism seems harsh.

UL has not been aggressive in helping importers. For example, it maintains a bare-bones staff—three or four persons in 1993—in Japan, who can arrange for specialists to be flown in (at great expense) to test goods proposed to be shipped to the United States.[29]

In many Asian countries, the relatively weak consumerist groups have organized to provide a mark—usually a variation of an S, which means it meets either a safety test set by the organization or recognized international or national standards. In essence, these groups are deeply influenced by the widespread use of known symbols in the Japanese system, where the government and private groups set conditions for use of such symbols. In so doing, consumer groups make themselves vulnerable to the inevitable charge that they tailor standards to secure fees.

In contrast, the strategy of the American consumer organizations has been to build membership and revenue around their informational magazines. Evaluative reports of products do not oblige them to endorse those products. (They have sued, with varying success, producers who use their ratings in advertising.) The Japanese and the Americans thus have quite different strategies.

The *Good Housekeeping* endorsement is intriguing in that it is accompanied by a guarantee, made necessary by the obvious fact that the magazine benefits enormously from advertisers who pay its very high page rates. Unlike Underwriters Laboratory or consumer groups, it is an avowedly profit-making enterprise whose main income comes from advertising. It maintains an operation to test product claims, but without the guarantee, it would presumably accept advertising from products that do not meet their tests. That guarantee raises the question of the efficacy of their tests, since giving a product a failing mark diminishes revenue in significant ways and might tempt the magazine to adopt latitudinarian standards.

Clothing is an area where labeling has always been important, since fashion design is built on names and symbols. The fact that many of the "big names," like Bill Blass, neither design nor manufacture most of the products bearing their name is known to many who buy them. Blass is assumed to have given approval both for appearance and wearability. (Similarly, import wine labels sport the name of American experts to indicate they have passed a personal, informed taste test.) Union labels in clothing indicate American origins, but by and large unions have been unsuccessful in conveying just what their arcane method of evaluating clothing products means. The ratings seem to be based on the amount of labor required rather than the skill.

The success of the all-wool mark has led other fabric industries to imitate it, though with conspicuously less impact. In those cases, an industrywide operation licenses use, but it is easier for consumers to accept the claim of "all wool" than a claim of "all safe" by the producer doubling as tester. The fiber indicator carries prestige but also gives directions concerning care and cleaning of the product.

An intriguing example of third-party logo certification occurs in the case of Jewish dietary laws. Kosher products command a premium since they may involve extra steps to comply with rabbinic law and always involve the extra cost of inspection. State governments have brought fraud charges against those who sell nonkosher goods as kosher; the court decisions generally have been supportive, but at the fringes such laws present constitutional issues. For example, the New Jersey Supreme Court held in 1991 that a state board—which by law included rabbis—set up to rule on what was kosher[30] involved "establishment of religion," even though the board had never been consulted by the enforcing inspectors. Further decisions, dating back to the first quarter of the century, have made it clear that supportable claims of kashruth (even when contested by persons who consider themselves more observant) cannot be suppressed. The Union of Orthodox Rabbis therefore developed the U logo over half a century ago, so that its adherents could know which products met with their approval. Other groups with different standards of kashruth have also taken up the practice. It is currently estimated there are over two hundred such symbols.[31] Some Muslims accept kashruth as equivalent to *halāl,* since the basic rules are very similar. As Muslims grow in number and affluence, they seem likely to develop their own notation.

Because most products are in themselves kosher, but are inspected to prevent intrusion of nonkosher contaminants, the automation of closed assembly lines in food production has made it extremely easy to certify such products. Manufacturers therefore acquiesce to the U or other licensure since they can add a new clientele at small cost. Alternatively, producers can assert their belief they are producing a kosher product by using the letter K, which, for historical reasons, cannot be registered.

The kashruth example indicates the flexibility of the logo certification method. Kashruth adherence is in general terms the same for all those observing it. But inevitably, some groups or sects differ in their emphases or interpretations. They can develop their own logo and adherents can in effect look for certification by their own authorities for their specific preferences. Others will find less guidance. Those Muslims who are more lenient in their rules on specific matters have no difficulty, but those with stricter standards take their chances. Strict vegetarians and those who are lactose intolerant may generally rely on a "kosher" ("pareve," containing neither meat nor dairy products) but run the risk that the item contains fish products. The system is in accordance with a code in both senses of the term—cryptic and legalized. The code is easily obtainable, an open book, but few actually wish to pursue the matter. Indeed, the whole thrust of the logo system is to say, "You know us. We do the tough work. We are identified with you. Trust us."

The difficulties in enforcement on a "voluntary" basis became apparent with the emergence of a publication devoted primarily to "customer alerts" involving clear or incidental misuse of kashruth designations. Since labeling foods kosher is a public function, the easy violations with little consequence offer unusual insight into the problem of voluntarism in this area—against the logic of the New Jersey Supreme Court which suggested even state enforcement of fraudulent claims was probably unnecessary, when logos could do the job.

The publication *Kashrus* appears five times yearly and offers ten dollars to readers who find a verified violation. The September 1995 issue lists twenty-eight new unauthorized uses of symbols, and twenty-five continuing abuses, some by major national companies. They list another forty or so problems of misleading designations at various levels of seriousness to the users; these are by national producers, who are perhaps unaware of subtle changes or are reluctant to change wrappers for a small part of their clientele.

In the areas of safety, quality, and durability, reliance on stamps of approval becomes almost as complete as that on brand names. Instead of trusting a profit-making manufacturer, we rely on expert engineers, consumerists, environmentalists—in short, on people like us.

The difficulty is that there is little room for gradations, which can be important in conveying information. Those who want tougher electric safety standards are not likely to agree on which particular steps are absolutely required; they do not have the cohesiveness of sects, who can organize to create small variations built on specific trust. It is easier (and probably more productive) to lobby Underwriters Laboratory to be more stringent than to attempt to duplicate it.

While those who would wish to develop specific targets, such as greater protection for the environment, have organized groups and could—like sects—develop a set of gradations in logos and a variety of stands, quality is even more difficult to represent and agree upon. In that area, the first organization to form tends to persist and its minimum standards dominates. Refinement comes with a restatement of the standards for conferring the logo, not with a multiplication of logos. For example, the EC has developed a symbol to designate products that have been produced, and that can be disposed of, in environmentally sound ways.[32]

Identification by symbol may be broad or narrow. Restaurants may use the heart symbol of the American Medical Association for dishes with reduced cholesterol levels. The American Dental Association approves cavity-reducing toothpastes and mouthwashes.

Succinct summary information need not be an endorsement or statement of quality. In EC countries, irradiated food products must be identified by a (rather attractive) green-white flower symbol. Irradiated milk is sold in the United States as well, with a shelf life of some weeks printed on the package; milk is the most common irradiated product. American consumer groups have continually fought introduction of such products, ostensibly because many consumers will not know they are buying irradiated products, but also because these groups are opposed to such products under any circumstances.

There is little opposition to identifying poisons or dangerous objects. The cigarette industry, which once vigorously opposed the Surgeon General's warnings about the dangers of smoking, now welcomes them as a defense against consumers' claims that they were not aware of the risks.

Controversy over dating perishable meat and dairy products has been stilled by the grocery industry's own studies indicating open dating (as opposed to coding) helps clerks in handling inventory, and saves as much money or more than is lost by customers who refuse to buy the less fresh, but still good, items.

Third-Party Evaluation and the American Consumer Movement

Consumerists were unhappy with the refusal by the Natural Bureau of Standards to publish product evaluations done for government agencies. This led them to become progressively estranged from that organization, and ultimately, there emerged two parallel membership groups, each publishing periodicals summarizing the results of their respective testing of products. The origins of the dual movement hinged on personalities and political affiliations, and originally, some differences in emphasis regarding the relationship to the cooperative movement and other nonprofit alternatives to consumer capitalism. Over time, both organizations concentrated on consumer evaluation processes; the main difference between the groups now is that the more prosperous *Consumers Report* can typically test more models and is printed more handsomely and on better paper than *Consumers Guide*. The two groups borrow each other's methods, have learned from each other's mistakes, and have grown more alike over time. *Consumers Report* has benefited from its superior profitability and has diversified to provide health and travel information, but both reports have become increasingly concentrated on automobiles and other middle-class purchases, far from their original notion of helping the small goods purchaser or average consumer.[33]

The original approach of the movement was muckraking, exposing "lemons" and false advertising in the mode continued by television's consumerist David Horowitz. The *Uncle Tom's Cabin* of the consumerist movement was a work by two of its leaders, Arthur Kallet and F. G. Schlink, *One Hundred Million Guinea Pigs*.[34] It was replete with horrors, such as the fact that a trapped German spy committed suicide to avoid questioning by swallowing a tube of a popular toothpaste. (It is possible to commit suicide by ingesting large doses of many normally safe products.) The implication of the book was that American products were designed solely to make a profit and to fool consumers, with utter disregard for the health and safety of the individual and the welfare of society.

Originally, then, consumer magazine ratings were designed to uncover and prevent threats to health and safety and to sniff out fraud. It encouraged consumers to "fight back" (the title of Horowitz's program). But testing led in a different direction. It was relatively easy for consumers to avoid poor products; by and large, major brand names were dependable. Consumer evaluations eventually took on a much harder task—maximizing value. Furthermore, by listing specific advantages and disadvantages of a product, they allowed consumers to choose the particular assets qualities they preferred. A magazine article could educate consumers regarding the range of qualities that experts valued and could make them more sophisticated in their choices. It could also provide summary evaluations—"excellent" or "poor"—and convey other facts. "Best buy" ratings represent maximum value for the dollar; the "best buy" may be the third-rated product, since the premium charged by the top two may be deemed excessive. Ratings may assess one type of car as superior for long-distance driving, another for braking, quick starts, roominess, or durability.

Obviously, a long and detailed article contains more information than a logo or brand name. Nonetheless, readers must rely on the honesty of reported results, and must trust that tests are reasonable evaluations of the quality desired in the product. In most instances, test procedures are reported so that knowledgeable people can evaluate the tests. There is an obvious problem, however. With so many different products, consumer groups can afford to test only one sample, or at most a few samples, of individual models. This assumes product stability and quality consistency, which may or may not be there.

The effect of such information on the American consumer has been quite different from what was originally intended. With all its imperfections (particularly susceptibility to sampling problems), testing results have been much more sophisticated than most other evaluative information. On the whole, the testing of the two organizations and their results over time show reasonable reliability and consistency. The underlying information, however, though indicating many anomalies in product lines, still shows considerable correlation between price and quality. In most instances, consumers were educated to want more from products—to seek maximum value from them—rather than to find the minimum cost product to do the essential job. It is possible to glean which is the cheapest workable product by considering the data, but that has not been the focus. In a consumerist society growing steadily more affluent, the magazines trained and informed people about the range of product attributes, e.g., truly high fidelity equipment or the newest photographic materials. To accommodate such a consummate readership, the reports concentrated on products where quality was not self-evident and where testing might reveal hidden problems. In short, they provided increasing evidence to inform the larger, more consequential, and less repeated decisions people make. They still evaluate dairy products, food products, paper goods, and cleansers, though with less frequency; they also increasingly note that the taste or appearance of food is a personal matter, not the result of the objective qualities of ingredients. Not only are the publications less shrill and moralizing, their subscribers are now affluent, sophisticated, and demanding, but they are still unmistakably consumers. Far from rebelling against or being estranged from the marketplace, they are its most avid devotees. Moralists do not need consumer reports. Buyers do.

No doubt the consumerist movement has raised product standards, but it has raised two or three generations of consumers with elevated and expensive tastes as well. That would surprise and probably disappoint the founders, who had a streak of moralist economizing in their makeup.

Grading and Self-Certification

The establishment of a classification or grading system with the actual rating of the product in private or regulatory hands can be an efficient form of government regulation, even though the system may be wholly or partly independent from government. Generally, government classification of goods one by one is inefficient. Enforcement through sampling, through consumer familiarity with the system, and through special sanctions for fraud and penalties for mislabeling can result in saving money.

Such systems may result from guildlike agreements to facilitate handling of goods. The number of carats in a diamond is precisely determined and is seldom misstated by reputable dealers. There are other factors that influence price—cut and brilliance—but carat numbers permit discussion around a stable factor.

More commonly, the classification is more subjective and more complex, and therefore likely to require government sanctions. The most familiar of those arrangements is U.S. government inspection and grading of meat and poultry. The grading system is highly politicized and subject to dramatic manipulation. Because inspection is theoretically individualized for appearances' sake, the system is less than an unqualified success.

The case of beef grading is a good example. For years, the classification "premium grade" required fine marbling—kobe-like, superfat beef from carefully nurtured steers, thus with a luscious and characteristic beef flavor. That grade was almost automatically sold to steakhouses and restaurants, seldom appearing in supermarkets or butcher shops. The remaining meat was also evaluated for other qualities and assigned grades indicating its ultimate flavor and texture. When Americans began to be more aware of the dangers of fat in the diet, the industry altered its own pattern of "finishing," i.e., fattening the animals for the market, to help assure continued profitability for a shrinking industry. The Department of Agriculture in effect adopted roughly the same strategy as the Soviet brand name ploy. It raised the grade label on each type of meat: commercial became good, and good became prime. Quite legitimately, it argued that it was reflecting a new emphasis on less fat in the diet. At the same time, it was now able to label more meat at grades whose classification was attractive to the consumer. This was primarily a response to the threat of losing even more cattle raisers if accommodation (and a rise in earnings) did not take place.

The system of grading each unit by government inspection seldom operates as intended. Deming argues that most item-by-item inspection is inherently self-defeating.[35] Government budgets inevitably skimp, and at some point, inspection becomes nominal. In the United States, poultry inspection, combined with assembly line procedures, are often seen as actually promoting contamination, while red meat inspection is essentially pro forma, but not ineffectual.

Grading and type classification combined with continual sampling is often a preferred method. In manufacturing, where units are much more interchangeable, sampling reveals virtually all defects present and allows for an estimate of their frequency. Since animal disease is more commonly unique to the animal, and since "dressing" animals is not typically the cause of disease, inspection by sampling will not yield the same level of information. Arguably, contaminant effects would be detected, but the risks from a diseased animal are different from those of a poorly assembled brake mechanism.

The advantage of such classifications and self-inspection is apparent in connection with type classification and self-certification of automobiles. Consumers can rely on manufacturers' inspection because of the visibility of misrepresentation and because of dealer and consumer vigilance.

Then, too, the system ultimately rests on the much-abused American liability system.[36] The threat of high-cost litigation and withdrawal of insurance protection keeps self-certifiers generally reliable, since liability increases astronomically with evidence of knowing misclassification. Nonetheless, neither the Europeans nor the Japanese share our enthusiasm for self-certification.

In our system, self-classification is routinely accepted, even with respect to imports and customs taxes. Adherence to domestic standards is accepted on the manufacturer's say-so, with occasional quality checks. In a sense, the manufacturer warrants the level of compliance and reliability. The savings on red tape and bureaucracy apparently outweigh occasional slipups, provided the inspection sampling is adequate to detect deliberate and systematic fraud.

Theoretically, type grading and individualized assignment of grades could be conducted entirely by the government, entirely by the producer, or by some mixed system; grades could be established by an industrywide committee, for example. But an all-producer system instills little more confidence than do brand names. Since grading is usually subjective, producers going through such a decision process in public add little to consumer confidence. Such a procedure is therefore infrequent, but both grading and inspection by non-government third parties are quite common. Large-scale sale of food supplies for animals or the wholesale sale of rice, beans, and other staples often fall under association rules that specify grades for quality and contaminant levels, and sometimes require industry association inspection. This is in addition to Department of Agriculture standards or other regulations involving foodstuff sales to consumers.

Grading involves more information than certification or noncertification. Its rationale is usually apparent, has educational value (if Grade A has less X than B, X is obviously an undesirable quality). This also permits gradations in purchasing use (grade A is for salads, C for baked casseroles). Consumers must rely on the grader, and this is often the vulnerable point in the process. If the inspector has fifteen seconds per item (which is not uncommon), the system may be a facade for random selection, much ado about nothing, as Deming argues. Self-certification may be a good method for making clear the discretion of the producer and for pinning the ultimate responsibility on the enterprise. It may also cover irresponsibility with the cloak of government or nonexistent third-party supervision. The control mechanism behind self-certification has leverage over front-load quality control as well.

Full Disclosure and Complete Ingredient Labeling

The consumerist movement has long had a preference for letting the public know everything possible about a product, allowing the consumer to make informed choices. Producers are not anxious to do this since it involves inefficiencies and costs and does not offer anything positive in return. Regulators are aware that consumers do not necessarily want or benefit from complete information, and therefore have both a reason and an excuse to mediate between the two claims. Regulators argue they are attempting to package information in a way that is meaningful to the consumer.

Theoretically, for example, the home buyer could master the complete architectural plan of a house, specifications for its components, and inspection reports on them. If fact, most purchasers are best served by a careful list-oriented personal inspection of layout and facilities and an expert inspector's report on especially good or bad aspects (deviations from the norm). An overflow of information does not help understanding. As Bismarck is often quoted as saying, "Those who are fond of laws and sausages, and wish to remain admirers, should not inquire too carefully about the ingredients in them or the process by which they were created."

Full disclosure is often counterproductive, a strong argument against it, but producers are also aware of its costs. Small changes in ingredients or modes of production could require extremely expensive relabeling. Consumers unfamiliar with ingredient names may be misled and negative rumors may hurt a product. Consumers quite often misread the names of chemicals (especially when they are similar), which leads to fears that a poison or carcinogenic agent is present. The names of unfamiliar ingredients may in themselves discourage purchase.

Consumerists have a powerful rejoinder. Most of the time, full disclosure may not be useful, but it is the buyer who should make the decision to be uninformed. A buyer even has the right not to buy foods or goods produced with a "safe" compound that is related to a dangerous compound with a similar name.

There is both a practical and a moral aspect to this argument. As a practical matter, consumers can use full information to form their own standard as circumstances change, to concentrate on their immediate concerns. Morally speaking, they should possess that information even if it is useless for understanding, because it gives them power and the problem is at bottom theirs. An interesting example of the moral view of consumerism arose when the Carter administration confronted a new automatic method for deboning meat that produced a uniform percentage of bone and gristle, on average lower than that produced by manual deboning, but higher than the most skilled human efforts produced. Consumer groups saw the mere existence of bone in the meat—it became a usual and inevitable ingredient—more significant than the actual level. Yet they did not condemn traditional processing, which could be expected to, on average, add more bone than the new process.[37]

Regulators usually take a more moderate, nonmoralistic course, in part because it gets them off the hook politically. They usually provide packages that give consumers maximum information without excessively burdening producers.

An example of this dilemma is found in the case of vitamin content. Producers usually wish to brag about it, and the basic cost of adding vitamins is quite low. Not only is there a list of vitamins and minerals on products, but dosage units and the percentage of the daily recommended dosage are given, not only on the packages of vitamin pills and supplements, but also on other food products, such as cereal and flour.

This would seem to be a consumerist dream—full disclosure of basic information and a standard by which to measure that basic data. Yet it tells very little. The "recommended dosage" of various vitamins and minerals is based on very imprecise knowledge. In any event, the crucial variable is how much of the need is likely to be met by an individual's regular diet. Not surprisingly to anyone familiar with Herbert Simon's Nobel Prize–winning arguments, full information, as it turns out, is not so simple a matter as it seems.[38]

Lists of ingredients ordered by quantity is an efficient method for some purposes. By law, "macaroni and cheese" appears on the label, since "cheese and macaroni" would be misleading. In some eras, it may have been acceptable to merely list "artificial coloring," because it was seen as inconsequential, but that is hardly defensible in today's atmosphere. The specification that a piece of clothing is made of a blend of 65 percent wool and 35 percent polyester is usually quite meaningful, since fabrics tend to have distinct properties.

Although lists accompanied by standards are not panaceas, they usually convey additional and useful information. When phrases such as "accepted by the American Dental Association" or "meeting or exceeding USDA standards" are explained in some detail, they may be the optimal solution in an imperfect world.

Misinformation, of course, can masquerade as standards. "Ninety percent fat free" looks great, but that level of fat content is excessive for most products; for vegetable products, "cholesterol free" is a meaningless tautology. The words "less sugar" should lead consumers to ask, "Less than what?" In that case, manipulation and sleight of hand are the result of an absence of standards, though that is hardly the only basis for misrepresentation.

In short, information can not only confuse but actually mislead if it is not embedded in some context of knowledge, some structure of standards. Conversely, reliance on standard setting without basic knowledge of the process leaves one at the mercy of the person who controls that process.

Part II

American Standards
A System That Just Grew

4 Standards in American History

AUTHORIZATION FOR NATIONAL STANDARDS ACTUALLY antedates the American Constitution, yet it took a century for Congress to use the clearly granted power. Under article 9 of the Articles of Confederation, "the United States in Congress assembled" had the "sole and exclusive right and power of ... fixing the standard of weights and measures throughout the United States." That power was never exercised.

A somewhat weaker provision was included in the Constitution's article 1, section 8. Under that enumeration of legislative powers, Congress was authorized "to fix the standard of weights and measures." It was, however, the restrictive admonishment of the same section (clause 1), that "all Duties, Imports and Excises shall be uniform throughout the United States," that impelled most of the action that occurred during the early decades of the Republic.

In 1790, George Washington's first annual message called for standardization as "an object of great importance." He repeated the call in 1791, suggesting that standardization was "no less honorable to the public councils than conducive to the public convenience."[1] Pursuant to House instructions, Washington's secretary of state, Thomas Jefferson, made extensive proposals in 1791. A Senate committee insisted on delay since both France and Britain were engaged in similar proposals. Although subsequent committees of both houses were more enthusiastic, only a monetary system resulted. Flurries of interest by committees (in 1792, 1793, and 1796), state legislatures (1798, 1804, and 1808), and the president (1816) all ended in inaction. A report by John Quincy Adams in 1817, in his capacity as secretary of state, was comprehensive and remains much admired to this day; but efforts at that time and a decade later remained ineffectual. Once again, the sole exception dealt with the monetary system: Congress accepted the British troy pound as the base for defining coinage in 1828. Subsequent changes have involved redefining the physical characteristics to set the standard but have not altered the basic commitment to troy weight.

In addition to these provisions, the American Constitution also recognizes Congress's power to establish standards indirectly by allocating responsibility to promote science and technology. The Founding Fathers were generally mercantilists, not laissez-faire economists. Jefferson was influenced by the physiocrats, but as ambassador in France, he had little direct influence on the basic document.

During the constitutional debate, Federalists and anti-Federalists alike believed the open-ended power to deal with interstate commerce permitted the national government to regulate even the incorporation of businesses. Not only was that power not implemented by Congress, but efforts to utilize it were decisively rejected. The sweep of the anti-Federalists' triumph in constitutional interpretive localism can be gauged by the opposition such a move would inspire even today.

A number of factors limited the development of national standards and prevented the inauguration of nationwide product regimes. The growth of the Jeffersonian-Jacksonian states rights philosophies and the importation of physiocratic economic views kept even the clear-cut standards provisions from having much, if any, consequence in the early history of the Republic.

Not only was business licensure seen as intrinsically local (except when dealing with means of transport), protection against interstate fraud, where Congress had much easier claims, was seen as abhorrent. Coinage regulation was surprisingly gradual given the total monopoly stipulated in various provisions of the Constitution. While the decimal system was accepted by Congress in 1792, it was not until 1828 that a standard of weights for coins was actually promulgated.

Even the adoption of more general standards for weights and measures— without any prescribed punishment for noncompliance—was resisted in spite of constitutional authorization. As noted, Presidents Washington and Madison, and (as secretaries of state) Jefferson and John Quincy Adams, urged a comprehensive system of standards. Recognizing objections and obstacles, Jefferson suggested phasing in such measures, first applying them to foreign trade. Adams would have explicitly left day-to-day enforcement to the states. Congressional committees were appointed to deal with standards in 1791, 1795, 1798, 1804, 1808, 1816, 1819, 1821, and 1826; all were without success.[2]

The wedge that introduced standards was not the desire for a national market but the constitutional requirement that excises and duties be uniform throughout the United States. Because of the lack of national standards, each customhouse had to develop its own way of assessing congressional tariffs, necessarily favoring some importers and regions. Secretary of State Adams found that no two customhouses agreed, even on what a bushel or pound was. Naturally, there were pressures on the Treasury to end those anomalies.

The Treasury had established a Coast Survey to undertake a geodetic study of the coasts in 1807, and its first superintendent was a Swiss-born meteorologist and engineer, Ferdinand Hassler. Hassler was not formally appointed until 1816, though he was engaged in preparations and necessary purchases under an 1807 authorization (which included a salary). Criticism of his slow progress from 1816 to 1820 led him to resign to farm and teach, from 1820 to 1829. In 1829, he was financially impelled to take a job as a gauger in the New York customhouse. He was then beautifully located when Congress, under pressure, called upon the Treasury to do something about inequities in the imposts and duties.

In 1830, Hassler was recalled to Washington to work on the problem of standards, and was placed, for want of a better locale, in his old office in the Coast Survey. Two years later he was reappointed superintendent, and the weights and measures project became a fixed feature of the Coast Survey. The disguised locus proved politically desirable, which illustrates the sensitivity of what he was now asked to do.

Hassler made a diligent study, and in 1832 the secretary of Treasury promulgated his recommendations of a series of standards for imports. These were relatively noncontroversial measurement definitions derived from European national definitions. Enthusiastically, Hassler pressed for a set of weights and measures for the country as a whole. In 1836 Congress temporized; it commended the standards to the states, authorized copies of Hassler's standards to be printed, and established the Office of Weights and Standards, but refused to adopt them in any formal way. A year later, it authorized that a standard set be duplicated for each state. Most states responded favorably, but the physical duplication of the standards took years.[3] Only in 1856 did Hassler's successor as superintendent of the survey and supervisor of the Office of Weights and Measures announce that sets for each state and most custom-houses had finally been crafted, though even then not all had been delivered.

Already the metric system was creating problems for the United States, and, beginning in 1872, conferences were held to reconcile the divergent systems. The United States subsequently joined a permanent International Bureau of Weights and Measures and accepted that organization's definition of "meter" and "kilogram" for limited purposes in 1893.

Other agencies necessarily dealt with standards as well. Tax authorities defined a "proof gallon" and the number of gallons in a standard barrel for revenue purposes. The navy adopted a standard gauge for bolts, nuts, and screw threads.[4] In passing, Congress provided for standards for various products in various statutes. Sporadic—even accidental—legislation of this sort did little to provide uniformity; such provisions might not be included in later versions of bills, or key definitions and specifications might be inadvertently omitted or altered.

The government's chief instrument remained the Office of Measures in the Coast Survey, but it was not granted an explicit appropriation until 1873, and it became a full-fledged entity only in 1882. The eminent philosopher Charles Peirce, who earned his livelihood in that office for much of his career, worked diligently for its formal recognition and for authority to deal with foreign countries in the standards field. Testifying in 1884 before the Allison Commission, the first major effort at structuring scientific efforts, Peirce urged a carefully circumscribed role for the agency, arguing it should eschew basic research and leave commercial standards to the states.[5]

The Allison Commission, which was considering a proposal to establish a Department of Science and a National Academy of Science, spelled out a bold plan. But the possibility of interference with business and individual enterprise was viewed as an obstacle to promoting research, let alone entrepreneurship. Peirce's careful approach was the preferred route and the commercial standards issue was avoided.

A still conservative proposal to establish an independent standards bureau was successful nearly two decades later. Austria, Russia, and Germany had already established such organizations, and the German laboratory had been credited with helping develop chemical and other scientifically based industries in Germany. Great Britain established a National Physical Laboratory in 1899, and that example precipitated a major and successful effort in the United States in 1901.

Secretary of the Treasury Lymen Gage, a McKinley appointee, found Samuel Stratton, a professor of physics at the University of Chicago, and appointed him "inspector of standards." A bill was drafted with support from the scientific, commercial, and industrial communities. The argument that the United States, alone among the industrial powers, lacked such an agency, and the contrast between the minuscule "Office of Weights and Measures" and the scientific prowess of the German Reichsanstalt proved irresistible. The major modification effected by Congress in 1901 was to change the name from the "National Standardizing Bureau" to the "National Bureau of Standards." When in 1903 the bureau was transferred from Treasury to the new Department of Commerce and Labor, the secretary of commerce eliminated the word "national" from its name. In 1934, with "bureaus of standards" proliferating in government and business, the original name was restored. In 1988 it became the National Institute of Standards and Technology (NIST).

After World War I the value of research and standardization garnered prestige and authority. Although fledgling organizations had been developed before the war, their scope in most European countries was deliberately vague. After the war they were officially given wide responsibilities and became standard setters, not merely developers. In the United States the bureau's enhanced responsibilities included a complex supervisory relationship with one of the many progenitors of ANSI, with power to set up "voluntary" systems. When Herbert Hoover became secretary of commerce and then president, he gave that system shape and vitality. His political muscle and standing with industry and commerce were important elements in that process.

The Early History of NBS

The creation of a federal agency does not usually end the debate that precedes it. Absence of opposition to the agency at the moment of its original legislation is sometimes a good portent, but it often also simply means the issue was not adequately joined. The Brandeisian compromise over the federal reserve system was, in the light of history, a huge success. However, a cosmetic verbal compromise Brandeis helped concoct for the Federal Trade Commission satisfied the politicians but has kept the organization floundering and unsure of itself and its purpose.[6] Even more appropriate to understanding the problems of NBS was OSHA (Occupational Safety and Health Administration). Created primarily in response to internal bureaucratic impulses with some (hardly overwhelming) backing from unions, OSHA sailed through Congress because no force was opposed to safety in principle. Once it began to promulgate regulations it found that its broad but thin support quickly waned, while opposition grew dramatically.[7]

Keeping up with major industrial rivals works well as a political slogan, as the Sputnik crisis and the call to imitate Japan indicates. Establishing the NBS was a reasonable response to German successes and also followed the American pattern of that time of echoing and aping British actions. The science community had long favored such a move. Industry had its doubts, but those who expected good results were vocal and the others disarmed by the clear achievements of the German laboratory.

After legislation the doubts resurfaced. NBS has been regularly controversial, but more important, it never satisfactorily carved out a clear niche from the huge domain granted it. It was at times very practical and industrially oriented, often the price of survival, but it exhibited longings for more basic theoretical concerns. Although respectable, its scientific accomplishments have not been in a league with the premier organized research organization of this country, the privately funded Bell Laboratories. Certainly it does not often have personnel vying to be Nobel laureates. As its mission has varied over the years, so have the groups supporting it, and sea changes are not usually a good political strategy.

Given the relatively small size of the organization, the bureau was heavily dependent on the initial recruitment of its scientists, which determined the direction of its efforts. On the whole, the retirement of employees has been used shrewdly through the years to end a program, or to advance or augment one. But, limited to twelve scientists in 1902 and to twenty-four two years later, its aspirations and programs were necessarily few in number. Today, its numbers, though much larger, still set a limit on its programs, since collaborative requirements in most scientific ventures are generally more stringent.

Periodic congressional reorganizations have also contributed toward confusing the purpose of the bureau. When housed in Treasury, it had a certain immunity by virtue of its anomaly. When it moved to Commerce and Labor, later remaining in Commerce, its practical payoffs became almost the total concern of the business-oriented individuals who usually head that department.

The earliest programs were especially concentrated. The unit placed emphasis on measures and weights, of course, but it also established programs in heat and thermometry. Stratton, regarded as second only to Michelson among Americans in this area, personally worked with two others in light and optics. The major commitment of the new structure was to electricity, and reflected the desire of Congress to maintain national preeminence in that field.[8]

The constitutionally mandated and politically useful emphasis on measurements inhibited basic research in most areas, especially since instrumentation and training of measurers, and communication with the state enforcement agencies, took up so much of the agency's time. But requests of government agencies for testing of materials and products, a purpose not even contemplated in the beginning, began to strain the agency's resources.

This had unexpected payoffs for the government, however. Bureau research found 75 percent of incandescent bulbs sold to the government to be substandard. The bureau tested cement for the Panama Canal Commission, paper for the post office and Government Printing Office, and the tensile strength of the cable used in the Washington Monument.[9] In the early years, the government had no other laboratories, so the NBS was heavily criticized if it refused to assist an agency, but curried considerable favor when it was cooperative. In 1908 alone, thirty-seven agencies had one or more of its products tested. This record unleashed an even greater demand. Manufacturers, especially those intending to sell to government, sought testing or advice on manufacturing or advice on how to set up their own quality-control mechanisms.

The bureau heads realized that in doing no more than respond to a multitude of requests the bureau left itself without a focus. But they also recognized that ignoring such needs would be impolitic and even unwise. The bureau developed a separate division to compile and systematize information on existing standards, measurement devices, and testing mechanisms. Literature searches also established areas of helpfulness without research commitments, and the bureau developed programs to aid sectors of the economy where the need was greatest. Many of these activities permitted the bureau to assess costs to requesting agencies, allowing it to grow beyond congressional budgeting levels.

The testing function grew exponentially in early years, and the size of the bureau tripled. It was always difficult to recruit, and even harder to keep, topflight scientists, however. Not only industry but also the universities generally paid better, so turnover was high, made higher by demands for routine service. Turnover led to a de-emphasis on basic research. The push to be useful was not sufficient inducement for top researchers, and this tension was evident from the outset.

An exception was the unit on electricity; there the historical timing of the inauguration of the agency meant the issues of unit definitions for the newly studied phenomenon were both basic and congenial to a standards agency. The mushrooming growth of the electrical industry and its needs also coincided with the development of NBS.

A similar confluence of events and the basic significance of calibration allowed NBS to contribute to the development of radio and other wireless communication. In other areas as well, fundamental measurement or specifications, e.g., a more precise figure for Newton's gravitational constant, or Silsbee's 1917 hypothesis on superconductivity, were obviously important basic scientific work. The institute still maintains an important role in work on superconductivity and is looked to for leadership on that major development.

In trying to find a voice, the bureau opened the results of its testing to the public. Reflecting some of consumerism's original backing of standards, the agency published circulars written for general consumers, beginning in 1915. Its leading publication, "Measurements for the Household," sold over fifty thousand copies and was hailed in the *Ladies Home Journal*.[10] It described basic home devices and, while avoiding brand names, indicated preference for product lines (e.g., tungsten filament bulbs). No other government operation had dared do such things, and ultimately, the bureau found the approach unnecessary, while at the same time consumerism found that a nongovernment voice was preferable.

Consumerism was an even greater diversion from the agency's growing desire to develop core interests at the expense of routine testing. It was also a lightening rod attracting controversy to an agency with little capacity to cope with it. Accordingly, the agency began to minimize its public release of testing information. But this not only lost the support of a former constituency, it actually incurred the wrath of the consumer movement. NBS stalwarts believe the AD-X2 controversy (involving bureau evalution of a battery additive as worthless) in the 1940s, one of the greatest wounds ever inflicted on the agency (even though the bureau was ultimately vindicated), demonstrated the wisdom of this withdrawal from public product evaluation, as opposed to standard setting.

World War I considerably increased demands on the agency for testing of materials and products used in the war effort. An emphasis on efficiency and conservation of materials led to government efforts to eliminate inferior products and to prolong the life of machinery. In the interests of quick and cheaper repair, a call for standardized parts and standardized design also attracted support. The atmosphere of national and efficient mobilization of all resources is best illustrated by the integration of virtually all railroad lines into a wartime system under a federal administrator, Joseph Eastman, a feat not duplicated even during the more massive war effort of World War II. The bureau had coincidentally developed a program for testing railroad track scales, and this and other scale-testing activities burgeoned during the war, as did its lucrative and controversial move into the production of specialized optical glass.

Inevitably, the war effort spread the bureau thin. It developed some expertise in aircraft, the use of aluminum in engines, special steel alloys, dyes in uniforms, the measurement of gun velocity, and problems with radios. Testing quality was improved for uniforms, cement, paper, leather, and sugar, and programs to find domestic sources for leather and sugar were started in World War I. The agency developed considerable knowledge about basic products, since war agencies urgently needed and supported quality and dollar-wise purchasing.

World War I also promoted the standards movement by bringing into prominence one of the greatest zealots for standardization ever to gain high public office, Herbert Hoover. As an administrator on the War Industries Board, Hoover was impressed by the savings incurred by eliminating multiple forms of the same items. He never seemed to understand that while this was more profitable in the short run, it could be deleterious to innovation and progress in the long run. Certainly it made absolute sense in a war situation, and for most products was sensible in long-range terms for the economy as a whole. While the American marketplace was centralizing, the production system was still a congeries, with many meaningless local variations of sizes and shapes and colors.

Hoover realized that the term "standardization" implied the elimination of the picturesque and the unusual. It had strong currency in technical literature, so he continued to use it, but he also introduced a new term in 1921, "simplification." It was more positive in tone, and he promoted it in popular forums, establishing a "simplified" procedure practice unit in the bureau, promoting a simplification project in a preface for a book on the topic by a friend, and lending all his power and prestige to that effort. Hoover used the fame he acquired as postwar administrator of international relief and his position as secretary of commerce under Harding and Coolidge to back an extreme form of standardization, a "crusade for standards," as one chronicler called it. That program was like many of Hoover's social solutions, oversimplified and rather cold-blooded. Ultimately, the proposals he backed boomeranged, somewhat discrediting the standards effort.

While still a private citizen, Hoover became the prime mover in a study of the Federated American Engineering Societies (FAES). Its findings of redundancy were incorporated into a report, *Waste in Industry*,[11] which advocated greater uniformity in technology. The same theme was incorporated into a work published by the National Industrial Conference Board (NICB), *Industrial Standardization* (1929),[12] written by Robert Brady, who later emerged as a major expert for the Temporary National Economic Committee

(TNEC) and a critic of big business. The report was his dissertation for Columbia University. His work on standardization also contributed to an interesting volume for the TNEC, for which he was a consultant. He was a contributor to the *Annals* issue of May 1928,[13] which remains a classic work on standards; with Schlink, he wrote a piece about the consumer's stake in standards, and wrote another article on his own in that issue on government standards. His ultimate major volume was *Business as a System of Power.*[14]

Both the FAES and NICB reports accurately noted the waste inherent in the multiple and incompatible mechanisms that characterize the American industrial system. Lack of uniformity increases costs for replacement parts, requires wider training or experience of repair persons, and entails confusion by operators and numerous costly errors resulting from complexity. The 1928 report estimated that most industries could cut costs by 30 percent by insisting on Henry Ford's any-color-you-want-so-long-as-it's-black approach. Savings would come from many sources: producers could avoid new design costs, including the debugging of new models, and could save on costs for replacement and for corrective training.

Obviously, there is a great deal to be said for such standardization, which avoids complexity for its own sake, as a sort of Gresham's Law of production. Some years ago, a major airline agreed to buy a fleet of planes from a builder different from its normal supplier; however, it insisted on Rolls Royce engines, which were not normally utilized by the new supplier but were used in the airline's other planes. That action saved the airline millions of dollars, since maintenance crews could operate with experience and expertise on one set of problems. Variations in size of packaging have been studied in industry after industry, producing great savings in inventory with little or no cost.

The difficulty with the approach is that, carried to its logical extreme, it is the archenemy of progress and represents the sort of dead hand paralysis so typical of Eastern European Communism, with its planned uniformity and reluctance to change. Even the airline later went back to the market to buy a small number of middle-range planes and found it could not drive the same kind of bargain in that situation. Therefore, it bought the best plane for its purpose, not limiting itself to a uniform engine. Ultimately, its mechanics had to diversify. Insistence on strict simplification and rigid uniformity has a clear tendency to impede progress and carries with it the real danger of costing society far more than the supposed 30 percent savings claimed. Ultimately, too, investment in human talent and a more skillful labor force is likely to prove to be sound capital investment rather than an expense. Again, Hoover's concepts were throwbacks to Chaplinlike assembly lines, human beings as robots, which are now easily recognized as restrictive and economically wasteful.

Even while the message of the report was being accepted, and major concerns were reexamining operations to minimize costs inventory and needless proliferation of mechanisms, the caveat was also made that standardization could easily be carried too far. Mindless uniformity has its dangers. The FAES report was seen as largely a mistake, especially by economists. The NBS, which had minimal involvement in propagating it, paid a price nonetheless, and was seen by some as a tool for dead hand capitalism rather than a force for innovation, as originally expected.

NBS as a Major Force

Stratton had managed to create a growing agency in his two decades as director, expanding the NBS to a workforce of 850. More important, he had straddled the diffuse possibilities of an ill-defined agency and moved it in different directions in successive eras, usually attracting political support from some important political sector or another. In 1923, he was designated ninth president of the Massachusetts Institute of Technology, a sure sign he was considered a success. In announcing Stratton's resignation, Secretary of Commerce Hoover also appointed him to the bureau's visiting committee. At MIT, he proved a successful administrator, establishing new programs that bore an uncanny resemblance to those of the bureau.

Stratton had maintained a high profile in basic research through flexible and positive responses to the interests of the staff. For example, two heat specialists were permitted to work on the quantum theory of spectra, and they published an important book as a result. He also turned to other agencies for funding, as a supplement to congressional appropriations, drawing on goodwill engendered by his responsiveness to agency requests.

His successor, George Burgess, who was promoted from within, was considered a more able scientist and a more participatory administrator, but one less inclined to permit boundary-crossing research. On Burgess's retirement, Lyman Briggs, also promoted internally, headed the bureau during the Depression. This was clearly a time when being housed in the Commerce Department was a political liability. The bureau was employing a staff of 1,066 in 1931, but lost 50 percent of its funding and a third of its staff over a period of only two years.

Its very future was uncertain from one day to the next. Reorganization and dispersal were suggested, particularly in the years when the secretary of commerce was Daniel Roper, who had little clout. On the other hand, Roosevelt seriously proposed transferring the National Advisory Committee for Aeronautics (the predecessor to NASA) to NBS, a move that would have put the bureau in charge of aeronautical research, as was the case for its British counterpart, the National Physical Laboratory. The bureau was stabilized, with neither growth nor severe curtailment, once Harry Hopkins, one of Roosevelt's closest associates, took over Commerce in 1939. Hopkins had other priorities—welfare projects at first, management of the war production effort later.

Still, the 1930s produced a reassessment of the role of the bureau. The artful dodging of the Stratton era unfortunately culminated in clear dissatisfaction with the program on all fronts. The result was to weaken the self-confidence of the bureau, even though it also produced a more coherent set of priorities.

The clearest break came with the consumerism movement led by Frederick Schlink, a former technical assistant to Stratton. His series of articles in the *New Republic*, coauthored with Stuart Chase and published as a celebrated book, *Your Money's Worth,*[15] argued that the bureau, with a limited budget, saved the government over 100 million dollars a year, but denied the public knowledge about product quality that could save consumers 1 billion dollars. *Your Money's Worth* was a Book of the Month Club selection and a runaway best-seller. It was followed by a series of works creating a genre of antiadvertising, antibrand-name books, typified by the volume coauthored by Schlink (with Kallet) *100,000,000 Guinea Pigs.* Other such works bore the titles *Our Master's Voice: Advertising, Paying Through the Teeth,* and *Guinea Pigs No More.* A leading consumerist refers to the genre as the "guinea pig" books, since the consumer was seen to be manipulated and experimented on by producers.[16]

The book contained great praise for the evaluative work of NBS and expressed anger that it withheld information from the public:

Which brings us to ask a blunt and necessary question. Why does a service run by tax payers' money refuse information covering competitive products to that same tax payer? . . . Release would make a disturbance—here and there—granted. Some injustice would be done—granted. But facts are facts. . . .

A scrutiny of the catalogue of one of the great mail order houses reveals the fact that on over half of the non-luxury goods listed, the Bureau has already collected essential information. . . .

With the Bureau's testing information freely available a great lever would begin to operate on the manufacture of shoddy and shady goods and on the selling of sound goods at exorbitant margins. . . . It would require more temporary confusion, and possibly minor injustices than could conceivably arise to offset the enormous benefits which would flow from a free release of the magnificent work now done by the Bureau of Standards.[17]

Schlink and Chase founded Consumers Research in 1926 (it was incorporated in 1929), in partial reaction to their claim that government was conniving at business fraud, and therefore, that NBS constituted a serious underuse of the taxpayer's money. Robert Brady, the eminent economist who later served with the TNEC, echoed the argument in one of the articles in the *Annals* in 1928. In the 1930s, consumerists pinned their unrequited hopes on another agency, the NRA, which made a gesture in their direction by establishing a Consumers Board.[18] Later, Consumers Research and the even more successful breakaway group, the Consumers Union, established highly successful consumer information magazines as major and commercially successful ventures. Much freer to form judgments (and commit errors), the private organizations established a niche in American culture which is quite strong to this day.

Consumers Union broke away in 1936, nominally over ideological issues. *Consumers Research Bulletin* evaluations were restricted to subscribers. The CU people proclaimed they would serve poor families and not evaluate luxury goods. But their slicker publications and innovations—especially the annual *Buyer's Guide*—made them commercially successful. Today, automotive and other high-ticket evaluations dominate their publications and it is clearly a middle-class organization. Still, their broad social commitment is best represented by their attention to health and insurance issues, not merely purchasing.[19]

A related but contradictory critique came from the American Engineering Standards Committee (AESC) which the bureau helped reorganize in 1919 to facilitate industrial standardization. This committee was representative of leading engineering groups and was convinced that the bureau had moved from scientific and government domains to commercial and engineering areas, which properly belonged to AESC, since it was a quasi-government unit rather than a government structure with potentially coercive power. The jurisdictional family quarrel expanded when the AESC reconstituted itself as the American Standards Association (1928) with a broader agenda and even weaker government links. Its executive secretary was a former bureau employee, and Schlink, the quintessential disillusioned critic of NBS, was its assistant secretary for nearly a decade. The anomalous and incongruent positions taken by different groups disillusioned with the bureau was in large part a product of its own earlier grandiose and contradictory aspirations.

The AESC-ASA critique was in many ways the more acute. As its leaders pointed out, the promulgation of standards and their application to concrete evaluations can become comprehensive regulation if done by government. They argued that separation of functions would encourage industry to accept voluntary standards more easily and without compulsion. On the other hand, the consumerist suggestion that government could be a successful consumerist evaluator seems naive, even dangerous, when viewed with sixty years' hindsight.

Clearly, the NBS's presumed base was eroding on both flanks. Industry was not showing it solid support. Indeed, ASA opposition was briefly buttressed by explicit industry voices. There had been little legislative warrant for NBS's expansion, and the bureau was accused of wasteful research. Even its good work was considered to be in competition with that of private research agencies such as Arthur D. Little, Inc. A Department of Justice inquiry found NBS's actions had been assets to industry. The Comptroller General reviewed specific complaints about the bureau engaging in actual manufacture of optical glass and special castings for the Coast and Geodetic Survey; it ultimately found those actions were "noncompetitive" and were needed by the agency.[20] But the criticism both inside and outside Congress continued. A 1932 congressional committee, looking into alleged excessive expansion of government activities in competition with business efforts, did not refer to NBS by name, but it criticized expansion of industrial research, not merely because it competed with private agencies, but also because government patents based on research "prevented exclusive development by industry." While criticisms of the bureau came generally from its business competitors, and congressional criticism remained muted, the really significant political fact was the absence of any strong industry voice speaking on its behalf. Stratton's empire building was too diffuse to tie significant support of manufacturing interests to the agency, but aroused vague regulatory fears and unadulterated envy.

The Roosevelt administration took steps early on to secure a firmer understanding, not just of NBS, but of the entire government commitment to science. It appointed a Science Advisory Board under the aegis of the NBS and NRC in 1933. Key figures in the research establishment, Karl Compton and Charles Kettering, for example, were members, and four of the nine members of the board were also on the visiting committee of the bureau. The same four were also on a committee Roper had appointed to evaluate all Department of

Commerce agencies, and all reports were ultimately folded into that of the Science Advisory Board.

The report suggested a retrenchment of NBS, on the assumption that its domain should be confined to scientific standards of a sweep government alone could undertake; standards for government purchases and operations; and broad programs not yet practical for private initiative. Commercial standards could be developed privately in conjunction with ASA. Basic research, on the other hand, was to be the province of private industry, universities, and private research organizations. Testing for other agencies was to be formally recognized and accounted for by direct appropriation, or overtly funded by billing to the agency.

The real curtailment of the bureau was inaugurated by budget cuts due to the Depression rather than a genuine programmatic decision. This is not unusual for a government agency. Since testing for agencies was only slightly curtailed, the cuts for other programs in real dollars were assessed at a punishing 70 percent. In addition, direct manufacture of products for other agencies was ordered curtailed by Congress, and Briggs had no choice but to comply.

Yet it was to Briggs that Roosevelt turned for advice when the famous Einstein letter called for atomic research; for two years, Briggs chaired the ad hoc structures supervising development of the bomb. Both units at NBS and Brigg's ad hoc operation made significant contributions to that development. Another major contribution of NBS during the war was weather prediction, so vital to many military operations.

After World War II, two subsequent directors sharply defined the new identity of the NBS. Edward Condon was the first theoretical scientist ever to serve as director. A vigorous and aggressive administrator, he was continually at odds with Congress, which found him too erudite, too involved in social causes for the McCarthyite 1940s, and too ambitious in his aspirations for the agency. Condon was also involved in a contretemps over Laetrile—a putative cancer cure—and failed to protect the agency from the AD-X2 battery additive issue, which temporarily forced his successor out of office. Condon himself resigned in 1951 when attacks over his political leanings seemed to him to be hurting the agency. By that time, however, he had successfully instilled new theoretical scientific concerns within the organization and helped revitalize it. In his years as director, Condon became ever more protective of the testing function of the agency as one vital to efficient purchasing by the U.S. government. He stressed the obvious convenience of a government laboratory undertaking testing at low cost. Congress found it frustrating that the bureau could engage in testing and then charge the agencies, because the practice allowed the bureau such budgetary freedom. But in the end, it did not believe it reasonable to curtail the activity. This was perhaps another reason for congressional antagonism toward Condon, who, they thought, wished to maximize the bureau's leverage to act on its own, ignoring congressional priorities.

It was, however, Condon's successor, Allen V. Astin, who was to become the (temporary) martyr and permanent role model for the bureau. After all, Condon was in his seventies when he was unceremoniously pushed to retire. Astin was in his prime when compelled to temporarily vacate the directorship, largely as a consequence of Condon's handling of the AD-X2 issue. But Astin was to return in triumph after the bureau was ultimately vindicated. More important, the incident altered the tone and style of the organization for years to come.

The AD-X2 contretemps, crucial to the attitude of the agency, warrants detailed treatment.[21] The bureau had tested battery additives and consistently found no advantage to them; oddly, motorists and even some tests suggested improvements in performance, but the bureau's careful studies found they were due not to the additive but to an accidental concomitant to the process. Dust was removed in the process of adding fluids, which resulted in cleaner contact points. That did improve start-ups. Obviously, good maintenance could accomplish the same thing and did not require additional purchases. Having reached that conclusion to guide government vehicle maintenance, the bureau mentioned it in publications on car care generally, carefully avoiding specific brand names. The manufacturers of the AD-X2 additive often pointed out that their product had come on the market after publication of the pamphlet, so it was natural for reporters to inquire, after an updating of the pamphlet, whether the study now included the AD-X2. The briefing official acknowledged that new products, including AD-X2, had been tested with the same result.

The company producing the additive had political influence to burn. A prominent senator was a close friend of the additives producer, and he accounted for most of the furor. Twenty-six senators demanded Astin's head, even though the matter had occurred on Condon's watch, since the new director vigorously defended his agency's conduct on the matter. The Eisenhower administration temporarily caved in, but ultimately, the agency was vindicated and their conclusions validated.

Once restored to his post, Astin adopted an even lower profile for the agency, emphasized potential scientific contributions, and further distanced NBS from making specific evaluations. He also cooperated with plans for broader devolution of standards accreditation and for delegation of testing by authorized and inspected laboratories in the private sphere. That program has been partially successful.

Yet the agency again was caught in pincer attacks from the right and the left in the Carter and Reagan years. Under Carter, the FTC sought new legislation that would have, inter alia, given the commission considerable power over the bureau. The FTC claimed the bureau was dominated by industry and needed a watchdog.[22] Standard setting would in effect have been declared suspect because of its cartelization potential. The first draft of the FTC report was quite harsh regarding NBS and standards, and its recommendations would have been crippling. The final draft was innocuous in tone and much more limited in its recommendations. Still, it asked for power to evaluate standards before adoption. Nonetheless, the report of April 1983 was dead on arrival to the Reagan administration, and probably would have fared no better with a liberal administration. It was obvious that the realities of international trade and the consequences of subjecting the process of developing standards to yet another government agency would have put the United States at a political and economic disadvantage. The FTC had labored on what was from the beginning a nonstarter. It is difficult to see how its proposed controls would have helped domestic consumers, and its rather skimpy list of purported abuses of standards was not commensurate with the harshness of the tone of the original draft or the call for considerable reform in the final report.

The commission's quixotic effort makes somewhat more sense given that, in its quasi-legislative capacity, granted by the original bill establishing the FTC in 1914, it was to have had authority over voluntary associations. This was one of the powers jettisoned to secure passage. Agencies, too, may have irredentist motivations.[23]

The Reagan administration and parallel congressional moves, largely a counterattack from industry, also were aimed at the agency. The bureau was particularly criticized for its failure to develop relations with nongovernment laboratories and to fully implement the concept of regional and sectoral testing organizations. In this attack, only a few years after criticism from the left, there was harsh talk of the agency thwarting (not colluding with) business, and suggestions that restricting it to narrow measurement, in order to free industry from restrictions, would be desirable.

For example, the Reagan administration moved to curtail by legislation the bureau's efforts to study fire and combustion in homes and industry, on the grounds that fire fighting belonged to state and local government. Similarly, the administration claimed research on home construction should be primarily local in nature.[24]

But the same considerations of international necessity protected the bureau from the rear, as it had done from the front. The major change was to rename the agency, now the National Institute of Standards and Technology. While emphasis was placed on confining the agency more strictly—this seems to be a perpetual issue—the very name change of the organization promises to liberate and protect it. By becoming the National Institute of Standards and Technology, the agency was legitimated in its pursuit of useful, and perhaps basic, research. Although a major component in its operation from its very inception, research is now officially acknowledged; Congress was subtly endorsing self-definition, change, and greater creativity for the organization.

In 1995, the institute was caught in the cross fire of Republican desires to achieve budget slashing and the vulnerability of the Department of Commerce, headed by a continually investigated secretary, Ron Brown. The department seemed headed for elimination until analysis showed most of the agency would be reconstituted as separate entities, transformed elsewhere, or reconfigured as a Department of Trade. The effort was summarized by a *New York Times* reporter as mainly endangering the sign in front of the building.[25]

After considering the abolition of NIST, House Republicans seemed to accede to a proposal of Congressman Robert Walker of Pennsylvania, himself trained in physics, that it be folded into a "Science and Technology Administration." From NIST's standpoint, the silver lining of the black cloud still hovering over it was its defense by twenty-five Nobel laureates, who labeled it "a national treasure and a vital scientific resource for the nation."[26]

The Formal System in Operation

Although open and public at first glance, NIST is a strange operation. It has accepted, and revels in, a closely curtailed role in standard setting, limiting itself to the scientific and basic standards adverted to in the Constitution, and which its own history, especially with Congress continually nagging it, suggests is the safest.

But the institute is quite mindful of its potential and its broader responsibilities. Clearly, it encourages the development of standards, especially indirectly. It actively participates in both the ANSI (the successor to ASA) and in other standards organizations. It houses some operations and encourages staff to join, maintain, and contribute to the growth of others. Lists of such employee participation are kept up to date and passed out freely, a wise bureaucratic precaution. The agency stresses the programmatic contribution employees play in standards, but there is defensiveness as well as pride of accomplishment behind this openness. The charge of hidden conflict of interest is much more damaging than open public participation.

ANSI itself is not a direct standards developer or standards enactor. It is rather a holding company that recognizes and validates standard-setting organizations. Like NIST, it also tests and certifies testing laboratories. Thus, it provides yet another political and legal buffer between NIST and individual companies, serving as an interfacer in which industry can play a largely masked role. Standards developed in accordance with its procedures may be published and disseminated under its name.

Those who are recognized by ANSI as standards setters vary enormously in type of organization and emphasis. Some are trade associations, others professional expert groups or entrepreneurships. They must agree to ANSI's rather elaborate procedures and promulgate standards in specific form with specified dissemination arrangements. Thus ANSI standards, recognized throughout the world by that name and regarded by most observers as the most objectively determined standards, are actually secondhand products derived in accordance with ANSI's complex procedures.

In general, American industrial standards are voluntary and noncoercive when they are promulgated by the developing organization. They may, of course, be enacted into law at an appropriate level. State legislation or municipal ordinances are common arenas for standard enforcement. In particular, housing construction is an area where local legislation adapts and enforces standards set nationwide, often by industry-dominated organizations. States often pass antifraud legislation with specific standards either enacted or indirectly adopted in any number of areas. National standards—regarding impurities in agricultural products, for instance—may also be defined by statute or regulation. Defense Department adoption of a standard has immense consequences for sales and purchases. The definitions are often based on established commercial standards, however they are arrived at. Even standards not enacted by either federal or local governments are given close attention by a prudent manufacturer or user, who is aware that courts and insurance companies are likely to turn to those definitions in times of controversy.

NIST has conscientiously tried to devolve much of its pioneering of standards to the appropriate network of standards organizations, once the groundwork has been done. This is easiest when a staffer who is an enthusiast on a topic retires or develops a new interest. For example, for years NBS had a scientist interested in precise specification of colors; his work was significant for the paint and tile industries and for many other home industries. The standards are now maintained by the Ceramic Tile Industry Institute, since precise definition of color tints is the key to lucrative bathroom design and sales.

While initial investment by NBS made sense, its continued use of government funds would have been questionable. Nonetheless, the institute continues a loose relationship with the ceramic tile industry.

Testing institutes are vital to the standards world. The premier organization is the ASTM (originally the testing laboratory of the Pennsylvania Railroad). It is well equipped for dealing with heavy machinery and materials testing, and has few rivals in its area of capabilities outside NIST itself. ASTM is also a standards developer and promulgator secondary to ANSI.

NIST also has responsibility for disseminating standards, acting both as a clearinghouse and as a sponsor of clearinghouses. In the former capacity, it maintains a library with a small expert staff to aid those—usually business people—seeking information standards of any type. In addition, NIST encourages and aids in the establishment of regional libraries and collections of promulgated standards. It maintains lists of locales, phone numbers, and addresses of such centers as well.

Congress seems to want a network of well-trained private organizations and laboratories, and seems disappointed that the institute has not been more successful in developing such a network. It is not clear how those goals should be furthered. Historically, NIST has taken a quite different route, and foreign organizations of a similar nature have also not followed that path. NIST remains a troubled organization with uncertain prospects and unfulfilled expectations.

While NIST has not really changed with its alteration in nomenclature, or adjusted particularly well to its assigned role of promoting independent laboratories and technology centers, it has been buoyed by increased support from the Clinton administration. While the Bush administration's interest in international trade helped protect the agency, the Clinton emphasis on promoting technology and infrastructure suggests that NIST could be a positive force. This was also suggested by the choice of a new director, Arati Probhakar, the first woman to head the agency.[27] Born in India, with a Ph.D. in physics from the California Institute of Technology, she brought government experience as a congressional intern and as head of the Defense Department Advanced Research Agency to a unit with vastly more scientific than political know-how. Her familiarity with Congress and the technological bureaucracy were seen as assets at a time when the agency seemed obliged to take on a strong role. She has emphasized her commitment to maximizing technology building and has shown less concern with standard setting, though perhaps the two are more intertwined than fashionable politics might desire. If the "new currents" she wishes to ride are more faddish and less novel than her favorable media coverage suggests, the desire to present to the public the agency's record and self-concept is in itself a positive step toward achieving a new role.

Among the new research programs praised by the media in recent years are DNA identification methods, superconductivity, a precise atomic clock preventing computer fraud and computer viruses, computer reading of handwriting, and the effects of electrical fields from power lines on human beings. Perhaps ironically, the *Wall Street Journal* of August 18, 1991, particularly praised NIST's work on preventing building and furniture fires—by a division Reaganites tried to abolish a decade ago. But this ambitious program is burdened by a legacy of neglect that must be rectified.[28]

5 The American "System" of Standards

Government and Private Standardization

TO THE EXTENT THAT ONE MAY SPEAK OF ANY American "system" of standards, it is largely shaped by weak government pressure from above and diffuse pressure from business and insurance needs from below. The avoidance of overt responsibility, the fear of antitrust, antibusiness, or antilocalism bias, is evident throughout.

The national government's avoidance of authority is all the more conspicuous in the light of the expansive power seemingly contemplated in the mercantilist Constitution of 1789. The triumph of states rights Jeffersonians, however, cast a pall over even explicit national powers that limited their exercise, particularly in the regulation of private endeavor.

The Constitution adumbrates an array of national powers. Patent and copyright authority are building blocks of traditional systems of standards. They are buttressed by exclusive authority over coinage and other money matters and by the power to establish "the Standard of Weights and Measures" (article 1, section 8, clause 5). But, as we have noted, the nineteenth century was marked by an avoidance of national claims. Far from government aggrandizement, it witnessed a national regime deliberately keeping out of even conventional opportunities assigned it under the Constitution.

Similarly, private organizations establishing standards have been reluctant to claim authority or assert governance. In this respect, the collapse of the

TABLE 5.1
Organizations with One Thousand or More Standards

1.	American Society for Testing and Materials	8,500
2.	Society of Automotive Engineers	5,100
3.	U.S. Pharmacopoeia	4,450
4.	Aerospace Industries Association	3,000
5.	American National Standards Institute	1,100
6.	Association of American Railroads	1,350
7.	Association of Official Analytical Chemists	1,900
8.	American Association of State Highway and Transportation Officials	1,100

Source: Robert Toth, ed., *Directory of Standards Activities of Organization in the United States* (Washington: GPO, February 1991), 5.

NRA and the doubts cast upon any partnership of government authority with industrial standard setting have reinforced the fears of antitrust suits and penalties. Triple damages, as Samuel Johnson noted regarding hanging, concentrate attention.

It is clear from an analysis of the standard-setting organizations identified by a continuing U.S. survey, *Standards Activities of Organizations in the United States,* the latest dated 1984, that multiple, if vague, pressures have nonetheless led to something of an organized system. Of a total of more than 750 organizations, 20 were found to have established 33,235 standards, an estimated 35 percent of the total. These organizations included 8 nongovernment structures, which account for 28 percent of the total enumerated standards and almost 3 percent of all estimated private standards. (See table 5.1.)

Obviously, the government is effective in directly creating standards, as it is in encouraging such programs, at least as far as absolute numbers are concerned. The paramount influence of the Defense Department also stands out. It is clear that while their standards, like other federal standards, are primarily developed in proprietary use—that is, for government purchasing purposes— they are often in the public domain and can be utilized by private purchasers.

The same general picture seems to be confirmed by the other organizations rounding off the top twenty in number of standards developed.[1]

9. American Petroleum Institute (880 standards)
10. Cosmetic Toiletry and Fragrance Association (800)
11. American Conference of Governmental Industrial Hygienists (700)
12. American Society of Mechanical Engineers (745)

13. Underwriters Laboratories (630)
14. Electronic Industrial Association (600)
15. Institute of Electric and Electronics Engineers (575)
16. American Oil Chemists Society (365)
17. American Association of Cereal Chemists (370)
18. American Railway Engineers Association (300)
19. Technical Association of Pulp and Paper Industry (270)
20. The National Fire Protection Association (275)

Eighteen of the twenty were also in the top twenty in 1984. Of the 1991 contingent, ANSI, the American Association of State Highway and Transportation Officials, and the Aerospace Industries Association were private but in essence governmentally induced. In total, the direct government standards, largely developed for purchasing purposes, outnumbered the estimated private standards in 1991.

A few private organizations (those relating to highways and pharmacopoeia) have clear and firm government roots and some, like those in the paper industry, are more closely linked to regulatory schemes than meets the

TABLE 5.2
(Estimated) Number of U.S. Standards and Their Developers, 1991

	N	%
Government		
Defense	38,000	40
Federal (GSA)	6,000	6
Other	8,500	9
Subtotal	52,000	55
Private Sector		
Scientific and Professional	13,000	14
Trade Association	14,500	16
Other Standards-Developing Organizations	41,000	15
Subtotal	41,500	45
Total	94,000	

Source: Directory, 4.

eye. The bulk of these are in industries which by their nature require precision; their standards were not developed for purposes of controlling and guaranteeing inventory, a common reason for setting standards. ASTM and the Association of Highway Officials among the giants, as well as some of the smaller groups, grew out of the railroad's need for safe, standard, and interchangeable equipment. But the Defense Department has been the ten-ton gorilla of the standards industry, directly engendering 40 percent of all standards and indirectly generating enough "private" and other government standards to bring it close to—or perhaps over—the majority mark. (See table 5.2.)

An analysis of the private sector shows that the number of directory-listed standards are rather evenly divided among the directory's major categories— "scientific and professional," "trade associations," and "standards developing agencies." Trade associations have a bit more, and "scientific and professional" groups a bit less, than the others. But analysis of all "nongovernment" listings in the 1991 standards directory of nongovernment organizations reveals a different picture of participatory activity. In number of individual structures, "trade associations" clearly dominate the landscape. Many of these are not so much standards developers as standard kibitzers, sending representatives to more active or more official bodies like ANSI, or to a group synthesizing standards for an industry. Others are highly specialized groups having a limited number of standards (half a dozen is not atypical), which they sell, and in rarer instances, police on behalf of a group.

The amorphousness of categories and self-classification result in some clear anomalies. The American Automobile Association (which has observers and participants in a variety of road and auto standards processes) lists itself as a "trade association," while the National Civic League and the National Easter Seal Society both call themselves "technical societies."

It is apparent by their own description that many, perhaps most, "technical associations" are formed and dominated by leading companies in an industry, and that genuine cooperative nonprofits (including laboratory and testing operations) have trouble fitting the directory's procrustean bed. Clearly, however, the predominance of the trade association would persist, probably even grow, if closer and more objective standards controlled the classifications. The breakdown is found in table 5.3.

The summaries in table 5.4 are based upon a keyword analysis of subject matter appearing in NIST's regularly published directories.

Apart from the Defense Department, standards organizations particularly emphasize building and construction materials and operations; this is evident

TABLE 5.3
How Standardizers Classify Themselves

Trade	387
Professional	90
Scientific	23
Technical	58
Miscellaneous	40
("accrediting," "not for profit,"	
"education," "consumer")a	
	———
	598

Source: Tabulated from self–classifications in Toth: *Directory*.
a. My own classification rather than the directory questionnaire breakdown.

from the many construction, concrete, and wood organizations. The very strong participation of government organizations in building and construction reflects the public interest in safety, planning, and other concerns.

The editors of the directory provide an index of the positive involvement of government in the construction industry—not merely as regulators in a passive sense—by estimating the influence of direct, government-developed standards on the construction industry as a whole (see table 5.5).

Eras of Standardization

Analysis of the organizations by founding year suggests some other patterns of interest. While a few organizations go back to the early nineteenth century, the vast majority were established or took on standards activities after 1890. This is in itself not surprising, for the last decade of the century was a period marked by formal associations of all kinds emerging throughout American society. On the whole, the organizations involved emerged slowly, growing in a surprisingly uniform manner over the years. Only 1942, at the height of the war effort, saw a clear diminution in that rate of growth, with only one such organization being founded. (See table 5.6.)

The major period of growth was the early and middle 1930s. It could have been anticipated that the "second" New Deal would engender such organizations, which in a sense privatized standard setting and took government out of the regulatory position declared unconstitutional in *Schechter Poultry v. U.S.*

TABLE 5.4
Number of Standard Organizations in Each Category

Acoustics and Noise Control	16 (2)
Aerospace and Aviation	16 (3)
Agriculture	35 (5)
Air–Conditioning and Refrigeration	14 (1)
Building	78 (7)
Business, Finance, and Insurance	27 (14)
Communications	49 (12)
Concrete, Masonry, and Ceramic Products	27 (0)
Construction	71 (8)
Consumer Products	55 (7)
Data and Information Processing	49 (17)
Defense	13 (1)
Education	21 (1)
Electrical and Electronic Equipment	36 (2)
Energy	31 (7)
Environment	23 (12)
Facilities Management	7 (2)
Food and Beverages	35 (12)
General	23 (10)
Government Officials	20 (1)
Heating, Ventilating, and Air Handling	19 (0)
Industrial Equipment	62 (2)
Instruments and Laboratory Equipment	18 (3)
Machinery	25 (0)
Manufacturing	45 (1)
Materials and Finishes	99 (3)
Medical and Health Care	41 (6)
Medical Devices, Equipment and Instruments	25 (4)
Office Products	11 (2)
Optics, Ophthalmic Products, & Eye Protection	7 (0)
Packaging and Paper	32 (5)
Photography	9 (1)
Plumbing	23 (4
Public Health	35 (4)
Quality Assurance and Testing	55 (10)
Recreation and Sports	26 (1)
Safety, Fire Protection, and Public Safety	104 (22)
Sanitation	24 (2)
Social Welfare	10 (2)
Textiles and Clothing	29 (3)
Transportation	52 (10)
Wood and Wood Products	35 (2)

Calculated from Toth, *Directory*. GNT numbers in parentheses are government standards–setting groups *included* in the category.

TABLE 5.5
U.S. Standards Used in Building and Construction

	Number of Standards
Private Sector	
200 Organizations	6,000
Federal Government	
GSA and Department of Defense	2,000
Corps of Engineers	1,000
Navy Facilities Command	750
Postal Service	350
Others	750
Total	10,850

Source: Reprinted from Toth, *Directory,* 6, table 3.

(295 US 495, 1935). As the NRA experiment with government control over industry played itself out as legal and administrative chaos, those functions were often exercised elsewhere. Some of that sense of the desirability of public-private partnership—of quality through regulation on the positive side and monopoly advantage on the negative side—did not die with NRA. Just as unions continued to press for industrial partnership after NRA, with the Guffey Act and Wagner Act, so did some industries persist in their standardizing, quality-building, or monopoly efforts.

What is most intriguing about this development is the strong evidence that the impulse for corporatism crested earlier, in Hoover's rather than Roosevelt's years in office. Of course, the Depression limited traditional business entrepreneurship after 1929, making organizational innovation more attractive. Hoover's own interest in corporatism was reflected during this period in the Reconstruction Finance Corporation. It is also likely that the notion of a managerial state, triumphant in Germany, Italy, and the Soviet Union, had its effects in the United States as well. The data suggest the intriguing possibility that the 1933–1936 "First New Deal" program, promoted by Raymond Moley, Adolf Berle, and other corporatists, followed rather than created the response of many industries to the Depression, to the more organized structure of foreign competition, and to the climate of the times.[2]

Two other patterns emerge from the organizational history of standards

TABLE 5.6
Years of Formation of Non–Governmental Organizations

Years	Organizations
1820–1849	6
1850–1879	15
1880–1889	13
1890–1899	23
1900–1909	43
1910–1919	66
1920–1929	47
1930–1939	97[a]
1940–1949	75[b]
1950–1959	72
1960–1969	59
1970–1979	47
1980–1989	31[c]

Source: Tabulated from listings in Toth, *Directory*.
a. Twenty-nine in 1933 alone.   b. But only four in 1941, 1 in 1942.   c. None in 1985.

structures: first, a period of strong growth was also experienced in the post–World War II period; and second, there has been a sag in the creation of new structures in recent years. Neither pattern suggests an immediate interpretation, though the Reagan-Bush rejection of a national industrial policy might have discouraged standards initiatives. It is intriguing to believe, however, that the political decision followed rather than created a grassroots rejection of any expanded "regime regulation" of new sectors of the economy. The prototypical multinational corporation of the 1970s, involved primarily with foreign trade, was logically unlikely to see national standard setting as desirable. Even on the international front, such organizations were more likely to play both ends against the middle than to rely on the U.S. market and the U.S. government to give them leverage in Europe. Only with the EU threat of a continental policy did any such efforts to unify the American base begin to seem advantageous. Even then, for most multinationals, a protean personality—a European identity and an American face—seemed the optimal program. Being an insider in the European Union was more likely to pay off than being a threatening American importuner from outside. No doubt corporations would have acceded to such a role in Japan if it had been reasonably available and reliable.

Changes in Standards Organizations

The standards world is fast paced. Between 1975 and 1983, the standards directory found fifty organizational name changes and fifty-eight dissolved or "unreachable" organizations. From 1983 to 1991 there were forty-nine nomenclature changes as well as thirty-five organizations that were defunct, merged, no longer involved in standardization, or unreachable. But forty new organizations were also identified in 1991.[3] The number of standards by non-government organizations was estimated to have grown from 32,000 to 41,500, roughly a 4 percent annual increase. But part of this was probably a product of better reporting; furthermore, as the editors note, "standards developers seldom inactivate standards once they have been published," even if their use dwindles.[4]

The listed organizations are generally stable and do not change locations easily; after all, headquarters stability is an asset. In general, there is a very heavy concentration of organizations on the East Coast. Washington has the most intense concentration, with New York second. There is considerable concentration in and around most major cities—Chicago, Cleveland, Dallas, and Philadelphia are especially prominent. Occasionally, an organization makes a genuine geographical move, as, for example, the American Institute of Aeronautics and Astronautics, which moved from California to Washington, D.C.

The organizations newly listed in the standards directory tend to be more remote from Washington, D.C., than organizations that appear repeatedly. Thus, the number of such agencies in the state of Washington rose from two to six and those in California from eighteen to twenty-one (despite the departure of the Institute of Aeronautics). In 1984, directory editors listed the locale of developers arrayed with top concentrations, as shown in table 5.7.

TABLE 5.7
Major Locations and Types of Standardizations, 1984

Location	Developers	Work With Others	Total
Washington, D.C.	140	72	212
New York City	41	18	59
Chicago	27	17	44
Philadelphia	7	4	11

Source: Reprinted from *Directory of Standards Activities* (Washington: GPO, 1984), 11.

"Location" seems to be defined as some sort of metropolitan area for the D.C. area, and as the core city for others. If Chicago suburbs had been included, the number in that midwestern hub would have rivaled New York, but, of course, some other definition of the New York City area might have augmented that total as well. In any event, the tabulation is not overly precise in its definition or enumeration. For example, the 1984 directory lists twenty-one organizations located in Cleveland, Ohio, nearly double that in Philadelphia, yet Cleveland is not listed in the compilation of top cities. These difficulties with figures—including inconsistencies—probably explain why the directory presents no cumulative data on location in 1991.

Enterprise-by-enterprise calculations show great stability, and it is easy to verify 1984 totals (except for the D.C. figures, which do not easily fall into any plausible category). These totals are compared to similar 1991 compilations in table 5.8.

The seeming drop-off in the District of Columbia is probably in great part a product of some oddity in definition of the Washington, D.C., area. This conclusion is reinforced by calculations of the number of organizations in 1984 and 1991. This shows a drop-off in organizations with a strictly District of Columbia address, from one hundred and fifteen to one hundred and one. But the net drop is clearly the result of relocations to suburbs outside the District of Columbia.

Two more organizations moved to the District of Columbia metro area than left it, and the newcomers were probably more significant as a group. The rather high turnover suggests that District of Columbia standards organizations might well be more entrepreneurial than the national group as a whole. (An alternative explanation is that NIST sources gain greater familiarity with District of Columbia organizations, and this results in inclusion of more ephemeral groups in D.C. than in other cities).

TABLE 5.8
Changes in Geographic Location of Standardizers

Location	1984	1991
Washington, D.C.	212	197
New York City	33	35
Chicago	36	38
Cleveland[a]	21	22
Philadelphia	11	14

Source: Reprinted from *Directory of Standards Activities* (1984), and Toth, *Directory*.
a. Not listed in directory tables, but data is theirs.

Most important is what did *not* occur. There was no dash toward Washington, no influx of organizations mobilizing a national effort or making a new attempt to cope with international standards. The data are inconclusive regarding whether the total in the D.C. area declined or rose slightly. A rise, of course, would be in accordance with the total national pattern. A fall would be mildly anomalous, though not especially significant. But in either case, there is a clear pattern, in that Washington did not operate as a major magnet of increased power and attraction.

This geographic inference is also consistent with the pattern for the founding era suggested in table 5.4. The fact that record trade years have witnessed neither the efflorescence of organizations nor their concentration in Washington suggests that mobilization to cope with foreign competition or for the purpose of bargaining with foreign governments is not a cause of organization. Once in place for other reasons, of course, an organization may assume new obligations and, like all organizations, alter its priorities and purposes.

A score or two of those private organizations have quasi-government purposes and structure. Thus, the National Metric Council and many of the public health structures were once firmly entwined with government agencies and have evolved to follow their own agenda while still maintaining some of these ties. The most dramatic form of this distancing is ANSI, clearly a government offspring, which the government now generally regards as an excuse for its own inactivity and as a mask for business's preference for nonregulation.

A host of organizations have probably come into existence because of regulatory regimes, and they are certainly shaped by them. Conspicuous here is the construction industry, which must concentrate and rely on existing local codes and standards for general construction and on U.S. government standards (Defense Department, NASA, NEPA) for more innovative types of construction. The genesis of the actual standards applied is usually more complex. Sometimes, industry proposes and government ratifies or rejects. But the Defense Department and other agencies may innovate or promote innovation, and neutral experts often offer new solutions to known problems. Here the influence of the insurance industry is felt; direct participation of commercial underwriters in drafting committees is common and of considerable moment.

Where the government regulatory regime is dense and comprehensive, an even closer tie is usually manifest. Lumber standards are sensitive to domestic inventory realities but also to international export-import requirements. Agricultural standards necessarily revolve around the regulations of the Department of Agriculture. The entertainment industry—especially television in its various guises—is manifestly organized to cope with the regulatory environment.

An interesting example of approved government involvement is the American Lumber Standards Council, which doubles as a committee of NIST and yet independently sets lumber standards for the industry. Established in 1922, it was upheld by litigation as constitutional by the Supreme Court and so continues to function in ways NIST is afraid to replicate in other areas, since doing so might present delegation or federalism problems.[5]

The bulk of standards organizations, however, seem to have evolved by necessity from the ground up, or as a product of industry protectionism rather than government paternity. Trade associations drift in and out of standard setting, but the larger ones cannot avoid the function. Some prefer to set up parallel technocratic "institutes" or research organizations, perhaps hoping to minimize interorganization politics, perhaps to avoid antitrust charges or public attention. A few have mechanisms to police standards, particularly in industries made up of many small companies, where purchasers have few inspection capabilities. In general, however, standard setting in the United States is largely a self-certifying system relying on complaints from within the industry (usually, allegations of contract violations), occasional government inspection, or the threat of loss of insurance protection. For small purchasers, the very weak mediatory Better Business Bureau (which in general copes with outright fraud rather than nonflagrant standards violations) or intraenterprise remedies (e.g., consumer ombudsmen) usually deal with complaints, though with varying effectiveness.

An interesting phenomenon is small conglomerates where entrepreneurial organizational managers appear to offer economies of scale to trade associations with heavy needs and limited resources. Under operation by a single director, a handful of organizations share offices (or suites) and all or some staff. Some of these sharing relationships seem to have evolved as spin-offs or more specialized services developed by a core organization. Usually, however, there is no such historical or even logical nexus. Such conglomerate offices operate in Arlington, Virginia, and elsewhere in the Beltway, but are also found in Cleveland, Ohio, and New Jersey. In most instances, the organizations were founded well before the current executive directors could possibly have structured them, but a few seem to reflect straightforward entrepreneurship by their present directors. All seem bona fide and forthright, and are well established. Indeed, some of these conglomerate organizations will soon be entering their second century.

The more usual situation is for a trade association to act as a holding company, performing a variety of services for the industry. The association may develop standards or represent the industry on ANSI, government, or other standard-setting structures. They may publish or distribute standards on their own or through one of the larger bodies. Publishing through ANSI is particularly prestigious.

In some cases, standards may be the actual nucleus of the organization. But when standards are the organizing mechanism of a structure, the organizations are more typically adjuncts spun off into research or technical operations, for the convenience of an all-purpose mother organization.

Leading professional associations enter the field in much the same way as trade associations. A small unit within the organization handles technical aspects requiring standards as part of their general benefits packages, which organizations supply to promote wider membership.

However, most "professional" and "technical" organizations seem to grow out of broadly shared concerns rather than the individual career patterns of their staff. The organizations involved may be managerial in style, but the organizational catalyst is often a technical topic or industrial concern. There is little evidence of standardization resulting from the hobbyhorse of disinterested professionals, and a great deal of evidence of entrepreneurial profit from desired trade standardization.

Many of the technical organizations exhibit narrower concerns. They develop highly specialized standards for narrow industrial sectors. Many are created by major industries as laboratories or public spokespersons for the industry—as, for example, the Tobacco Institute or the Resilient Tile Institute. Many, in other words, are really trade associations seeking presentability. These narrow operations lend themselves to entrepreneurial efforts. A standards developer can accrue many advantages as a standards tester, though only a small number of organizations maintain such dual roles.

Other organizations in the spectrum are those of officials who enforce standards (official and unofficial) or who professionally establish them. Among the associations of various engineers and design specialists are the Standards Engineers Society, the Society of Automotive Engineers, and the American Institute of Mining, Metallurgical, and Petroleum Engineers.

Paralleling them are such organizations as the National Association of Building Codes Officials and the American Association of Motor Vehicle Administrators, which allow enforcers to participate in the process of defining standards, though they do not directly create them. Many of these organizations seek out members or observers in standard-setting groups where they articulate enforcement realities.

A Profile of Government Standardizers

Seventy-seven federal units describe themselves as having standards responsibilities. Almost half the units are in four cabinet-level departments: Commerce (fourteen), Transportation (nine), Agriculture (eight), and Treasury (five).

The Department of Agriculture has important regulatory power over grain, livestock, and fiber products. The Agricultural Marketing Service sets over four hundred standards (and gradations within most of these). While most are voluntary, some, such as egg handling (including imports), are mandatory, and certification of enforcers and testers is possible in most areas for a cost-based fee. Grain and livestock standards are similarly administered by the Federal Grain Inspection Service, the Food Safety and Inspection Service, and Packers and Stockyards Administration. These groups also prescribe measurement devices. Other agriculture agencies deal with GATT standards in agriculture, wood products, rural electrification, and internal management communication.

The Department of Commerce has even more diverse concerns. NIST itself has independent programs on computer technology standards, crime laboratory technology, wood products, and soft drink bottles. Its largely voluntary program includes weights and measures, and promotes and authorizes testing laboratories. The department has several agencies working on weather measurement and atmospheric control, with responsibilities both on domestic and international fronts. Telecommunication, fisheries, and international trade coordination are other foci. The patent office alone has four programs trying to develop standardized invention and trademark classifications.[6]

The Department of Transportation has within it agencies standards for aircraft, highways, highway vehicles, pipelines, boats, and other watercraft. Treasury prescribes testing methods for alcohol and tobacco as regulatory treasures, and the customs services, the original font of standardizing in the United States, continues to function domestically and internationally as a standard setter, but also as coordinator in international affairs for customs purposes.

Most of the remaining forty-one agencies play roles similar to these. Many, like Health and Human Services (three programs), are essentially regulatory agencies so far as standards are concerned. As in the Department of Labor (Mine Safety and Health Administration and OSHA), their standard setting and enforcement are intertwined. Even "voluntary" aspects may be subtly coercive. GSA's Public Building Service, for example, is devoted to accessibility of federal buildings, which no doubt sets models for other structures under the federal requirement for accessibility to the handicapped.

Today, much standard setting is a tool of communication and management. The Joint Congressional Committee on Printing, GSA's Information Resources Management, and four Library of Congress programs deal largely with communication, and GSA's Federal Supply Service is involved in management.

International involvement runs throughout many agency responsibilities. This is paramount in the U.S. Trade Representative (an office with major GATT and WTO involvement) and in the postal service's relationship to the International Postal Union, but also in the many U.S. agencies involved in communications or computer technology.

The federal government has principal influence as a purchaser or facilitator, however. The Department of Defense sets technological norms when it prescribes new standards or simply adopts existing "voluntary" standards as contract requirements. Often the latter practice means the product will be produced to meet those standards, since they dictate the only economically feasible manufactured form of the product, or simply because economies of scale maximize profits. Ultimately, subsidies from federal resources and purchases dictate nuclear reactor designs as much as does direct regulation. If Fanny Mae or Sally Mae refuse to repurchase a mortgage based on the house's design, housing contractors will give up on the design as well. HUD committees and programs are also vital to most housing developers.

The core of standardization is also dramatically indicated by the anomaly of the old continuing listing of a joint Department of Justice and the Executive Office of the President venture called the "Interdepartmental Screw Thread Committee," once housed in the Defense Department. In fact, that interdepartmental committee, the successor to the "Defense Industrial Supply Center," deals precisely and exclusively with the matter of screw threads. Such simple but crucial basics lie at the foundation of national defense and demand extensive attention to a ridiculously tiny detail. For want of a common screw thread, after all, a kingdom can be lost. This is a continuing historical problem, not merely one of nomenclature.

Industry Standardizing: The Transport Groups

Specific industries may develop safety standards and provide standardization for economic reasons and for the purposes of producing interchangeable parts. The railway industry was a bellwether organization, historically well timed, which manifestly benefited from standardization, including interchangeability.

The railway industry was a major font for standardization and the American Railway Engineers Association is an example of the industry's continuing concern with technology. The Railway Tie Association concentrates on a narrow but crucial aspect of the railroads; the Association of American Railways (AAR) has a membership of 108 railroads and, as a peak organization, tries to coordinate safety and interchangeability. It publishes a manual, distinguishing between "specifications," "standards," and "recommended practice." It tries to keep members abreast of rule changes, communication and signaling advances, and data techniques, among other matters.

The Aerospace Industries Association is a trade association of producers, not operators, but like AAR tries to develop standards and act as an intermediary with appropriate government organizations. These organizations are larger and their functions more obvious (in a semiregulated safety-conscious environment) than, say, the Tile Council of America, but their purposes and modes of operation are quite similar.[7]

Consumerist and Semiconsumerist Standardization: The Case of Underwriters Laboratories

Founded in 1894 as an effort by insurance companies to reduce fires and resulting payouts, the UL earned a reputation that allowed it to become an independent, nonprofit, for-fee certifier of product safety. While it has a core identity in electric, heating, and fire extinguishing equipment, its expertise also leads it into other areas, such as life preservers. UL writes and publishes the testing standards it uses and has operated as a standards publisher since 1903. Many competing laboratories certify that products meet UL standards.

UL itself tests prototypes and monitors quality control, a growing field for the organization. It popularized the technique of certification by publicly recognized initials; manufacturers paying for testing and monitoring who meet required standards are permitted to use the UL symbol on their labels. Consumer recognition and the structure of the organization arguably give UL more freedom than some other standardizers or certifiers. While regarded by consumer groups as cautious, it is also generally considered to be more public-minded than trade standardizers.

In contrast, the American Gas Association Laboratories, certifier for gas appliances, is a subsidiary of the trade association. It relies on ANSI standards rather than developing its own, arguably a superior practice.[8] However, Cheit reports that the relevant ANSI committees are of necessity largely drawn from the gas appliance industry.[9]

Ralph Nader has criticized Underwriters: "They are a very meek, lowest common denominator type operation." A report by the Federal Product Safety Commission in the mid-1980s was more pointed. It found that UL had poor quality control requirements, so that producers were marketing dangerous versions of UL-approved models, including improperly crimped wire connections and knobs that, with little extra pressure, could twist or fray wires. The commission criticized UL's test for heaters—igniting cheesecloth—which its engineers found inadequate as early as 1969, because of increased public use of more flammable synthetics. Yet it took two decades and outside pressure to give UL enough leverage or courage to change the standard. It also resulted in a belated requirement (effective in 1991) for producer quality control enforcement of heaters, an issue the Japanese regard as much more significant than prototype approval.

At the same time, UL did on its own raise standards regarding safety of heaters. In 1976 it adopted requirements protecting against fire if heaters fell over, and in 1984 required more resistant electric plugs. In general, UL's defense has been that it has to judge whether greater safety is worth the outrageous cost for minimal, not maximum, results.

UL is responsive to many pressure groups, including *Consumer Reports,* toward which other regulators have a standoffish attitude. Cheit concludes it is rather more independent and public-minded than most standards organizations—more than theory and "progressive" critics suggest—but is not courageous.[10]

The States and Standards

The great terra incognita of American standards is the state and local government arena. Here the bulk of enforced standards on housing, on business practice, on fraud, and on contracts is enacted or implemented. Yet this arena has been little explored or studied except by lawyers detailing minutely prescribed admonitions.

Very simply put, that is because the states are largely standards users rather than creators. There are very good reasons for this state of affairs, which exerts powerful centrifugal and centripetal influence. There are good Madisonian arguments to explain why states behave as they do and why a federal role is a necessity to keep the "system" from disintegrating. In general, the nonsystem is seldom chaotic, permits local diversity, and is constrained by technological and financial imperatives. That allows federal control to deal only with relatively central efforts, which the states avoid, in part but not wholly because of that federal control.

States are seldom true standards developers or testers, since most are too small to afford such expensive services.[11] The larger ones recognize this as a "free rider" problem: they would pay the freight if they set up the research and share the benefits if the federal government acts as tester and setter.

On the whole, there is little justification for multiple government roles in research. To the degree that an issue is technological, there is no "federal" or "West Virginian" or "Hawaiian" slant on most physical properties or tendencies. A good machine operates well in all fifty states. To the degree that an issue is policy oriented—has regulatory options of special benefit or cost to different social groupings—different governments may use the findings in slightly different ways to promote the ends of diverse populations. On the whole, basic findings are the bedrock of standards and efficacy, and deviation occurs from that norm.

It is efficient to avoid duplication of standard setting, which wastes taxpayer money. Even more than the federal government, states are subject to local pressures to arrive at locally convenient truths (e.g., the superiority of butter over oleo in dairy states, or vice versa in cottonseed-growing states). The standard set elsewhere, the distant, presumably more objective standard, is often politically less questionable and gets the state political structure off the hook. Few state governments can afford the highly professional staff and the ultraexpensive equipment that modern standard setting increasingly requires. As we have seen, even the federal government has difficulty in that respect and in some eras (and no doubt, areas) falls short of the mark.

Even in such an arena as criminal research, which has relatively low overhead costs, the 1970s and 1980s demonstrated this. Money was available to both local and national agencies to conduct or authorize research on causes of crime or methods of containing it. While federal research money was often not well used, some important work, both theoretical and practical, was done. State efforts were basically weak and uninteresting, the type of research best described as not even wrong. A notable exception has been the work of the California corrections department, which had a tradition of closely tracking inmate population and recidivism, and which permitted outside researchers to develop interesting theoretical interpretations. Like much California exceptionalism, that tradition now appears to be history, a victim of bad leadership and increasingly poor financing.

The absence of state activity does not necessarily create a genuine monopoly for federal efforts, however. There are, of course, competing standards developers in governments everywhere. More important, private agencies, primarily of a business nature, abound throughout the system. The specific funding by federal developers is in general abundantly examined and challenged. Private researchers may also be retained as independent scientists for the specific purpose of developing or testing single aspects of a standard of the standard in its entirety.

While state and local governments are poor developers, they have great latitude in choosing from competing standards proposals where they exist. Furthermore, many standards can be adjusted without great cost or research. It required no great creativity for the state of Michigan to conceive of demanding 1 percent less fat than permitted by federal law in chopped meat sold in the state, relying upon the measurement of fat content developed in compliance with federal regulations. (Ultimately, the courts ruled federal meat regulation "preempted" any contradictory state regulations.) Similarly, when many federal environmental rules were in themselves arbitrarily chosen, states found it easy to develop programs more closely chosen to protect their specific geography and resources. States may not be *more* pollution-friendly than the federal requirements, but courts have found that federal legislation generally permits more stringent regulation, and a number of states have developed such programs.

Inevitably, some states become tough regulators while others are more lax. Delaware is notoriously generous to corporation management; Pennsylvania has strict sausage and potted meat regulations, and virtually all national and regional products of the sort therefore meet the Pennsylvania standard. New York, Pennsylvania, and California have at various times established benchmarks for state regulation of insurance, traditionally a state preserve. Pennsylvania has lax bar admission tests, California and Florida tough ones. California has strict auto emission and new-car construction standards, though these are triggered in part by federal emission goals, which are difficult to achieve, given that state's heavy reliance on highways and the automobile. California's building codes understandably contain unusually stringent antiearthquake and anticombustible requirements as well.

There are constraints on deviant practices, however. People and businesses vote with their feet, particularly if neighboring states are easier to live in. Modern businesses notoriously find it more and more easy to pack up and leave. There is resistance to excessive information costs imposed by localism. Increasingly, for example, states have been giving up the luxury of embedding local concepts of equity in their income tax, and are taking the easy road of complete, or virtually complete, piggybacking on the federal return and its system of forms. This is easier on the taxpayer and also makes noncompliance easier to detect.

The state of Louisiana affects great pride in its tradition of civil law and the Napoleonic Code. But it requires only a little coaching (largely in formalities and amenities, rather than substantive law) for graduates of out-of-state law schools to effectively litigate there.[12] That is hardly the case for English lawyers in Scotland, for example, who must deal with truly diverse common and civil law systems. Certainly, Louisiana would experience considerable economic hardship and corporate flight if it seriously followed the civil law tradition of absolute liability rather than the common law negligence tort law.

States also operate within the limits of a legal order where the federal system has supremacy. For over a century—from perhaps 1800 to 1937—the Supreme Court created a zone of state autonomy similar to federal supremacy—dual federalism. Today, the domain of state authority exists only in the absence of direct or indirect federal assumption of control.[13] Because congressional legislation, in contrast to the situation in the nineteenth century, is now virtually a day-by-day process, the proliferation of the bureaucracy and of the federal judiciary, and the nationalization of law (and therefore of federal standards) are also much more prevalent than they were half a century ago. It is more difficult for a state to introduce an outlying regulatory measure without scrutiny and challenge from federal agencies, often at the behest of affected regulatees. This is not to gainsay that such state regulations are a fact of life. When reviewed, they may be judged within the purview of local authorities; or they may not come under review. Nor are federal constraints always applied with anything approaching an even hand.

Still, the general effect is to flatten out local deviations. Extremes attract attention and opposition, and hence review and control by federal authorities.

Variations in local standards may simply result from the idiosyncrasies of decision makers, but are much more likely to reflect differences in political alliances and advantages. Standards users—those who negotiate the final enactment from among competing proposals—are generally consummate consensus balancers, deriving their authority from the consent of those closely regulated.

There is therefore the danger, if not the probability, of differences in interest influence from state to state, and difference in influence between those intimately involved and those remotely affected, who may be unaware of policies or outcomes.

In general, states are permitted the deviations suggested by differential interest aggregation; that is indeed one of the essentials (perhaps the essential) of federalism. Federalism is subject to congressional regulatory or judicial control where a national coalition has framed an implied or direct national policy.

The specter of a manipulative minority gaining advantage through regulation haunts the process. Standard setting is quintessentially open to such efforts. For half a century federal judges exercised some control over such matters under the rubric of substantive due process. That ended in 1937. Some control is exercised through prohibition of undue burdens on interstate commerce. Some states have retained "substantive due process" or its equivalent under their own interpretation of their state constitution, but that practice is declining.

Antitrust Enforcement and Federal Control

Antitrust remains an obstacle to regulatory schemes even when they meet with government approval. In *Parker v. Brown*,[14] the Supreme Court recognized that when governments regulate production or sale of goods in cooperation with private parties, they are in some sense cooperating to restrain trade. In *Parker,* the state created the Sunkist monopoly,[15] and the quota system installed was not only under California's aegis, it was in pursuance of federal legislation. Indeed, aspects of the program had to be approved by the secretary of agriculture. It made little sense to suggest that the Sherman Act (or other antitrade laws) preempted actions sanctioned by later congressional legislation. Indeed, if the case had been so construed, the courts would have had to follow the logic that the later statute implicitly repealed the older legislation, in whole or part.

The courts, however, construed *Parker v. Brown* as saying much more. Regulation means inhibiting something, and antitrust laws are not to become new "due process clauses" limiting state regulations, even those regulations that do not have direct federal approval. Cities have been permitted to grant exclusive franchises for cable TV, for example, over challenges on First Amendment grounds as well as monopoly grounds. Similarly, a city may regulate billboards, even though one consequence may be to favor some companies over others, and even though city officials may demonstrably be friends of owners of the favored firm.[16] Wisconsin's Bar Association regulations requiring members to have health insurance were upheld, even though all lawyers practicing in the state had to join the association.[17] A broad view has been established that the state may regulate through a chosen instrument—an association, a committee, a foundation—and endow it with reasonable power and authority.

Standard setting is a clear beneficiary of "government immunity" to monopoly prosecution. Standards are restrictive; when enacted into law, they are absolutely so. When the standards are legislatively enacted or promulgated as regulations, the fiction might be maintained that the standard setter was the legislator, rather than the expert or consensus body that set the basic parameters. Even that facade does not exist when municipalities or states incorporate by reference codes adopted by organizations, so that changes by the private group instantly become law. Nonetheless, government immunity is still applicable.

Since the 1991 decision in *Columbia v. Omni,* courts no longer allow juries to decide on allegations of government collusion with interest groups through antitrust. Antonin Scalia's majority opinion in effect identified all regulation as in some sense a coaptation of government by interested parties. But interest groups may not use a purported political effort to persuade government as a vehicle for publicly assailing competitors. This is called the "sham exception" to the "government action" immunity from antitrust. Essentially, the Supreme Court majority in *Omni* found antitrust a poor vehicle to deal with the involvement between the legislature and interest groups and the proper boundary of interaction between them. This seems in keeping with Marshall's reasoning in *Fletcher v. Peck* (6 Cranch 87, 1810) and its progeny. Not only would it constitute an intrusion by the judicial branch on legislative power, it could subject each and every action of "the people's branch" of government to such inquiry. The jury's intuition would be a limit to legislative action. There are more appropriate remedies to collusion, such as criminal action, which entails less risk to legislative effectiveness.

The Court was able to move easily to preclude such "collusion" cases precisely because it almost simultaneously moved to require regulatory schemes to be actively supervised by a state or local government that established those regimes. In the absence of the government's direct involvement—where, in effect, there is a private regulator whose action is ratified by a public action at some later date—special scrutiny by the courts is in order. Particularly vulnerable are price-fixing arrangements. The Court was led to this position by evidence that California liquor dealers had been following their association's pricing for long periods before California state "regulators" adopted the same limits. Since price fixing is classically considered restraint of trade, the obvious lack of supervision effectively made the government action an endorsement of monopoly, not a true regulatory policy of the type envisioned in *Parker v. Brown*. In *California Retail Liquor Dealers Association v. MidCal Aluminum*, the Court formulated its requirements: "A State law or regulatory scheme cannot be the basis for anti-trust immunity unless first, the State has articulated a clear and affirmative policy to allow the anticompetitive policy, and second the State provides active supervision."[18] The second stipulation was still assumed to be met by minimum review until a 1992 case involving four states that gave their approval to fee fixing by title companies. Justice Kennedy took a strong stand on what "active review" entailed.

Where prices or rates are set as an initial matter by private parties, subject only to a veto if the State chooses to exercise it, the party claiming the immunity must show that state officials have undertaken the necessary steps to determine the specifics of the price-fixing or rate-setting scheme. The mere potential for state supervision is not an adequate substitute for a decision by the State.[19]

The logic of *MidCal* is in essence a protection against continued regime control by an interest group. It does not prevent government favoritism toward a group, but makes its actions answerable either to a genuine regulator or to the courts.

This logic affects standard setters when their actions are automatically endorsed by governments (as in incorporation by reference), and they are subject to greater judicial scrutiny. The more particularized the group (e.g., AGA, an evaluator of its own heaters, most of which it produced and installed) the weaker its regulatory inspection and the greater the scrutiny.

By confining the inquiry about "supervision" to antitrust litigation, the courts avoid delegation problems and the tough, primal government problems of legitimacy, dealing instead with a complex spate of intricate exceptions and exceptions to exceptions. On the whole, this is very good social policy, challenged primarily by Naderites on the left and very purist separationists—much purer than Justice Scalia—on the right. In general, if a state delegates broad control to a private regulator (e.g., bar associations) or assumes responsibility for regulation, it is not regarded as engaged in any restraint of trade under federal law. Enforcement of private, decision-making "mixed regimes," where public authority is in effect under private direction, is suspect and impeachable, particularly when pricing is involved.

Setting standards and requiring a set of specific characteristics, even if that clearly limits access to the market, is lawful regulation, provided efficiency on safety or similar public concerns are served. Nonetheless, the courts have not given blanket immunity to such regimes, one reason there is still so much tip-toeing around responsibility for standard setting by both public and private agencies.

The situation is equally complex with respect to maneuvers prior to legislation. In *Eastern Railway President's Conference v. Noerr Motor Freight*,[20] questionable but legal political activity by a group to secure legislation was held not covered by antitrust regulations. The railway interests had formed supposedly independent lobby groups and shrouded their own control. Those puppet organizations made public charges, allegedly derogatory to the reputation of the trucking industry. The district court awarded damages based for loss of reputation, but not for the costs truckers incurred working to convince the governor to veto the legislation.

The Supreme Court reversed the decision and dismissed all damage claims. The justices reasoned that since congressional legislation punishing such political activity might well be in violation of First Amendment rights of petition and association, courts should not impute any legislative intent from vague antitrust prohibitions against "restraint of trade." This logic became known as "Noerr immunity" from Sherman and Clayton Act prosecution or damages.

The Supreme Court, however, differentiated between political activity to lobby a legislature or other government entity and maneuvers to control a "private association," even when the standard setters' actions were rubber-stamped by city councils and state legislatures. No right of petition applied to such actions, only normal everyday speech and assembly standards.

The bellwether case was *Allied Tube and Conduit Corporation v. Indian Head, Inc.*[21] At stake was the emergence of a new plastic conduit or hollow tubing for sheathing electric wiring. Manufacturers of steel sheathing organized to control the 1980 meeting of the National Fire Protection Association, at which time a committee report approving the safety of the plastic tubes was to be voted on for the 1981 code. Many governments automatically accept such code revisions, which occur every three years in that particular association. The 1981 code was later adopted in full by twenty-five states and the District of Columbia. Nineteen others adopted it with minor changes.

The steel companies recruited and paid for the memberships and expenses of 230 persons to become "new members" and pack the annual meeting. These members sat together and coordinated actions through walkie-talkies and hand signals. They advanced no arguments or reasons to reject the expert committee report. The vote was 394-390 to return to committee. An appeal to the board of directors was unsuccessful. That body found that what was done was not a violation of the rules, but only of its spirit, and felt it had to accept the vote.

In 1983 plastic tubing was approved for buildings of less than three stories and in 1986 (for the 1987 code) for all buildings. The meeting-packing maneuver had bought a three to six year advantage for steel manufacturers, no doubt a good return for their $100,000 investment. They conceded their actions, but claimed "Noerr immunity" because they were engaged in lobbying.

The district court judge sent the case to the jury to assess under a "rule of reason" with the burden on the plastic manufacturer to prove that the anti-competitive actions outweighed the advantages of standard setting. The jury found that the actions, though not prohibited by the rules, did "subvert" association procedures. Although they found the actions were based at least in part on an honest belief by the steel tubers that plastic was unsafe, the methods were not "the least restrictive means of expressing opposition" and clearly restrained trade. The jury set damages of $3.8 million. The district court subsequently overturned the jury award on the grounds that the association was "akin to a legislature" and that therefore Noerr immunity applied. The court of appeals reversed the decision, rejecting both the logic that the association was "quasi-legislative" and the argument that the tactic was an indirect step in legislative lobbying.

The Supreme Court, by 7-2, upheld the court of appeals. Justice William Brennan's very careful opinion was further constrained by an explanatory footnote in response to a dissent by Byron White, joined by Sandra Day O'Connor. The latter two justices would have conferred Noerr immunity, on the theory that the ultimate target was legislation. The dissenters argued that the court decision endangered the "over 400 private organizations preparing and publishing an enormous variety of codes and standards" contributing "enormously to the public interest."[22]

Brennan argued that the behavior in *Allied Tube* was sufficiently egregious and exceptional that it created little danger of subverting the standards industry. The activity involved was at heart akin to normal collusion, aimed not at convincing or converting but at controlling options by stealth. The decision, he adds, is expressly limited to a standards organization in which "an economically interested party exercises *decisionmaking* authority in formulating a product standard" (emphasis in original).[23] Only those organizations that contain self-interested decision makers are subject to this level of scrutiny. NFPA did not have reasonable procedures to protect against the hijacking of its quasi-legislative authority and the hijackers cannot therefore hide behind what might otherwise be viewed as the public interest in encouraging standard setting. As with most Brennan formulae, there is no indication which of these criteria is indispensable or even primary. NFPA has taken steps to correct the problem, specifically authorizing the Standards Council to overrule decisions and bring into play more review when claims of improper decisions are advanced.

Brennan's opinion was also informed by a rather more scandalous event, culminating in the antitrust verdict in *ASME v. Hydrolevel Corporation*.[24] Essentially, the chair and subchair of an ASME subcommittee helped draft a request by their employer for interpretation of the Boiler and Pressure Vessel Code, which was worded to suggest fault in a competitor's product. They then drafted a clever reply, insinuating the principal feature of the competitive product was not in conformity with the boiler code. The letter was sent out under the committee secretary's name, and was used by salespersons in the subchair's company with great success. Hydrolevel—the upstart company— was sold for salvage, but sued when the *Wall Street Journal* and a congressional committee uncovered the facts. The culprit and company settled out of court, but ASME denied responsibility.

ASME pointed out that it received twelve thousand requests a year for interpretation of the boiler code alone. There is a strong public interest in vigor and frankness in replies about standards. (There is some evidence that the "privates" are in fact more forthright than government enforcers.)[25] Interpretations are sent to designated individuals in the structure, but ASME argued that monitoring sufficiently to discover hidden abuse of authority such as occurred would be inhibiting.

The fact that ASME had not taken elementary precautions, such as requiring all drafters to be identifiable (if only for internal purposes) did not help their cause, though in truth the complex facts needed to understand the trickiness of the interpretation would probably not have been clear to anyone but the perpetrators. There were later events—requests by the Hydrolevel Corporation for reevaluation—that might have triggered some scrutiny, but since even Hydrolevel did not then suspect chicanery, ASME did not feel remiss in not looking for it.[26]

But the fact was, since the perpetrators acted as ASME agents and under normal principles of law, ASME was held liable and paid dearly. Its indifference to the damage done Hydrolevel also gained no kudos for the organization. More important, it illustrated how easily the committee structure lends itself to subtle manipulation. The discovery process in the suit revealed the offending company had valued and rewarded the employee precisely because he had over the years demonstrated his ability to shape ASME standards to help the company.

The application of antitrust triple damages provisions to ASME was viewed with dismay by Rehnquist and other dissenters as a crippling blow to vigorous standardizing and the intrusion of government into a system that did not need fixing. Taken together with White and O'Connor's dissent in *Allied Tube,* this might suggest considerable government intervention into standardization. On the other hand, these two events might suggest that not only is there a great potential for manipulation—obvious to anyone observing the loose structures involved—but also that this was the "tip of the iceberg" and that there was considerable corruption and semicorruption.

Almost certainly, neither conclusion is justified. The government's use of antitrust is predicated largely on actual conspiratorial activity, which is difficult to prove. Even price fixing, though somewhat more patent, is not always easily inferred. The courts have not attempted to draw antitrust implications from either too strict or too loose safety or other technical standards. They give "objective" groups a very wide berth, and "mixed" groups one that is only slightly narrower. Trade associations (like AGA) get the closest scrutiny.

In general, the most effective protection against judicial intervention into actual standards drafting has to do with the question of expertise. The trier of fact—the judge—will usually be inferior in knowledge to the original decider; even more compelling is the fact that the witnesses are likely to be no more expert or disinterested than most standardizers.

The extreme unwillingness of the courts to intervene in standard setting is exemplified in *Radiant Burners v. Peoples Gas* (1968).[27] As a standard setter, AGA is strictly trade association controlled. Its gas seal of approval is roughly the equivalent of Underwriter approval for electric goods. But AGA is also the trade association for gas supplier and equipment producer companies. Often, these companies are one and the same. An equipment producer claimed he was improperly denied a seal of approval, though his heater was both safer and more efficient than that produced by the gas companies. Without AGA approval most gas distributors would not hook his equipment to their lines. In some instances, local codes required AGA approval; in others, the company acted on its own.

Essentially, the standard setter, the competitor, and the crucial supplier of gas were a single entity. Yet both the district court and the court of appeal refused to hear evidence as to the arbitrariness of the denial of approval. That action was viewed as a difference of opinion, a view that ignored the fact that the decision was used to deny the producer access to markets by the very people who controlled the rating.

The Supreme Court reversed the decision, holding that the facts alleged would, if proven, constitute an antitrust violation, and rejecting the lower court's suggestion that the challenger had to prove injury to the general public. Given the classic and comprehensive monopoly situation represented, it is remarkable that it took a Supreme Court decision to allow the producer a day in court. It was, after all, a trade association, with absolute power in most markets and its own authority in most jurisdictions. The gas companies subsequently reached an accommodation with *Radiant,* so no trial on the merits—which might have caused great embarrassment—ever took place.

In both the ASME and *Radiant Heat* cases, the Department of Justice filed amicus curiae briefs urging court action against the standard setters. In *ASME,* the solicitor general suggested that not holding the association responsible would promote even less supervision and more abuse by volunteers. In *AGA,* the government's brief contented itself with criticizing the "public damage" requirement as crippling to antitrust regulation.

On the whole, product certification presents more immediate potential distortions than the current standard-setting procedures, which are predominantly consensual and therefore usually visible to questioning eyes. As the various antitrust cases indicate, there is less countervailing machinery at the end of the process than at its inception.[28]

Cheit's fine study concludes that safety standards are generally not an aspect of regulation that restrictors are prone to manipulate, inasmuch as price is not likely to be affected. Nonetheless, he concludes that voluntary standards are often minimal but provide reasonably adequate consumer protection. Government regulation is more rigid and demanding, though in two of his inquiries the government set standards to meet new situations with surprising flexibility, rapidity, and wisdom. He found no inherent superiority of one mode of standard setting over the other.[29]

The response of accused regulators, on the other hand, seems tied to the standard-setting structure. The companies and AGA, a proprietary association, settled to avoid further embarrassment. NFPA restructured itself, even hiring Robert Dixon, formerly a major Department of Justice official, professor of law, and author of a prize-winning volume on representation, to suggest reforms.[30] With a complex constituency, NFPA had to reassess its balance between internal and external authority. ASME, whose membership is nominally individual, but which relies on advertising in its publications and on other corporation backing, persisted in a curious defense, both in litigation and thereafter. No wrong was done by its volunteers, it argued, and if it was, ASME knew nothing about it and had no obligation to look into it. Even after being severely taken to task by court after court, ASME refused to admit any fault. Indeed, if a recent publication (by an independent writer for the association) is typical, the association is angrier at the *Wall Street Journal* for revealing abuses than at those who misused its processes.[31]

Comparing Systems

The clear centers of standard setting in European countries have long been the national standard organizations, usually government or, as in Britain and Germany, semigovernment nonprofits. Germany somewhat resembles the United States in having regional organizations as well as a national standard setter. Private nonprofits are also incorporated into the system. In all of these, some initiatives are undertaken by trade associations or large enterprises, as in the United States. However, the level of business standard-setting activity is considerably below that in the United States.

While Brussels became a focal point for interest groups as the EC became prominent, the most conspicuous change from the One Europe program was instituted with the American influx; this was systematic, concerted professional lobbying, as opposed to the discreet, quiet, personal, and classic style of European presumption of power. Conspicuous, too, in the new situation was the weakness of many interests, especially the consumerist sector. Until recently, environmentalists were also conspicuously weak, but that is rapidly changing, as politicians all over Europe attempt to steal the issue from "green" parties, and environmental groups begin to operate as interest groups.

The presence and perceived activity of nongovernment groups in the American system is not only considerably greater, it is also formally different. Such groups are the first-level promulgators of standards, the consensus builders, the aggregators of knowledge and opinion. Government authorities may then ratify the standards, making them official and similar to laws, or the "voluntary" standards can be accepted sub silentio with hidden teeth—tort liability, for instance—or even left genuinely voluntary.

In general, NIST conspicuously avoids promulgating standards; it can therefore be increasingly expected to become "the national institute of technology and oversight over others who do in fact set standards." In most countries, the Institute of Standards still promulgates and publishes approved standards with varying degrees of coercive power.

At first blush, ANSI picks up the slack. It publishes approved standards of worldwide repute. It is close to ISO in its international reputation for objectivity. But curiously, ANSI publishes standards others have promulgated. ANSI certifies "objective" structures that follow careful and elaborate rules, and certifies standards which those structures advance, in accordance with

ANSI's equally elaborate procedures. These include appeal procedures, public announcement, careful documentation, and expert evaluation.

The American system therefore radically separates expert, objective standards from government policy and market purchase standards. These are often reunited in practice when legislation embraces standards. Where no official ratification of standards occurs in the United States, the private organization may operate virtually untrammelled, but with full knowledge of antitrust risks.

The line between self-regulation, e.g., the promotion of a quality mark or maintenance of safety through product specification, and improper restraint is not always clear. If a local government, for example, enacts an association's standards, the claim that the original promulgator was unduly influenced by free samples might be subject to litigation. The threat of litigation (even when there is little likelihood of a court victory) is a considerable deterrent to action. Thus this control may actually discourage valuable use of standards.

American voluntarism also goes further in permitting a large measure of self-certification by manufacturers. This simplifies inspection and is a logical extension of labeling, specification of ingredients, and the like. To many regulators, this is like an honor system in testing: cheating can be expected. Even many of the largest and most reputable of the top five hundred American firms have been found to take advantage of self-reporting, particularly in defense contracts. Self-certification is almost exclusively an American practice and on its surface is unenforceable.

Close examination suggests there are strong deterrents to violation, however. The criminal penalties for fraud and violation of regulatory rules are similar to those of preinspection violations, based on the reality that government units do not generally inspect everything. Ultimately, the sanction is that the consumer would have a perfect case. The vaunted generosity of American liability law is the greatest insurer of proper self-certification.

It is hard to defend this arrangement as coherent, rational, or efficient. It minimizes government interference in the formative stages and casts a legal shadow over everything else. It keeps the system working without direct governmental controls, and that must be assessed positively. The system is less than attractive to many Americans and to foreigners, who deplore our costly and arbitrary liability system or consider antitrust policy inefficient and meddling. Certainly, it is a system at cross-purposes with itself.

Part III

Other Systems,
Other Functions

6 Standards in the European Community

Building Blocks Toward Integration?

Eliminating Parochial Standards

THE EUROPEAN COMMUNITY HAS BEEN A powerful influence in the growth of interest in standards. This is paradoxical, since the focus of Community attention has been not on the formation but on the elimination of parochial standards, "nontariff barriers," by a process of "harmonization." But in replacing country-by-country standards with a "harmonized" Community standard, the Europeans drew attention to both the positive and the negative aspects of such regulations.

When the Community moved to its "EC 1992" plan—which was designed to lead to "a single Europe"—it highlighted standards in yet another way. The older form of controlling incompatible standards through bargaining among the members, "harmonization," under attack as nit-picking and as an endless, thankless job, was supplanted by a more flexible approximation of the American system. The free flow of goods was affirmed as the rule rather than the exception. Essentially, restrictions were to be enacted only through community control and therefore minimized. As of 1993, when such a community standard could not be arrived at by consent of all nations, all goods legal in any member country were presumed to be legal when sold elsewhere in the Community, a "full faith and credit" principle for products.

This step was arguably less of an advance than it appeared, since, in the 1979 case of *Casis de Dijon,*[1] the European Court had already upheld the notion that the principle of free movement was immanent in the basic treaty. Arguably, the Single Europe Act merely implements the principles articulated in that decision. Indeed, the commission argued that mutual recognition was already Community law.[2] Furthermore, it remains to be seen how far the European Council and courts will go in the inevitable process of accommodating local measures, for example, restricting inherently dangerous goods, analogous to the old American constitutional doctrine of the state's policing power. This is prefigured in such Community operating principles as the Commission's Note on the Differential Application of Community Legal Acts of January 18, 1978, which attempts to give "leeway in the joints" based on local needs, even in implementing Communitywide directives and regulations, while maintaining Community dominance. More basic still, article 36 of the treaty exempts regulations for reasons of vital national interests (such as health) and the court, even prior to EC 1992, had already developed a reasonably clear set of cases based on these notions.

Of course, neither regulation nor harmonization deals exclusively with product standards. Discriminatory regulation establishing tariff barriers and parochial nontariff barriers can involve regulatory aspects that are different from product standards. Exclusionary tactics can center on modes of production, basic raw materials (however transformed), and other aspects not involving product specification or even production standards.

In the early decades, the court interpreted Community preeminence broadly and local power narrowly. As Henry G. Schermers writes, the court considered the prohibitions against obstacles fundamental. "Accordingly the exceptions to these rules specified in the Treaty which allow unilateral action by the Member States for the protection of national interests have been interpreted narrowly."[3] Faced with a comprehensive control system by the Community, the court could now continue on its old course—consistently, or for political reasons—or it could emphasize a broad interpretation of state power, since such interpretations are easily overridden by new Community legislation.

Still, in practice, the new program was a major step forward. By essentially "occupying the field" in defining European standard setting, the Community took a giant step toward furthering a single market greater in population than that of the United States. This was a dramatic and well-publicized example of the leverage that standard setting has in forming, defining, or disrupting markets, and presumably, even societies.

The point was not lost on American companies and trade agencies, both official and private. To the nations of Europe, EC 1992 was a program for removing internal trade obstacles. To outsiders, it underlined the importance of the Community's power in creating a single European barrier, erecting obstacles for nonmember nations at Europe's border, and at the same time eliminating them for internal markets for Europeans.[4]

The United States was a godparent to the European Coal and Steel community, and naturally saw this step as bittersweet. It had benignly encouraged integration of the European communities as an extension of the spirit and purposes of the Marshall Plan and as reflected glory in what was viewed as the sincerest form of flattery, imitation. Numerous works echoed the theme that the United States was the first common market. Europeans as well as Americans took up the chorus. The European Court, for two decades the most fervent of the Community institutions in pursuit of integration, openly cloaked itself in the mantle of John Marshall, guardian of a new federated society. In the early years, an economically strong Western Europe enhanced American foreign policy as a powerful bulwark and even a showcase against the Eastern bloc. The EEC was in many ways the civil face of NATO, with largely overlapping membership; the two organizations, though they had different structures and different delegations, were nonetheless housed in the same city, and were both aimed at thwarting any contagion from the East. The nerve center of the Community in Brussels, where the bureaucracy is headquartered, was known as a "French house" during its early decades (later a French-German condominium), but throughout the years it was also an anticommunist house. The Russians cemented that bias by rejecting all efforts to work with the Community and by creating its own rival structure, COMECON.

By 1985, much had changed. The evolution of the Community quickly involved paths unparalleled in the history of the United States. The Community's economic growth, though relatively stagnant for a decade, had been conspicuous in the early years. Competition with the economically moribund East was no longer a primary consideration in economic policy, or, to the world's amazement, in foreign policy.

The stark realization that American industry might again be on the outside looking in at an integrated and barrier-entrenched Europe was tempered by strong countervailing forces. The largely American multinationals were already well ensconced in Europe. Indeed, it is only a decade or two ago that Europeans, especially the French, were raising alarms over the threat of American takeover of all industry. With strong European coinvestors, American industrial giants were not only in position to take advantage of a freer enlarged community, they were also in good position to help shape the regime standards for products of the Community. Under the new rules, failure of emergent standards leaves them free to find a government permitting them to produce as they wish, since by and large laissez-faire in the Community will mean, at least on paper, laissez-passer.

For the bulk of American manufacturers engaged in European trade—who do not have such automatic entry—the traditional, continuous, durable, and inert force of the European bureaucracy provides its own reassurance. As a hedge against the worst and a token of potential for the future, branches of American legal firms mushroomed in Brussels.[5] This deluge of lawyers has already established regular conduits to the Community, a core of expertise, and familiarity with Community ways and means.

A flurry of congressional hearings in the late 1980s saw American business representatives and congressional figures suggesting that Europe had an obligation to provide American representation on standard-designating committees. Obviously, such guarantees would not be forthcoming unless mutually agreed upon, and WTO provided guidelines. Obviously, like the United States, other nations or communities have a choice of standards. While accommodating strong external forces, industry and government are the dominant presence on standard committees in every country. The recognition that overt and crude pressure was not going to carry the day, but that accommodation would prove easy enough in most areas, has left American business as hopeful as they are fearful.[6]

All this highlights an awareness of the significance of standards in the process of controlling trade. Tariffs are now too visible an instrument to be used extensively without retaliation. There are quasi-legal international mechanisms—WTO and its close relatives—that cannot be easily flouted. Hidden subsidies and tailored standard making are less visible and are based upon complex and more defensible claims; therefore, they are increasingly the devices of choice. To resort to international mechanisms to battle such violations requires a complex and intricate assemblage of data. This not only buys time for the violators but fogs judgments and makes outcomes uncertain.

At the same time, however, defense of even contrived standards educates the public in the positive uses of standards. The shield of proper usage masks the doubtful uses. Popular discussion of what is and is not appropriate conveys that reality. Standards become visible even when the issue of improper standards is highlighted as a problem of international coexistence.

The Growth of the EC

Europeanization has developed in several discrete stages, with clever and attractive tags for each stage. The creation of the Community has been largely the dream of a thin stratum of elites with a sense of mission, impatient with popular sentiment and enthralled by neofunctionalist international theory. That school of thought has emphasized that constructing unity requires building blocks, a series of positive steps and progressive accomplishments.

The essence of the strategy, according to Monnet, was to stick to technical, functional matters as much as possible, for technicians from different countries would generally be able to agree on a technical solution to a problem, while politicians could be relied upon to make a mess of things. However, as their appetite for complicated technical dossiers was known to be limited, there was every chance that the experts would be left a free hand to "build Europe."[7]

By amassing achievements, the Community was to gain public adherence. It would not only develop its own self-confidence to absorb new function but would also win the hearts and minds of its beneficiaries. Yet the verdict today—with the Community operating at a much higher level of achievement, however—is an echo of the summation of Emile Noel, one of the heroes of Europeanization over a decade ago: "In the economic sphere we have succeeded beyond our wildest dreams, but politically we are almost where we started. Perhaps that is because businesses seldom become governments."[8]

In its first guise, the Community was the European Coal and Steel Union, an anticompetitive cartel designed to ruthlessly deal with excessive world capacity in coal and steel by cutting back below world competitive standards. Its vaunted efficacy in closing mines and factories inspired confidence among trans-European elites and laid the foundation for later phases of the Community. It also left an enduring suspicion on the part of the left that the purpose of the Community was to rescue an effete business elite whose own willingness to compete and innovate was seriously in decline. The working class continues to have the feeling that it has little or no stake in the "Europe of the Trusts."

The success of the Coal and Steel Community at least in part validated the functionalist approach, by providing the launching pad for the new European Community. This was a decisive step, for, unlike the clearly defined Coal and Steel Community, the EC is avowedly protean, and, as time has demonstrated, it has the potential for continually broadening social, political, and economic capabilities. From the outset, it was far more than a customs union or even a continentwide cartel; on paper, it was a sort of federalist state in the making. Although the grasp fell far short of the reach, progress was the pattern of events.

The pace of Community development has characteristically been one of fits and starts, involving maddeningly recurring diplomacy to repair periodic setbacks. The structure of the new Community was a peculiar amalgam of a typical international organization and a national federal government, thereby encapsulating some of the ambiguity at its core.

The European Commission and the European Court became the principal repositories of the "European dream." With a highly limited bureaucracy, an expansive program was difficult to carry out, and thus had to be federalized. The emphasis was on specified areas where a small staff could make a big contribution, thus creating leverage. The role of the Prussian bureaucracy in the German Empire may have been an unconscious prototype, while to some degree that of Germany's current decentralized administration was a visible model.

Numbering only about fifteen thousand, Eurocrat employees can hardly be the ubiquitous pests suggested in many newspapers. Of those, approximately 10 percent are translators working in multiple languages and approximately 20 percent are employed at research centers. The majority are employed at headquarters in Brussels.[9] Of necessity, the EC relies for enforcement on national structures and paper trails. The former is unavoidable, and the latter may well have become an addiction.

The Old Harmonization

By 1980, for example, inter-European tariff walls were essentially supposed to have come down. But this achievement was less successful than hoped. The elimination of tariff barriers, not surprisingly, made nontariff barriers more significant than they had been. Indeed, national parliaments and bureaucracies proved their ingenuity in moving to new arenas. Page estimates that such barriers—largely local standards—rose from 1 percent of value of goods to 16.1 percent between 1974 and 1980.[10]

The other "costs of non-Europe" were adumbrated in the Cecchini Report of 1988, prepared for the commission, and in the Albert-Ball report of 1983. These negative aspects included failure to act to eliminate barriers and to promote and invest in the common market.[11]

What these studies all demonstrate is that the actions of European governments in concert are not always the same in purpose or fact as the sum total of actions of the individual governments. While the EC may decide to move in one direction, the individual members may operate at cross-purposes or in direct contradiction. The EC's complete dependence on the individual state bureaucracies exacerbates the dilemma. As quickly (or more accurately, as slowly) as the EC moves, a dozen centers of contradictory legislation and a dozen bureaucracies thwart it—including the very instruments it is dependent on for enforcement.[12]

So, like it or not, the Eurocrats must rely on precise written edicts—community standards—to control constituent members. In addition, they are continually faced with redrafting edicts to cope with ingenious government efforts. If federalism is, as Bryce said, synonymous with legalism, quasi-federalism seems to entail hyperlegalism.

The effort that came to typify integrative policies prior to EC 1992 was the process of "harmonization"—a logical and necessary step to its supporters, a mindless bureaucratic churning to its critics. The term "harmonization" is applied to any process that reduces multiple state laws into one European law, but has special application to the defining of standard products—including agricultural and processed foodstuffs—for the Community market.

Similarly, while the Community pursued standardization directly through traditional organizations, it had to work around the relationships those standardizers have with national governments. In many instances, these organizations were created by national states or act as arms of them. EC 1992 reaches out aggressively to embrace such structures and actively encourages development of multiple standard setting and testing.

The old process of harmonization was generally convoluted,[13] set in motion by the council or the commission for a particular field or product. The process centered on teams of experts from each member country meeting to compare existing regulations and to negotiate a common position. The national delegations themselves have varied enormously in degrees of cohesion; for example, the French would typically arrive with an agreed-upon position coordinated by a powerful figure in the premier's office, while the Germans—in part a consequence of länder federalism—often came as participants with quite diverse views. The laborious process, when successful, produced something of a consensus. Final negotiations were often left to the member states' permanent (nonexpert) representatives to negotiate from among options presented by the expert committees or Community staff. It has been suggested that these legal-diplomatic representatives sometimes ended up with compromises on paper that had no physical referent, that is, with a verbal standard unworkable in the real world. While this critique seems plausible (since a diplomatic process is used to solve technocratic problem), no examples have been put forward to justify this claim. The complex elitist diplomatic process of harmonization seems to have produced no more inherent problems than does more monolithic and expert-dominated standard setting. It was in essence an internationalized and more cumbersome process, beginning from existing national standards and achieving international reconciliation by painful negotiations, but otherwise was not in principle different from the process most countries operate with domestically.

A more common criticism—with considerable anecdotal evidence to support it—is that harmonization was bound up in trivia and thrived on red tape. Inherently, the process required the staff (and ultimately the commission or council) to write standards of astonishing specificity to dominate already specific national requirements. This created a situation with tremendous potential for satire. Efforts to find the least objectionable common denominator from elements of detailed standards already prescribed in a dozen countries almost always required ineffably tedious and minute compromises. Hence, the harmonization process resulted in—or at some stages of deliberation considered—such matters as the size and stitching of buttonholes in suits or the noise level of lawn mowers. Particularly ill considered were efforts to standardize prepared foods. Trying to define bread in terms of size, shape, and composition created consternation and some merriment in France, particularly at the thought of using English loaves as models. Given the diversity and tenacity of French food concepts, and the strong culinary cultures of Italy and Germany, the effort was not merely unsuccessful, it was ill fated and ill advised. The media have seized upon such examples as the essence, rather than a consequence, of the process.[14]

Since harmonization was aimed at eliminating unfair competitive advantage, the goals sought were sometimes unclear. Agricultural and food product regulation worked better generically than it did in product-specific measures (e.g., prohibiting additives). The definition of standard products was made more complex by the Community mission to ensure equal competition among countries.[15] The often repeated example of regulating noise levels of lawn mowers was justified neither as a grab for power by the union nor as a genuine regulatory or beneficial step, but as an attempt to eliminate a price advantage for poorly insulated mowers in countries not regulating noise. This type of harmonization led to complex casuistic reasoning; harmonization involved not merely tedious legalism, but occasionally, incredible or audacious claims of interconnectedness. These could easily be interpreted as power grabs or arrogance on the part of the Brussels bureaucracy, which was interfering with freedom of choice, dictating lifestyles, and inflating costs by unnecessary rigidity and the proliferation of paper trails. Sometimes, of course, the criticism was right on the mark.

Where harmonization worked well, it was quite successful. The European

Court resolved the issue of protectionism for whiskey in Britain, beer in Germany, and wine in France by making the level of alcohol content the uniform basis for taxation.[16] In order to eliminate any advantage that a country might gain through speed regulations for freight haulers, the Commission required that tachometers be installed in trucks and that a printout of each trip be filed. The resulting control and its effect on safety far exceed the effectiveness of patrolling. The elimination of unnecessary agricultural barriers is strikingly apparent in the availability of food products in stores throughout the Community. This is especially noteworthy in winter and among those who remember the highly restricted availability of fruits and vegetables only a few decades ago.

An interesting example of an early EEC success through wider markets was the diversification of "white goods," small electric utensils, especially for the kitchen. In earlier years, nontariff barriers had meant limited production in each country. Opening up the market enhanced the already respectable German industry but also permitted the Italian industry, with its attractive styling of goods, to compete in Europe and abroad. Unit costs dropped when a stronger market permitted greater competitiveness.[17]

Benefits from the harmonization process, however, hit the wall of diminishing returns. The best targets were generally dealt with earliest, and later moves were resisted more fiercely. Enforcement problems provoked adverse comments and horror stories reminiscent of anecdotes about OSHA in its formative years.

Not surprisingly, a good deal of the criticism came from the English, who joined the Community in what is referred to as "the first enlargement." David Vogel has argued that the English style of regulation is strikingly less legalistic and less closely linked to precise standards than the American system and most continental regimes.[18] Rather, the English have depended on goals and aspirations conveyed to the regulated and on continual nudging by the supervising bureaucrat.

Harmonization is especially repugnant, irritating, and even strange to the English, who are unfailing in their recitation of outré anecdotes regarding Brussels's preoccupation with trivial pursuits and ultrarigid methods. Since two of the most influential media interpreters of the Community are English—the *Financial Times* and the *Economist*—such anecdotes are well circulated and widely known. Although often exaggerated, they are certainly based in reality.

The criticism of harmonizing excess was only part of the growing problems the Community faced in the 1980s. The Common Agricultural Program was piling up both surpluses and financial deficits at a record pace, giving the Community the worst of both worlds. Perhaps even more fundamental was the slowing of industrial expansion.

Surprisingly, it was the very accumulation of negatives that provided the impetus for the next stage of Community development. Undoubtedly, the force of personality of a new, ambitious, and visionary commission president, Jacques Delors, had much to do with the more aggressive stance. He and his allies successfully argued that the Community had begun to stall and might grind to a halt without strong positive steps. The achievements of the Community justified these steps, and its very failures now required further progress. On the economic front, a truly unified European market was to be achieved through EC 1992, a program to eliminate barriers by January 1, 1993, primarily through simplified standard setting. Progress in the marketplace had to be paralleled by political progress.

By 1993, it appeared that the Europeanists had drastically overplayed their hand. The initial rejection of the political charter—the Maastricht agreement—by voters in Denmark, followed by a narrow approval in France and hesitancy in Britain before ratification, required reassessment of the political thrust and exposed much more popular dissatisfaction than had been anticipated. Denmark's approval in a second election was a Pyrrhic victory, especially since it involved numerous exemptions from the political unity supposedly at stake.

The New Harmonization: The Planning Stage

But EC 1992, the economic program for the movement of goods, has proceeded more or less on schedule. In formal terms at least, it is surprisingly close to its greatest aspirations. As to the political problems, they seem to be similar to the cyclical crises and retreats that the Community has confronted and in time surmounted.

Since 1992, the unequal pace of politics and economics has continued and even accelerated, producing anomalies. Goods may travel freely in the single European market, but the incompleteness of political accords has maintained the restrictions on personal travel among the several nations of the EC, though checking of passports is nominal.[19]

In short, the development of the Community continues to be ragged but continuous, discouraging but hopeful, on schedule in some matters, behind but progressing in others. The Community has survived setbacks at the very moment of greatest exhilaration, but, having witnessed quick efforts to repair damage when setbacks occur, Europeans and outsiders are nervous and increasingly leery about the pace of change.

The New Harmonization: The Complexities of Implementation

Among the jewels remaining in the battered crown of EC 1992 are its new approach to harmonization, its push for Community standards, and its new affirmation of the Community's commitment to the free flow of goods. It is in this area that the EC, through the sincerest form of flattery—imitation—makes its clearest acknowledgment of its debt to the United States. This is not surprising, even though Europe's problems, its political history, and its culture permit virtually no reasonable analogy to those of the United States. Nor does the state of industrial development in the struggling American communities of 1789 provide much guidance for how and when to integrate aspects of the industrial complex developed—some say overdeveloped—by European postindustrial economies in the last years of the twentieth century.

In economics, the study of unification has been stylized by the work of a giant in the field of international trade, Jacob Viner.[20] Essentially, he argues that customs unions do create advantages for member states, but some of these amount to trade divergence, that is, the process of finding new partners for existing relations. Other trading changes create new products, new opportunities, and new productivity.

The EC is more than a customs union, of course, but at minimum it is that. To some degree, it merely diverts trade from Australia to Britain, for example, and replaces it with European trade to the advantage of Danish agriculture. But it also permits industrial development and investment of a new type. For example, most Danish industry cannot exist and would not justify capital investment on the basis of its domestic market. It is therefore dependent on EC's openness. With that base it can also produce quite profitably for the United States or other world markets. Furthermore, interindustry trade is unleashed, which can dwarf both the diversion effects and the initial creation of new international markets.

Using refinements of Viner's approach and methods of estimation derived from its specifics, economists have claimed that the incompleteness of the free market in the late 1980s—that is to say, trade barriers—cost the Community perhaps 8 percent of its total potential inter-European trade. In addition, the simple existence of multiple standards cost another 8 percent.[21]

The known political costs involved in the old harmonization were an added burden. On the one hand, the achievements of harmonization were diminishing. After decades of effort, there were still twenty-nine types of electric outlets, ten kinds of plugs, and twelve types of cords commonly used in the Community. British chocolates were not acceptable in many countries because of differing definitions, and carrot jam was rendered salable only by defining carrots as fruit.[22] On the other hand, tremendous negotiation time and political capital were expended without real results. All too often, the EC "standard" was an agreement to accept the status quo—that is, to simply Europeanize all national standards. By 1985, most observers were willing to accept Jacques Pelkmans's verdict that the old harmonization approach was a disaster. Scrapping it was both logical and popular.[23]

The strategy of EC 1992 was outlined in a commission white paper in 1985, "Completing the Internal Markets," and was followed by the Single Europe Act of 1986. A modification of the Treaty of Rome, the act was approved by the governments and parliaments of member states. It has strengthened qualified majority voting in the council and endorsed the economic objectives of the commission's 1985 paper. In debates in the House of Lords, Roy Jenkins artfully pressed the point that Margaret Thatcher had rammed the Single Europe Act through Parliament, and that in many ways it was even more pathbreaking than Maastricht (which she opposed, even breaking with her successor on the issue).

The Single Europe Act included 282 legislative proposals and a timetable for implementing them. Many of these involved defining areas targeted for standardization. According to the commission's evaluation, they have been most successful in eliminating parochial protective standards, and, when fully realized, the elimination of these nontariff barriers was supposed to increase the total gross product by 8 percent. The commission claims it had 90 percent success in its total economic plan before 1993.[24] Furthermore, in early 1994 the commission issued what was intended to be the first annual report on progress in the internal market. It reported that, of the 282 white paper measures listed in 1985, 265—or 95 percent—were adopted by the end of 1993, and all but 2 were already legally in force. Of the remaining 17, half a dozen or so were in draft form before the council, and only a few of the remainder were described pessimistically as blocked.

Of the 265, fully 222 require "national transposition measures." Only half have been "transposed" by all states, and roughly 75 percent have been adopted by ten of the then existing twelve partners. Denmark and the United Kingdom lead, while Spain, France, and Ireland have lagged behind in passing implementing legislation.[25]

Mechanisms to monitor and pressure nations toward compliance have been established. A set of peak advisory committees to deal with new technical problems has also been created, though many of the regime-specific committees have been delayed.[26]

In the standards field, "some 150" new mandates have been implemented, 20 in 1993. The European Committee for Standardization (CEW) is working on 3,000 items engendered by New Approach directives, and about 100 more are in process by electrotechnical and communications standardizers. All this will ultimately require national "transposition," as will many aspects of quality control.[27] Many of these measures have stipulated deadlines of 1996 or later. Still, the usually critical *Economist* has declared that the process was essentially complete in 1995.

The commission has also sought to minimize local provisions that have a defensible purpose but where overlapping or even conflicting standards add to costs. These were roughly estimated to add another 8 percent to the gross product. These rational but burdensome standards include conflicting health and safety regulations among different governments, quasi-legal voluntary codes by different organizations (some within a single country), and different (and often exclusionary) testing methods that empirically define standards. Standardization of testing and measuring standards is itself a major issue.

The commission's proposal encompassed topics and standards agreed upon by the end of 1992. Where no community program was agreed upon, compulsory standards could be implemented at the national level only with respect to safety or other essential matters. Such standards must be filed with the EC commission, which also has the power to freeze introduction of any such measures. Products prepared in accordance with Community standards or—where there is no Community regime—produced in accordance with the originating state's standards, are presumptively salable anywhere in the Community. Some of the cases testing the limits of that approach are described in the council's 1993 *Annual Report*.

The newly established standards regimes vary considerably in specificity and delegation of authority, but they bear witness to considerable effort at simplification and flexibility in relation to the past. The language of most of the documents is even more cordial and user-friendly in style and tenor. Self-certification—an American preference—is possible in some instances and the burden of proof is on the manufacturer or distributor only on those occasions where substitute but equivalent standards are being opted for. Existing voluntary standards organizations are overtly recognized and the Community now contracts with such established bodies for standard setting or test certification, depending on the domain. National administrative and enforcing bodies are given relatively clear missions and their obligations and areas of discretion are well articulated under most regimes.

The attitude represented is as important as the details, though that attitude must necessarily be translated into concrete operations. Rightly or wrongly, the populace regarded old harmonization as exemplifying the old joke about rigid regimes—everything not permitted was forbidden and everything permitted was compulsory.

There is abundant evidence of a desire to drastically increase voluntary, nongovernment, and quasi-government organizations, not merely as testers and certifiers, but as establishers of more flexible—presumptive rather than prescriptive—regulations. Given the resources of the Community, this might seem to be an obvious strategy, but it goes against the grain of European regulation. As a document of the European Commission noted as recently as 1988, "unlike the situation in the USA and Canada where several hundred organizations publish standards, each in its own fields, the European countries have centralized structures, although largely for historical reasons, the electrotechnical sector is an exception."[28] The current encouragement of pluralistic standards is a recognition of the complexities of a continent-sized economy and a tacit acknowledgement of an overrigidified past. It is the EC's form of deregulation, in recognition of a world trend and of Europe's overregulation.

Localizing and Pluralizing in the "New Harmonization": Theories, Realities, and Fears

The "new standardization" also represents a spirit that has come to be known in the Community argot as "subsidiarity."[29] The importance placed on that principle is reflected in the fact that it is a coined word, thus entirely free from any "false connotation" from previous usage. Essentially, "subsidiarity" asserts that all decisions should be made at the lowest level of Community life capable of dealing with the problem. There is strong sentiment in favor of giving the principle juridical life, to operate as an equivalent of the nineteenth-century American use of the Tenth Amendment.

"Subsidiarity" has two guises, as is often the case with legislation or court decisions, a Janus-faced aspect of broad, vague principles. Like court decisions, fundamental constitutional formulae can be read for "all their worth" or "for little worth." "Subsidiarity," like the Tenth Amendment, was carefully crafted to minimize juridical interference and to emphasize a political spirit, a mode of interpretation. It is rather like British "constitutional conventions," expectations of the game resting on gentlemanly nonviolation on the part of Parliament. Even the most elitist Europeanist, however, intent on securing acquiescence to a united Europe without actual concession, must be aware that the intriguing notion of "subsidiarity" has the potential for being enlarged and expanded, even in the European court system. A court creative enough to develop a jurisprudence of taxation and punishment built on "proportionality," a concept not in any of the working documents of the Community, might well create a vigorous system of controls with the term "subsidiarity." Adopting the term, it is clear, was the price of acceptance of Maastricht and ancillary agreements.

Mindful of this history, and of the fact that the Canadian antidote—the granting of express powers to the provinces and all residual powers to the central government—has generated a malaise of its own, the espousers of "subsidiarity" have attempted to distinguish sharply between deeply embodied principle and legal enforceability. Yet they must recognize the potential for both political and legal expansion of the principle, and know that, far from being mischievous of necessity, the principle of subsidiarity may be, as the Tenth Amendment was in fact, the bridge between parochialism and integration.[30]

Standards are not simple in a system as complex and diverse as the EC, and instituting sweeping change carries hazards. For example, eleven different directives were found to contain contradictory, inconsistent specifications of use of the CE symbol, including the basic question of whether it was to be "CE" or "EC." The Eurocrats quickly detected this, but the process of correcting their own failings was necessarily as complex as enactment of the original provision. The problems were finally reconciled in late July 1993, months after the system was to have been in full operation.[31]

In many instances, "debugging" the new system has similar, though perhaps not so fundamental, complications. Many "framing directives" simply call for supplemental rules. Even the allowance of a good deal of time hardly assured that a small staff could complete all the tasks assigned them by a large number of diverse and essentially independent high-level negotiators. This was especially the case where agreement on principles was reached just under the wire, or indeed at any time in 1992. The availability of particular specialized staff could not be planned, and when the principles agreed upon were different from past practice, the transition was often complex.

The old harmonizing units could start the promulgated process whenever they thought the issue was resolved. The new negotiators all too often handed an agreement on principle to the commission staff, with a January 1, 1993, deadline for working out exact language. Often that deadline was impossible to meet, and interim arrangements—usually the status quo—were announced with embarrassment. Further postponements have had to be announced for many other programs, for these and other reasons. One unanticipated snag has been that some of the requirements for naming advisory committees to deal with new products or methods are complex, and some committees will not be in place until as late as 1997, requiring makeshift arrangements until then.

In some instances, drastic, substantive changes were effected, particularly in applying standard European law to Britain's looser business practice. For example, stricter rules have been applied to agents of companies, regarding such aspects as termination of a relationship, delays in payment, and compensation for termination. The rules were adapted from those in Germany, where such relationships are so concretely defined that agreements for agency have been accepted by banks as collateral for loans. Apparently, the British negotiators concluded that legal precision, where loose and unstable practice had prevailed, would avoid disputes and not disadvantage British trade.[32]

In this and many other aspects, smaller businesses complained of greater paperwork and strain. The actual shipment of goods is now free of many government payments and fees—crossing a border does not in itself trigger VAT (value-added tax) payments—but the process necessitates registration for "Euro-passports" for goods. Small businesses particularly have found this increased paperwork burdensome, but it is hoped this is an adjustment problem, not a permanent one. A simplification of the VAT is promised in the future.[33]

The single Europe project was certainly ambitious; in U.S. history only the National Recovery Act was comparable in scope, though breakthrough programs such as the Clinton Health Plan suggest some of the same complexity. Theoretically, the new approach emphasizes mutual recognition of each nation's standards. In practice, the bureaucracy has focused on the product regimes outlined in the master plan. In essence, the threat of free circulation of goods was leverage to obtain an agreement to standardize and harmonize an enormous number of products and processes at a dizzying pace.

The Eurocrats employed a great many new and flexible devices to meet the 1992 deadline. Actual drafting of standards was farmed out in creative ways to experts.[34] Meetings were streamlined. The new rules of the game allowed "qualified majorities" in the Council for measures already approved by the Parliament, instead of the old unanimity procedure.

On the whole, the Community did very well in meeting most of its deadlines. The commission and council were nonetheless bottlenecks that slowed matters in spite of their more community-oriented views. This was obviously expected, since it is at these levels that intensity and political interests coalesce to make last stands. That was true under the old approach and, in modified form, continued under the new.

The problem with postponement is that it invites further lack of confidence in the process and uncertainty about the competence of the bureaucracy. The intent was to simplify and homogenize regulations simultaneously. All in all, the result has been problematic.

The media made their usual jibes at Eurocratic solemnity and lack of humor: The official decision to refer to the paperwork permitting agricultural goods across borders as "a plant passport" instead of, for example, a "transit certificate," was perhaps the perfect example. But these gaffes primarily underscored the complexity of what was being undertaken, and on the whole, matters went as smoothly as could be expected. The incompleteness and vagueness of some aspects sometimes helped in the transition. The seven-year lead time proved more or less adequate, but certainly not excessive.

Reading compilations of EC directives on EC 1992 provide a staggering demonstration of the diversity of efforts that economic regulation in the modern state entails. The Community wisely sacrificed consistent (or even similar) forms of effort, so that the maximum number of areas of economic life could be appropriately regulated. A mixture of EC directives (requiring and ordering national steps) and regulations (which have "direct effect" on individuals) are used. In general, the basic or "framing" directives specify the degree of freedom the member states have, rather than rely on any definition in the Single Europe Act, which could never have approximated the precision to deal with all aspects of that crucial issue of local authority.

This results in a considerably more jumbled situation than verbal and generalized descriptions suggest. Nonetheless, it is a dramatic simplification compared to the old patterns.

All this is hardly without cost. Small companies find the new state of affairs difficult to fathom, let alone comply with. While conceptually simpler, new patterns of compliance must be learned and may ultimately prove more burdensome. Self-certification or type certification frees businesses from bureaucracy but requires new paperwork. The big companies adjust much more easily, and thus have an abiding faith that ultimately all will be adsorbed and the benefits will become evident.

More precisely, new standards now take shape at several levels. These include: communitywide standards for most common goods and agricultural products; national legislation required by Community directives and not in contradiction with Community norms; "voluntary" or "presumptive" standards contracted by agreement between the Community and the network of national and regional standards makers, which can be replaced by those manufacturers having equivalent or superior results; responsibilities of manufacturers at the individual or enterprise level; and conformity to these requirements by distributors, who then affix the "CE" labels permitting transshipment. Enforcement against improper use is not the exclusive responsibility of governments. Businesses may go to court to claim that a rival is not meeting requirements, whether these are Community standards or lower-level ones.

A set of more than two hundred directives has established a varied number of regimes and standards. Some are broad, others extremely specific. In some cases, a single directive may be both broad and specific.

Most "framing" directives outline the Community's interest in a product area and its purpose in regulating it, and define what member nations must do to implement its requirements. They also often define the leeway that national governments have in dealing with products. Less frequently, they define the roles of standards organizations or of individuals. Specific standards contain definitions and function much like ANSI or ISO standards in prescribing technical requirements.

The Community has defined eight "modules" that specify ways that manufactured codes can achieve compliance. Framing directives specify which modules are available to producers and delineate any additional requirements.

Essentially, five modules (A, C, D, E, and H) are self-certifying, while the other three involve authorized testing and verification. The difference in these modules lies in how the certification is established and verified. Different regulatory regimes offer options. In some instances, the individual countries have a choice of which modules they choose to adopt. States also have considerable power in defining acceptable certifiers. Three of the self-certifying systems (modules D, E, and H) require that a quality mechanism be in place; thus, certification of the system by an authorized certifier is needed.

Agricultural product regimes are of necessity more individualized but work in analogous ways. The paper trail required is, if anything, more complex, since it entails health, veterinary, and foodstuff regulations. Again, the *Annual Report* promises simplification and acknowledges that the first specifications were too restrictive.[35] In addition, many of the dozen or so blocked proposals are in agriculture, where national politics is strong. The complexity is underscored by the fact that Spain and Portugal have commitments under their accession agreement that were not to end until 1996, and accommodation had to be worked out. The post-1992 enlargement had complex phasing-in provisions for the new members as well.

Given the multiple documents that had to be worked on by overlapping or totally diverse drafting groups, it was inevitable that contradictions should develop. No terrible consequences have been reported from these imperfections, though individual manufacturers and distributors have borne financial and psychic costs, even after the most conspicuous of these wrinkles were ironed out, in late July 1993. In addition to the CE mark, some equipment must have GS or safety marks.

The Community is also developing a set of "green marks" indicating environmentally sound products, as well as subsidiary marks for irradiated foods and other products consumers might be leery of. The "greening" of the Community and its current interest in consumerism is an effort to create new loyalties and dispel the image that it is serving big business and defending the trusts.

The "eco" label will be voluntary and, it is assumed, attractive to consumers. As of 1993, Denmark was asked to be the "lead country" dealing with paper products, textiles, and building insulation (it has developed a proposal on some paper goods). England was asked to develop proposals on "white goods," hair sprays, antiperspirants, and light bulbs, and has forwarded proposals on most of these. Germany was the "lead country" on detergents, and dishwashing and household cleaners, while France, Italy, and the Netherlands also undertook assignments. The first standards actually approved—in early 1994—involved dishwashers and washing machines.[36] Progress has been slow on others.

With respect to express Community standards, the drafters of directives have been at pains to anticipate national reactions and to tailor national discretion to the complexity of the regulatory domain and the flow of innovation. For example, in automobile manufacture, national governments have the power to challenge new developments when producers certify that their products fall within a previously granted type of approval. These governments, however, are constrained from closely regulating carrots or corn, for example. Quite understandably, even when the Community has promulgated a European standard, different rules of subsidiarity are to be followed depending on the product involved.

When there is no specified norm, goods legally produced are presumed legal everywhere in the Community. But might not pressure containers safe in warm climates be hazardous when subjected to northern European winters?

Do not contamination problems of foods vary? The domains of local "police regulation" have unexplored possibilities and will be clarified in the future.

The "police power" doctrine was the vehicle by which American courts permitted a good deal of local authority, even over matters directly entrusted to the national government—immigration, for instance—not to mention matters "inherently" local—fire laws and restaurant licensing—or boundary issues, such as control of insurance companies. The vigor or laxity of national enforcement of Community standards (as opposed to enforcement by commercial competitors) is yet another variable to be taken up in the future. Experience has shown that these variations in enforcement can promote national interests and can have an impact on the effectiveness and professionalization of European bureaucracies.

Since the Community is almost completely dependent on the national bureaucracies for enforcement policies, it will be a long time before Europe sees reasonably consistent enforcement of its standards. National bureaucracies vary enormously in competence and parochialism, and in their desire to enforce European standards. Populations also vary in their respect for the law and in their enthusiasm for the Community. The public's enthusiasm for Europe is at approximately the same level as the bureaucracy's, though not in every country. The willingness of private citizens—generally, importers or exporters—to avail themselves of the right to sue has generally reflected the bureaucracy's attitude toward those businessmen who have recourse to courts. Not surprisingly, in those countries where officials visibly resent such actions and take unofficial reprisals against them, fewer cases are filed, even under pre-European conditions. This pattern seems likely to continue.

The Shift to Nongovernment Standards

It is conceivable that, in the future, the less articulated and much less publicized new relationships with the network of standards organization will be viewed as an even greater break with the past than the more formal changes of the "new harmonization." By arranging new testing and certification procedures and entrusting semiformal and provisional standard setting to professionalized groups, the Community is transcending the structure of an international organization—which recognizes only national states as subjects and individuals as objects—by incorporating subnational units into its processes.

To be sure, the EC has long since established that regulations (and even some directives) have a direct effect and that, nominally at least, its legal reach is partly federal rather than confederate in nature. Brussels is headquarters for an increasing number of interest group delegations from within and outside the Community. Those delegations are easily taking up the slack resulting from NATO's decline at the marvelous expense account restaurants of Brussels. Generally, however, lobbyists came to the bureaucratic capital of the Community quite some time ago. As standards experts and informal legislators, they worked at the national (or, in West Germany, at the länder) level and, where permitted, participated in national delegations. They are increasingly visible, but their presence itself is not new.

It is clear that the Community is becoming increasingly important for major interest groups. The proliferation of offices in Brussels has been a logical consequence. These relationships, however, have not created popular support and have aggravated suspicions among labor and consumer groups that they do not fit into the technocratic, closemouthed, even secretive bureaucracy, whose Gallic style has been to avoid attention and public accountability.

The neofunctionalist model is being subtly challenged by the shift to a quite different style of bureaucracy, reflecting changes that began with the first enlargement. The British style of openness in interbureaucratic involvement has had the effect of progressively loosening the tight-lipped, brilliant, Gallic-Italian "coup" approach to decision making. Co-optation of interests is increasingly accepted as the preferred mode of operation, and, though not always practiced, it is ultimately appreciated as necessary. The basic reality of the staff-to-general-population ratio ensures that the Community is unable to effectively police what its programs require. The budgetary restraints on growth of any real magnitude suggest there will be no real change in this picture for quite some time. If the Community is to govern the fundamental economy—not merely a thin layer of goods at the top—co-optation and voluntarism must play the major role, not merely for ideological reasons but as a daily practical necessity.

The Common Market was a product of a European neoliberalism, which emphasized the elimination of artificial barriers. There was an incongruity between that goal—simplifying, breaking down barriers—and the means, which has been to pile on red tape. The minuscule size of EC staffs, the growing sense of discordance between ever tighter regulations and little effective follow-up, and the evidence that national obedience is quite different from one state to another have underlined the need for new sources of loyalty and new forms to achieve compliance.

The direct use of standards organizations is a low-level change that depends on expertise and does not necessarily offend or challenge national governments. Only time will tell whether it is a breakthrough or simply an administrative convenience for all involved, but it clearly moves in the direction of broader means of implementation.

The semiofficial setting of presumptive standards also changes the process, by involving processes of validation beyond simple legislative fiat. The rationale for setting a standard is no longer merely that it is the best compromise possible among competing states; the claim may now be that it is technologically sound. This will almost surely continue to push the Community to accept greater "transparency" in standard setting, as it has already been forced to do under international pressure. "Transparency" is GATT-speak, not Eurobabble. "Transparency" requires known procedures and open decisions, particularly to protect foreign interests. It has also operated as a catalyst for internal reform in the EC, much as it has done in Japan. This opening has encouraged American technical and commercial groups to feel they are being accorded a fair hearing, whereas they once felt they were not. More important, it suggests a role for European consumer safety and labor groups which, combined with greater say in Parliament, might elevate the average European citizen's sense of belonging and contributing.

Since regulations of the Community are, by constitutional definition (in the Treaty of Rome), applicable to the individual citizen, and since directives, though aimed at national authorities, have long been held to confer rights of litigation, the new harmonization's emphasis on the right of competitors to bring complaints underscores as much as expands standing to sue. Many of the implementing directives specifically define a right to litigate if the CE sign is misused. Arguably, this will automatically eliminate a need for litigation over the issue of standing. Whether outcomes of cases could also be affected by this provision is a matter of speculation at this point. The right may be broadly or narrowly interpreted, both procedurally and substantively.

By definition, however, the new approach also grants more power to individuals and firms to certify their own compliance with necessary requirements. In complex areas, like automobile manufacture, the Community still does not accept self-certification (largely an American preoccupation), but does accept type certification, and should allow it to cover minor variations or improvements on the manufacturer's say, much like the Japanese practice.

In other areas, where performance or design standards are precise and simple, the producer is in effect a self-certifier of compliance. The directives and regulations are often quite specific regarding the burden of proof and who may inspect for the producer. At least on paper, this results in great decentralization.

The Community encourages voluntary certification and standards in most areas. As in many other systems, distinctive and distinguishing marks, confirming adherence to standards, are found in many parts of Europe. Many have a long history in their regions or nations. The CE mark is supposed to be highlighted and these other marks less prominently displayed.

Summary

In recent decades, the growing perception of harmonization as a means of social legislation, or as the camel's nose for Community expansion, detracted from the economic force of the process. Splitting off the economic issues of the single European market from the political impact of the Maastricht agreement refocused attention on the economic consequences of harmonization. The special attention paid to standards, with the strong claim that the elimination of conflicting standards and testing could reduce prices by one-sixth, cast a spotlight on standards as never before.

The strategic effects of EC 1992 may have been fully intentional or largely accidental. Certainly, the EC's political program—the Maastricht Treaty—has operated as a lightening rod for the combined venture of a more integrated Europe. The economic program was accepted without real opposition, almost without a murmur. And the drive to comprehensive, but no longer minutely detailed, standards reversed a course that would have created more problems the longer it prevailed. Avoiding this paradox, the Community has sidestepped the growing unpopularity of overregulation and, it is hoped, has gained the advantage of flexibility.

Federalist theorists have more or less accepted the position that the unification of disparate states has always occurred as a product of war (conquest, resistance to conquest, or, in the outlying case of Australia, as a misperceived anticipation of a war that never came). The Soviet presence constituted such a threat of war; even in Europe's gravest hours, however, political and military will was manifested in NATO, while Charles de Gaulle insisted on France's sovereignty and the separation between the economic community and NATO. The paradox of Maastricht is that the push for political enhancement of the Community coincided almost precisely with the unraveling of the Soviet Empire. Subsequent events suggest the timing was misguided.

For all its fanfare, EC 1992 was an almost invisible milestone. By January 1, 1993, the bulk of the key directives were a year old or more, and much domestic implementing legislation was also already in place. The new openness was a legal, but in many instances not a commercial, reality, since new patterns of shipping and deal making were yet to develop. Sold as a program for individual initiative, new entrepreneurship, and prosperity, it seems to have avoided the animosity elicited by Maastricht and did not prove a prominent target for oppositionists.

The seeming success of EC 1992 promises growing homogenization of standards and economic integration with significant payoffs. But will that lead to continental cultural standards and joint understanding? The alarming disintegration of economic and political communities in the past decade suggests that neofunctionalism overestimates material and administrative factors and vastly underplays political and symbolic ones.

The nagging fears are twofold. The first fear is that petty standard setting will continue to predominate over bold, imaginative, delegated regulation. The habits of bureaucrats might persist and therefore fail across a much wider area. The second fear is that EC's limitations in personnel and politics will doom the program, even if it is carried out with imagination and verve. Enlargement through the incorporation of nations skeptical of the EC, which have bargained hard for exceptions to Community law, suggests that political obstacles are growing and that advantages are waning.

In a sense, EC 1992 was bound to succeed in approximating its goal of putting its common expectations on paper. Some of these "agreements" are face-saving, and not at all real. Others may prove unworkable. Others will not integrate much of anything. The number of types of electric plugs in use within the Community has not diminished since 1992, and unification of standards in the real world is tested by reality, not by the promulgation of official decisions. The Achilles' heel of the Community remains its lack of enforcement mechanisms. As it expands its focus from controlling governments to enabling individuals, its capacities are strained still further.[37]

The lack of adequate Community enforcement mechanisms has led to ingenious and interesting efforts to co-opt other organs, notably standards organizations, to help. In addition, it has forced the EC to insist on voluminous reports and registration procedures that may become as unpopular as the old harmonization effort. The EC proved it could do what it has always done well—draft standards and embody them in documents. It has made its decisions, but now it must do what it has not done very well in the past. The time has come to enforce those standards, and that task may well be beyond the capacities of the Community.

7

Standards and the Japanese Miracle

The Politics and Economics of Quality

I N ONE SENSE, THE STORY OF JAPANESE POSTWAR industrial success is a chronicle of standards. Facing a postwar need to recover from a disastrous war, a felt need to become industrially the prominent power it had failed to become militarily, Japan was handicapped by an image as the producer of shabby, inferior goods. "Caveat emptor" was not a good strategy in export policy, because substandard products reinforced the negative image of Japanese products generally. The solution was to turn to vigorous national quality standards. In its most precise formulation, quality control, controlled sampling, and methodical step-by-step precision would ensure that quality was built in, checked over, and instilled in the psyches of workers and managers alike. In standards there was the promise of success, of redemption. Quality control became an obsession, almost a religion, as Japan rebuilt itself from wartime devastation.

This fervency was not merely expedient, wise, and successful, it also fit cultural patterns and the Japanese character. Assuming responsibility for successfully carrying out a task, emphasizing regularized and carefully planned actions, and sharing decision making are all characteristics that observers and regional specialists have noted in both prewar and postwar Japan. The Japanese are risk-averse, preferring strong training and process over individual innovation, even in drama and other arts. Quality in all its manifestations—even in the presentation of food—is also a cultural consideration. Thus, these impulses combined in a profound, harmonious, and effective way.

The regulation of quality and safety is a total commitment of the Japanese government, which undertakes protection of the consumer and theoretically guards against improperly conceived or risky products. It is not merely that an organization needs government approval; licensure power exists because the government is in loco parentis so to speak, charged with the responsibility to protect consumers. This noble stance, sometimes cruelly belied by experience, nonetheless undergirds the system of regulation. A bad product reflects on the government even more than on the manufacturers. This age-old attitude too meshes well with total quality commitments.

A Tradition of Regulation

The tip of the standards iceberg is manifested in a number of government, quasi-public, and privately granted quality marks, many of which are widely recognized and therefore believed to be effective local selling points. Some of these marks seem essentially designed to favor Japanese products in the domestic market.[1] Many are aimed at assuring quality for export markets as well. All participation in securing such markings is deemed "voluntary." However, in such areas as plumbing, ministry regulations adopt trade association evaluations in such a way as to make hookups to public water and sewer lines depend on compliance. Most ministries also accept the principle that products adopting the government standards (JIS and JAS) should be given preference for public purchases; thus, there are clear, competitive advantages to conforming to "voluntary" requirements. Japanese government agencies had clear instructions to buy Japanese products until 1972, and the GATT-induced change at that time was ambiguous regarding whether the old order still applied absolutely to such items as computers.[2]

In addition to these quality standards, the government assumes a vigorous regulatory role for products affecting consumer health and safety. This creates a paradox: the manufacturer has little or no liability in terms of actionable litigation, but the government takes on a highly theoretical liability. Once the Japanese government permits a product on the market, it is presumed that the manufacturer has satisfied virtually all legal elements of responsibility to consumers with respect to basic design and safety. There is a strong expectation that individual "lemons" will be serviced and that the producer will provide remedies, especially during an undefined initial risk period. Hence, there is an emphasis on the need to know whom one is dealing with and whether the manufacturer is likely to stay in business. Those responsibilities to assure a serviceable product, however, are social and commercial obligations that are not enforced by law. (In one instance, where products are granted the semipublic "S" mark for safety, the producer pays a tiny royalty for each item and the nonprofit certifying association has a fund for those proving damages. Those awards are both infrequent and very small by Western standards.)

Government Marks of Quality

The government-sanctioned marks are the JIS (Japanese Industrial Standards) issued by the Japanese Industrial Standards Committee and supervised by MITI, and the JAS (Japanese Agricultural Standards), supervised by the Ministry of Agriculture and the Ministry of Health and Welfare.

JIS marks are issued after a rigorous inspection, both of a product prototype and of the factory involved.[3] Quality control at the factory is the key issue. As an MITI official observed in an interview in 1992, "It is no big trick to produce a high-quality model." Regularized quality is perhaps even more important than product design, and is rigorously investigated.

The requirement that plants be open to government inspection, both when the original JIS mark is granted and subsequently, still operates as a strong deterrent on non-Japanese companies' use of the mark. Until the Tokyo Round and the subsequent "Action Program" era, there was no provision for inspection of factories outside Japan, and even today the costs of such inspections to the producers make it impractical for most foreign companies and products. Of course, this is an inevitable problem if the factory is to be inspected, and no one argues that the Japanese are unfair in assessing the costs of sending inspectors abroad. These costs are inherently high and are reasonable only for high-volume or high-price commodities. At the same time, the government maintains a complaint service where consumers may bring a suspected lemon and, if inspectors agree, obtain a substitute.

Many foreign, especially American, companies also feel unenthusiastic about inspections, even of plants located in Japan. They fear a breach in product security, reflecting a conflict between Japanese and Western views of the relative value of "trade secrets" and "intellectual property." This conflict also manifests itself in concern over the Japanese making publicly available patents that, in the American system, may be kept confidential as trade secrets. Grants of such protected patents are published in Japan as a routine matter; only applications are protected.

The JIS process is rigorous and few Japanese products go through it. An estimate derived from interviews at MITI is 3 percent of such products. While some have speculated that only larger companies can afford the process, an MITI official reported that the majority—perhaps as much as 60 percent—of all such marks are granted to companies employing fewer than three hundred employees, which is MITI's break point for "small and medium" enterprises, as opposed to large companies.

Since the Tokyo Round, foreign companies have officially been qualified for the JIS mark. Like the Japanese enterprises, they are not required to seek it, though where government purchasing is an important factor, they are sure to do so, since in practice government agencies usually require them in their purchases. Positive approval of basic procedures also makes approval of product changes and variations comparatively easy; once a complete inspection process is positive and the inspectors are confident of quality control, new products are easily, even routinely, approved. It is widely believed that there still exist remnants of favoritism to Japanese, as opposed to foreign, producers, with respect to what agencies choose to define as a wrinkle and what they call a "new product" requiring recertification.

The JAS mark is conferred on agricultural products and foodstuffs generally. Most of the popular fruit juices sold in ubiquitous vending machines carry a JAS mark, and many are American brands. Prior to the Action Program era and the government's easing of restrictions, no American agricultural brand had a JAS mark. In several instances, American produce was incorporated into a Japanese product (e.g., tomato paste into ketchup) with a JAS mark, but the Japanese firm was the identifiable final form producer. Since production facilities or methods of preparing foodstuffs are not usually at issue with such foods, and inspection of basic facilities is needed only for sanitation, not design purposes, that exclusion was especially resented. At present, many products of American origin sport the JAS mark and generally boost the image of American agriculture, which is quite high in Japan.

JAS and JIS requirements are similar to other Japanese processes of certification, though more stringent than they. At least four ministries had standards of their own in 1991. Further incorporating these principles, the consumer group NGO (Non-Governmental Organization), which issues the "S" or safety mark, charges a very nominal royalty for products as insurance against claims. While nominally the equivalent of absolute liability, this private structure of recompense actually pays small and infrequent awards of reimbursement. The "S" mark is apparently esteemed by customers more for the rigor of its guarantee than for the expectation of any recompense. Few claims are reported, and even the government officials directly responsible for quality control were unable to enlighten me about how to file a claim. (In fairness, this is endemic in Japan, where crossing organizational barriers is not easy.) Figures were not easy to obtain from Japanese sources and direct studies, but I was able to get them for two years from an OECD study, and there is every reason to assume these figures are typical. In 1985, twenty-seven complaints resulted in compensation totaling 6.5 million yen; in 1986, nineteen cases netted a bit over 1 million yen. This is pocket money, especially in comparison to American awards.[4]

The Vulnerability of the Japanese Consumer

There is a myth of the demanding Japanese customer and the protective Japanese government; in fact, however, consumerism is extremely weak and protection inheres largely in personal relationships—the customer knows the seller—and in the broad availability of alternatives. This came into the open as a political issue in 1993, when the weak consumerist movement tried to enact legislation aimed at legalizing consumer rights.

Because it is relatively easy for an established concern to inaugurate a new variation of an old product line with government approval, the resulting protection or immunity of the firm is considerable in proportion to the slight expense. On the other hand, new enterprises, especially foreign firms, may experience disproportionate hardship. Thus, in a sense, the Japanese domestic market can provide a safe and largely exclusive laboratory for new products produced by old companies, with little probability of any liability at all. Newcomers have a different and much tougher row to hoe.

In one sense, Japanese business is dominated by its setting of standards and by the government, which permits products to reach the market in the first place. As with almost everything in Japan, appearance and reality intertwine in complex ways.

The Vulnerability of the Importer

Dealing with the Japanese used to be—and largely, still is—a flashback to a different era. Permission to do business, sometimes requiring a Japanese sponsor, is a prerequisite, though paradoxically, formal incorporation of a business entity is quite easy. Among other obstacles, product quotas used to be assigned to established manufacturers or distributors for some goods. The identity of the firm and amounts assigned it were generally a closely guarded secret. So were the rules. For example, some unused quotas were believed to be annually transferrable; others apparently were not.

Complaints about inspection processes are legion and sometimes outrageous. In one extreme case, meat was refused entry with the demand that the names of the actual slaughterers be given. Cake mix was held in storage for "inspection purposes" for months, until worms appeared. Inspectors demanded information on the exact roasting process for coffee. Whiskey containers had to state the amount of duty paid abroad, and currency fluctuations made it difficult to give correct information in yen.

Particularly galling were persistent arbitrary actions. After long delays, officials asked for more and more details. Often, after one of the many reforms of the process, officials would still demand documents that had been officially proclaimed unnecessary. An OTO (Office of the Trade Ombudsman) study in 1982 determined that in fully 10 percent of cases where entry was denied, no valid restriction was in order.[5] In many instances, approval or appeal had to be requested by the importer, who was not necessarily equipped to deal with the issues or provide the information requested.[6]

The direction of Japanese regulation is largely toward the removal of obstacles. A 1991 study by an American consulting firm found 55 percent of regulatory developments to be easing barriers, 40 percent to be stationary, and only 5 percent to be worsening. Among the areas where no progress was seen were hiring and partnership restrictions. Among those improving were tariff and standard regulations, processes, and restrictions.[7] However, it is strongly suggested in the media that a more restrictive turn occurred with the recession and the move toward the elections in 1993. The winning parties, however, campaigned on the principle of eliminating preference for specially favored rotten borough districts, a key stronghold of the long-entrenched Liberals.

As part of its culturally indicated paternalistic policy, the Japanese government assumes formal responsibility to prevent dangerous products from reaching the market. With a purposely weak, small, and slow court system, liability law is for practical purposes not part of the business picture. Commercial transactions take place with reliable, steady individuals or with firms that stand behind their products. The government reinforces this by assuming a somewhat fictitious legal responsibility for having permitted faulty products on the market. Thus it has both a regulatory and a financial stake in maintaining high product standards. Conceptually, it would not only be failing in its duty to its citizenry if it permitted poorly conceived or dangerous products on the market, it would in theory also expose itself to financial loss. (In the *SMON* case in 1979, the government in fact paid damages for not instituting adequate safeguards for monitoring the dangers of a new drug. In several others, settlements were paid. Thus, historically, this liability is not completely theoretical.) In practical terms, that risk is almost nonexistent; but a bureaucrat, fearful he might someday be held to have been lax in permitting a product or foodstuff to reach the market, will be cautious.

The most consistent drive in Japanese culture is toward avoiding error rather than achieving overwhelming success. Even an experienced clerk will not generally sell a product without a clearly marked price, for example. Taking on responsibility is not sought out anywhere in the system, though responsibility that is accepted must be fully, faithfully and loyally discharged. The bureaucrat thus sees granting product approval as a personal as well as a government act and, as a form of self-protection, may seek evidence that is unnecessary or even impossible to obtain.

Since, in general, the Japanese bureaucratic style rests on pragmatism rather than universalist principles, implementation of standards will vary according to bureaucratic relations. Reliable producers are given greater leeway and are asked for less evidence than the unreliable or unknown dealer. Under these circumstances, the stranger, and especially the non-Japanese stranger, operates at a clear disadvantage. In addition, since the standard by which the product itself will be judged is generated by a relatively inbred and largely unprescribed and hidden process, the non-Japanese dealer is even worse off. Both standard setting and implementation are unconsciously—or worse, consciously—biased against new faces in the system. The dramatic changes in the past few decades are moving to eliminate that glaring bias, but the malady lingers on and the memory still embitters people who are old hands at dealing with Japan.

Some industrial products can go on the market with less stringent processes of inspection. Where only the product (as opposed to the plant process) is inspected, the sampling may be batch by batch; at any rate, such detailed attention is justified because of the more ad hoc process.[8]

Product Liability in Japan

In general, liability standards require proof of gross negligence before the manufacturer is deemed at fault. This includes a systemic failure to produce at a proper standard, knowing failure to follow through on potential dangers, or persistence in producing a knowingly defective product. Accordingly, litigation is rare and judgment of liability even rarer.[9]

It is estimated that perhaps 150 liability cases have been filed since 1950. Published opinions in liability cases are said to number only about two score. In two famous cases, the government was held responsible for failure to require follow-up studies on a powerful drug introduced as a cure. In less than a handful of cases, manufacturers have been held liable for negligent behavior. In the most notorious manufacturing pollution case—involving proven and palpable fraud by the company's representatives during twenty years of proceedings and settlement—the awards were of up to sixty thousand dollars per person, plus medical and other expenses.[10] Because of the personal and environmental ruin for the entire community, the egregiousness of the company's conduct, and the ultimate political and legal triumph of the victims movement, the settlement was unprecedented. Typical awards are much smaller, yet filing costs alone often exceed three thousand dollars.[11]

This, of course, is a major deterrent to litigation, but it is only one of many. The absence of contingency fees and crowded schedules of barristers contribute to relatively high legal fees for collecting small awards. The absence of a jury, it is suggested, makes verdicts for plaintiffs problematic and awards small.

Tort cases are thus infrequent and product liability proceedings unlikely. For example, a crash of a Japanese plane resulted in a proportionately smaller number of suits filed on behalf of the Japanese victims, who were in the majority, compared to foreigners. And surprisingly, products with known defects, for which Japanese producers have been forced to pay compensation in legal actions abroad, have not been a basis for lawsuits in Japan itself. A prime example is a Japanese diet supplement that produced payouts of more than $600 million in the United States.[12]

The weak consumer movement in Japan seeks perennially to alter the system. A new law was passed as one of the few achievements of the reform movement of the mid-nineties, which may become important in implementation. While lawyers are significant players in Silicon Valley and contribute to American entrepreneurship, Japanese lawyers are not consulted often enough by Japanese producers for them to recall their participation in the creative process. Rather, it is the American lawyers employed by the Japanese firms that must be consulted to avoid trouble in the United States.[13]

Not surprisingly, Japanese industry has tended to support the system. While, theoretically, new products are severely restricted, that is not always so in reality. A new product has a burden of proof of safety and reliability, and that theoretically means that anything not permitted is forbidden. In practice, this is not so draconian for minor and uncontroversial products or those that seem similar to existing ones or that just seem safe. Often these are accepted at face value. The need to justify is not usually elaborate for variants of existing products, especially for experienced enterprises that know the ropes. Even so, neither the broad, open claim of liability in common law—in its most extravagant form, that is, in the United States in recent decades, or in its more modest form, in English law—or the continental system of absolute liability for major products (hedged by strong limits on litigation) has made real headway in Japan. Industrialists feel they can innovate only a shade less rapidly in Japan than elsewhere, but without clouds of potential losses hanging over them and without having to foresee totally unexpected negatives in the distant future.

Product Standards and Protectionism

In another sense, there is a darker side to Japanese product standards. Foreigners in particular believe that the standards serve as key devices of Japanese protectionism and autarky. The charges of overt and covert manipulation of standards to exclude foreign products have been part and parcel of American-Japanese relations for decades. As with much else in Japan, there is a ritual of announcing new trade internationalization and liberalization, followed by regression to the old autarky. There is a grand occasion when heads of state or at least ministers of foreign relations announce yet another new, dramatic set of ameliorative steps, which turn out to be rather less sweeping than first suggested and often grudgingly administered. There follows a round of high expectations, some disappointment expressed over the actual implementation steps, and finally new acrimony over the limited improvements that ensue. Both sides emerge even more frustrated and angry with one another.

Accusations of unfairness have centered at least as much on the process of administration as on classifications and official categorical exclusions. Categories of forbidden goods have clearly been reduced over time. But at heart, "Japan bashers" continue to claim that, pragmatically, little has changed. In general, most careful authorities—observers of international trade or Japanese studies experts—reject that conclusion. Most see enormous progress in procedure and in overt standards, and trace the difficulties of market penetration to the industrial structure, other interrelationships between financing and ownership, and especially, to the intricate, highly personalized distribution system. Breaking through those hard-core, characteristically Japanese systems requires long-range commitments, personal involvement, and the forgoing of quick profit in favor of a piece of the pie in the long run, all qualities not typical of Western business style. But where those businesses have found a distinctive niche and cultivated the market with cultural sensitivity, Western enterprise has had some significant success.

Initial difficulties encountered by Western businesses came as another shock and represented a type of business regulation generally archaic and forgotten in the West. Enterprise was legally permitted only when authorized; the tradition of monopolies and government prerequisites was supplemented by exclusion of foreigners from specific enterprises. To this day, a non-Japanese resident must have a Japanese "sponsor" who guarantees support or employment. The island character of Japan and its historic isolation, even the classic historical permission to foreigners to undertake selective business in selective ports, all carried over into a situation where foreign business found itself treated as exotic and potentially suspect, and rightly felt oppressed. This was epitomized in the suggestion of Tsutaoma Hata, some years before he served as prime minister, that American beef should be totally excluded because Japanese intestines differ so radically from those of foreigners.[14] Somewhat disingenuously, the powerful Japanese business federation has for some time maintained that since secret lists of forbidden imports and other bureaucratic archaisms apply equally to Japanese and foreign firms, the latter have no special grievance. There is certainly a grain of truth in that: The system has been vexing to all businesses, including local ones, but it is especially difficult to understand for the neophyte from another culture, and the pragmatic, even arbitrary use of bureaucratic regulations permits the continued favoring of domestic enterprise in critical ways.

Because power and authority are not coterminous in Japan—indeed, Haley argues that typically they are deliberately placed in different hands,[15] it is often difficult to pinpoint exact regulations. A maddening list of prohibitions abounds, particularly with respect to foodstuffs. This has permitted cabinets and prime ministers to produce long laundry lists of deregulated products on various state occasions. Many of these prohibitions are historically based and exist as internal memos that respond to specific problems: for example, after the poisoning of a member of a love triangle through tampering with a soda bottle, screw tops were forbidden in imported soft drinks. Jams, ketchup, and condiments continue to have screw tops, apparently on the conviction they will not be vehicles for poison.[16] Such ad hoc (and often secret) regulations might be overlooked or deliberately ignored for small shipments but invoked for large ones, especially when a Japanese firm applies pressure. Such chancy bureaucratic behavior is consistent with the general enforcement culture and can therefore easily accommodate a desire to limit imports, or it can be the direct result of local competition's pressure.

The cosmetic and drug industry, both foreign and Japanese, has had to cope with a formidable secret list of forbidden ingredients. Again, it is not clear why the administering agency has operated so close to the vest, but it appears to be the result of its lack of confidence in its own standards, its fear the list could not be rationally justified. Bureaucrats in Japan often use such evasive devices to avoid conflict. Since Japan has agreed under GATT not to operate through covert lists, has promised to advance "transparency," the government has gradually been publishing partial and progressively inclusive lists of these forbidden substances. Given the strong position of American and German companies in the cosmetics and drug areas, this past restriction cannot be said to have been targeted at foreigners by any means. Rather, current efforts to impact GATT standards of "transparency" operate to benefit upstart companies, both foreign and domestic. It has always been reasonably possible for any long-time cosmetic producer to deduce the nature of most forbidden chemicals, simply from bans and approvals,[17] though direct hints might have also been dropped to manufacturers with a special rapport with government. By making such lists known, the Japanese apparently strengthen the position of upstarts; that practice could at least theoretically help Japan's domestic producers in one of the rare and hard-fought areas where foreign firms have actually forged ahead and established dominance.

In most areas, however, bureaucratic arbitrariness has historically operated to disadvantage imports. This is far more typical than the cosmetics situation. Anecdotes abound of overly formalistic application of rules that unnecessarily cause delays and result in rotting of perishables, of sudden changes of classifications without explanation or advance notice (this can have devastating consequences for procedures or tax rates or both), of surprise invocation of unpublished and unattainable regulations. Foreigners, especially Americans, complain of their sense, perhaps a paranoia, that a comprehensive battery of hidden and arbitrary controls was invoked whenever the foreign company was beginning to have some success, that their Japanese competitors could somehow through political clout intensify constraints whenever the foreigners achieved a degree of acceptance with customers.[18]

Most of the complaints, however, refer to the past and are increasingly becoming history. By the time of the acceptance of the Tokyo Round, it had apparently become clear to the Japanese leadership that it had more to gain from accepting universal standards with respect to exports than from defending an autarky in dealing with imports. It is difficult to say to what degree it still thought it could carry water on both shoulders. It is possible for a nation to be hypocritical, advocating open exports and closed imports. Japan is hardly unique there.

The Japanese System and International Trade

The GATT-WTO standards are in the tradition of international criteria of exquisite ambiguity, featuring goals more than bright line boundaries. With respect to many specific practices, an importing country may even argue, with complete sincerity, that they are a violation of WTO principles, while the perpetrator insists with perfect innocence that they are in conformity to those principles. In agreeing to the Tokyo Round, the Japanese leaders must have been aware that they would hardly be strapping themselves into a straitjacket. Yet increasingly, the vague principles of GATT have been transformed into full-scale regulations, even moving toward the ultima thule of performance standards, because it is abundantly to the advantage of Japan to play the world standards card as often as it can. For example, Japanese airlines have agreed to adjust to world standards in providing compensation for crashes.[19]

It is not that there are no examples remaining of Japanese exclusionism. The rice policy, a total monopoly for domestic sources, which is estimated to triple or quadruple the price to Japanese consumers, is a symbol of the preservation of trade barriers. Even the 1992 relaxation, based on an acute shortage, was announced as a temporary measure, and the 1994 allotment seems little more than a gesture. Still, economists and other experts in international trade calculate that the degree of exclusion is no more—and is probably less—than that of other industrial countries, including the United States, and that most of the remaining obstacles relate to Japan's intricate informal organization and distribution system. Some complaints reflect the Japanese inclination to do business with Japanese, and even more, to prize reliability over price.

It is clear that the Japanese do value continuity of services and supply and that they minimize competitive pricing. The American Chamber of Commerce in Japan, one of the severest critics of Japanese exclusiveness, conceded in a 1979 report that Japanese firms regularly pay a premium for dependability and business compatibility in domestic and foreign trade.

In the 1990s, there have been clear signs of a stronger Japanese interest in pricing competition and an acceptance of the discount distributor who promises less than full follow-up. In the light of growing evidence that the "responsible" servicer and guarantor was partly mythical and of a growing impersonality in Japanese society, that willingness to pay a clear premium for hoped-for service can be expected to decline. The even more dramatic decline in lifetime employment suggests that some of the other linkages are being weakened as well.[20]

There is also no doubt, however, that government has exhibited special responsiveness to agriculture, especially for farmers in "rotten boroughs" exercising political clout. Not only is the price of rice kept artificially high, but when Japanese production of rice became excessive in the 1970s farmers were exceptionally rewarded to convert to wheat, soybeans, barley, or sugar beets.

At a maximum, a farmer could have received a return from combined sales and subsidy of between thirteen and fourteen times the cost of imported wheat.[21] Clearly, agricultural policy has been anti-import, and remains so, though in diminished form.

Another area of clear discrimination has been the hostility to foreign investment. The legal and political order reinforces Japanese practice, which encourages relations in which investors are trading partners—purchasers and perhaps also suppliers or distributors—creating families of businesses hostile or cold to strangers. Such banking-trading groupings are called *Keiretsu*.[22] Increasingly, however, Japanese industrialists are borrowing abroad and are unable to raise all capital from a small circle of business associates.

Still, business familialism of this sort, which includes a distribution system, is generally believed to account for much of Japan's continued low rate of import of finished products.[23] While some continue to emphasize unfair government behavior, careful studies have shown no unusual tariff favoritism. Gary Saxonhouse has argued that, generally, protectionism in Japan is remarkably similar in extent to that of other industrial nations, and he questions the conclusion that importation by Japan is atypical.[24]

The so-called Japan bashers, led by Clyde Prestowitz, suggest strongly that it is practice, not nominal policy, that is crucial in Japan. They reject the argument that removal of barriers has produced little improvement only because of basic internal factors in Japan and the United States,[25] an argument advanced by Fred Bergsten and William Cline inter alia.[26] Discrimination is, they believe, still the vogue. The reality is hard-nosed protection where it counts, in day-to-day administration, and only equal muscle applied in return is effective in their view.[27]

Evidence suggests, however, that existing standards are increasingly enforced objectively and with a commitment to "transparency." Thus the process of setting standard definitions becomes relatively more important with respect to the government's role, which, though increasingly circumscribed, is not inconsiderable. Standard setting becomes more vital when enforcement is evenhanded and "transparent."

The Creation of Standards

The process of standard formation in Japan, as elsewhere, is complex. In some areas, the bureaucracy seems to operate with autonomy and even, as we saw in the cosmetics industry, with considerable vestigial arbitrariness. But most product standards are set by ministry committees containing members from industry as well as members with a bureaucratic perspective; sometimes there is even a smattering of "public" or "consumer" perspective. Consumerism is organizationally weaker in Japan than in most Western countries. "Public" members may be experts in the field, unaffiliated professionals, or political figures. While such committees have weaknesses, they are leagues ahead of past practice, where shadowy, often anonymous experts ratified decisions already bureaucratically set.[28]

As usual in the arcane world of Japanese regulation, who is using whom, or who is in control or showing power, is at best problematic. The notion that government calls all the shots was long promulgated by foreigners and was vigorously denied by MITI and other ministries for decades. In recent years, the government has finally acknowledged that central direction comes from the ministries. Some commentators have rather shrewdly suggested that as the balance of power has shifted *away* from government, the ministries have been as eager to assert authority as they once were to deny it. The admission that they do give direction to the economy is therefore interpreted as a sign of weakness, not strength.

There is a great deal of this semihidden exercise of power in Japan, since it is almost axiomatic that leadership posts there are ceremonial and that true power is generally exercised at a lower level than formal power. Appearance and reality sometimes coincide, but cultural experts agree that in Japan they are much more likely to diverge. Such experts disagree about the particular instances, however.

When a government-sponsored standards committee is established, whether dealing with imports or domestic products, the ministry forming it has a free hand. At most, there may be regulations requiring "public" representation. Practical constraints may well come from political power, the economic sweep of the key industries involved, and, of course, the pool of talent needed for the committees. In reality, in Japan as elsewhere, these constraints require accommodation with major firms in most industries. The exact combination of political, economic, and technical leverage any leading firm may have is difficult to ascertain, even in relatively open bureaucratic structures; it is virtually unstudiable within the Japanese bureaucracy, given the highly formal and defensive posture typically taken.

Participation in a standards committee is, as in most of Japan's extended government structures, an honor carrying neither salary nor reimbursement for expenses. Membership confers dignity, power, and—not the least important—information. This is especially significant to industry representatives who not only shape standards and work with those who enforce them, but who will be perceived as leaders. Professors, lawyers, engineers, or other independent professionals may gain standing or insight, and that makes membership clearly worthwhile financially in the long run. Service is less attractive to consumer or "public" representatives, who may not have clear personal, or even organizational and sectoral, reasons for engaging in the process.

Individual tasks, especially first drafts of standards, are still typically assigned to trade associations or companies.[29] Since one of the major benefits of being on a standards committee is the expertise it confers, this privatization of drafting is a double bonus: the drafters gain both technical knowledge and special insight when using the legal information. (An analogue is the highly lucrative practice of Thomas Corcoran, chief legislative draftsman during the "Second New Deal" period of Roosevelt's second term. He won only a few cases arguing that statutes had esoteric intent—a notion courts reflexively reject—but was more effective in making such claims at the administrative level, to the benefit of clients.)

Characteristically, Japanese committees work by consensus building and interminable discussion. It is expected that everyone will have ample opportunity to articulate goals and objections to any policy. Some accommodation, at least of a face-saving nature, is expected to be made for even tiny minorities. The technical nature of standard setting also invites, or even requires, long, painstaking discussions and reconciliation of diverse points of view. Thus service on such committees requires many meetings, usually involving considerable time, often during working hours, and generally travel to or within Tokyo. This is difficult, of course, for a disinterested public observer, but easily (and rather invisibly) subsidized by a firm or private practice (engineering, public relations) where it is in fact an investment with future advantages. (In making these observations, I should note that much the same can be said for the pattern of participation in most U.S. standards groups, especially by "voluntary" standard setters.)

Typically, staffing for such a committee will come from the ministry or be shared with industry. The pacing and direction of the task force will usually be determined by the bureaucrats. Ultimate use and enforcement are the ministry's responsibilities—thus, realistically at least, some accommodation of its views must take place.

It is, of course, not the responsibility of the Japanese government to compensate for advantages or disabilities foreign companies bring to Japan's shores; it must simply not deliberately aggravate them. It should be expected that formal meetings in Japan will be conducted in Japanese and that regulations will be printed in that language as well. There are pressures both to improve translations of circulated drafts of regulations and to make documents available at a stage that allows for intervention. While Japan lags behind many countries in such consultative processes, its improvement has been impressive.

Japan's insistence on type approval rather than self-certification is in fact more universal; American self-certification is nearly unique. Arguably, it is ultimately and intimately connected to our tough liability laws, though strict liability would seem quite compatible with self-certification as well. The EC's gingerly acceptance of self-certification in EC 1992 does not seem risky to threaten much abuse of consumers, so it would be in Japan, since government oversight seems minimal anyway.

The blandness of the Japanese consensus standards process masks a reality, which might not always be apparent to participants, let alone pellucid to outsiders. Almost certainly, patterns of control by industry, experts, or the bureaucracy exist in various parts of Japanese economic life, as do instances of shared influence. In Japan especially, large self-financing, profit-making ventures with strong political connections are not shy about flexing their muscles.

The Japanese require early retirement from the bureaucracy, at age sixty, which makes employment in the firms it regulates an appropriate place of refuge, whether before or at the age of compulsory retirement. There are many ways to curry favor and feather a nest for one's future.

The Impact of International Standards on Policy

On the other hand, where national policy demands export advantage or new capital flow, the government has both a direct and an indirect advantage. Normally, capital is obtained from banks and other companies linked in *Keiretsu*, the famed Japanese cooperative approach to growth and interconnectedness. But in other instances, with small companies or in areas of close government control, the ministries are also capable of taking charge. There is ample precedent in Japanese bureaucratic culture for government to be active well beyond its nominal mandate. The persuasiveness of the police in modern Japan is a constant reminder that the core historical tradition of the society is a paramilitary, direction-from-the-top, closed and closemouthed enterprise. Where power collides with power, a modus vivendi reached behind the scenes, rather than a public clash, is the preferred outcome.

Both international pressures and the requirements of a complex industrial system operate to regularize standard setting and to move away from the historical pattern of casual collusion with industry. By and large, the Japanese government still does not operate its own testing facilities, but it can and does deal with independent operations, whereas it once permitted dominant companies in an industry to "objectively" evaluate products and function as the government testing laboratory. Although it resists self-certification by companies and accepts limited forms of it most grudgingly, the Japanese bureaucracy now recognizes some foreign testers and for many purposes will permit testing abroad, though (as is customary everywhere) at the producer's expense. Here again, the clear mandate of GATT helped create these options, which are usually feasible only for high-volume concerns.

Information about the establishment of a standards committee sponsored by the Japanese government and details of its purposes are now published; generally, announcements of such efforts are sent out in English as well as Japanese. The Japanese have essentially decided to deal with all foreigners in English, which is almost a second official language. In all instances of dealing with government, however, the Japanese text alone determines rights. Volunteers are now solicited, though most announcements remind potential participants that meetings will always be in Japanese, will take time, and will involve unreimbursed expense. While, in fact, fewer foreigners can overcome these problems than, for example, Japanese businessmen in the United States, these problems are not unsurmountable, and it hardly seems incumbent on the Japanese to make up for Westerners' lack of facility in Japanese, a language gap that in any event is shrinking. Non-Japanese are infrequently chosen for such committees, but presumably, a high proportion of those who can meet the requirements are appointed, since so few qualify or are willing to serve. In any event, public announcements also permit major players—including Western importers, manufacturers, or potential dealers—to request formal appearances and to make interactive written statements and iterative continuing comments on aspects of a standard important to them. In many instances, this can be as effective from a policy standpoint as personal participation.

Even while touting these highly important advances toward universal expression, the ministerial announcements normally bristle with reminders that the ministry has the power to choose members, that Japanese is the official language of the committee, and that the Japanese text of the announcement is controlling if a disagreement over intent occurs. Quite usual, too, is a redundant reminder that the committee will determine and control the terms of appearances before it and a rather brusque suggestion that the number and length of written communications may be limited. The process is taut and the reality still unfriendly toward strangers.

In short, the use of "nontransparency" is rapidly diminishing in the face of foreign criticism (and even truculence), which is actually more clamorous now than when artful dodging by the Japanese bureaucracy was considerably more common. As these sleight-of-hand efforts diminish, foreign importers are increasingly frustrated by and vocal about their failure to significantly improve their market share. The Japanese insist that the complainers are cry-babies and the foreigners, especially the Americans, insist the old tactics are still operative, but more hidden.

The Japanese do have protectionist arrangements, but they are also universalists. A MITI official informed me that, on the basis of personal research, he had estimated Japanese use of international and ANSI standards in 3 percent of its products, compared to American use in 1 percent. To the experts with whom I have discussed the matter, this seems to be a reasonable estimate. Since the United States relies strongly on ANSI-approved standards and since, in the majority of cases, ANSI's standards are also regarded by world trade experts as objective and virtually international in sweep and tenor, the Japanese commitment to international standards is considerable. Although comparison is difficult both in principle and in practice, that commitment seems to be somewhat greater in Japan than in the United States. Still, the dominating force of noninternational regulations—the remaining 95 percent plus—constitutes a broad and open arena, leaving many opportunities for tailored standards.

And, of course, those importers faced with protectionist standards will find the slow drift of Japan away from overt or covert protection scant consolation in a day-to-day sense. The substance of standards recommendations does reflect committee composition and procedures. Since Japan has only very recently and quite slowly moved to make such selection proceedings and outcomes "transparent," there remain many relics of past standards, past implementing regulations, and past practices, which only slowly—very slowly—are being replaced by more "transparent" rules and procedures. Protection for foreign concerns remains less intimately effective within the machinery of Japanese government than in most societies, for cultural and geographic reasons not directly produced or easily curable by simple legal efforts.

Since directly prohibited imports by foreigners are now limited to a tiny and negligible area, quotas, import duties, and standards are the main areas of interaction. The requirements of the WTO and other international pressures operate to squeeze out most overt discrimination, and make the arena of standard definition the primary focus for government-sanctioned protectionism, especially for Japanese companies defending their advantages. The response to this should be growing foreign understanding and participation in the basic process of standards, with both membership opportunities and participation more fully utilized. This will strengthen big U.S. firms at the expense of smaller ones, but that seems inevitable, given the situation. As with the cost of offshore inspection, there seems no easy solution short of Japanese government subsidies of small foreign company representatives. Representation by American trade officials might help, but there are too many problems to actual membership of U.S. government officials on such committees to permit that or even a U.S. subsidy to private members for their participation. Perhaps a group of firms in one category could pool resources to back a full-fledged participant, since it is clear that membership on such a committee affects outcomes in Japan at the very least as much as it does in the United States.

Hardball Versus Universalism in the Reform of Japanese Standards

Since government-enforced protectionism is now only a small segment of the import problem, little magic will occur. Much of the restrictive import process is deeply embedded in patterns of capitalization, mutual purchasing, and distribution in Japan, which are changing (perhaps disintegrating), but at a glacial pace. There are dark hints that the government, under its own initiative or in response to entrenched interests, sustains the internal tendency toward autarky, but, except for its key role in creating new major industries, there is little overt evidence of a commanding control. Foreigners have been clearly helped in making inroads by the ministry, the political system, the bureaucracy, and even by court decisions. In some areas, Japanese consumers have clearly opted for foreign products. The relative success of German business, which early on studied the culture and cultivated Japanese-style relationships, has led to the assessment that some limited growth can be expected by other countries that adapt similar methods and approaches. Texas Instruments is known to have followed that strategy to the hilt and has become a sojourner for the long haul. According to Prestowitz, it has also frequently and vigorously called upon the U.S. Trade Representative (and even more leveraged American political figures) to make its case. It has on occasion pursued its remedies in Japanese courts and won. It understands Japan, knows when to play hardball, when to concede the tough shots. It is considered by all to be one of the major successes in Japan. Yet a high legal counsel officer for TI told me that a decade ago an MITI official indicated that TI would not get more than a specific share of the Japanese market. Its share peaked and leveled off just below that figure. This could be coincidence. Understandably, the lawyer does not think so.

Summary

Japan is attempting to alleviate world concern over its trade practices and is increasingly eliminating clear and overt ugly practices of the past. It continues to defend an area of protectionism that both economists and trade protectionists believe is roughly comparable—and probably a shade less significant—than that of its Western counterparts.

It remains a difficult trading partner because of interwoven financial controls, in which enterprises that invest and primary customers and distributions systems are highly intertwined. Regularity of supply and quality is valued more highly than price advantages. The role of government in maintaining a system with strong autarkic elements allegedly exceeds that in other countries. But, evidence suggests that central direction is focused on new major industries rather than on maintenance of past advantage. The government in the past half a dozen years has shown some willingness to go beyond its slow abandonment of old arbitrary practice or overt discrimination and actually promote foreign interests, in order to redress the imbalance. Foreigners, however, remain frustrated by what they read as failure of the Japanese to grasp the need to accept some measured responsibility for an international equilibrium, and by what is internationally seen as dogged pursuit of advantages that will bring down everything and everybody. To the outside world, Japanese accommodations are slow, grudging, and inadequate.

Standards played a key role in establishing the new image of Japan as quality conscious, and are now interwoven into its internal economy as well as international trade. Japan's commitment to international standard setting makes great sense for a country with ambitions as an international supplier. Japan may well emerge as the foremost advocate of such an approach, since it seems to have the most to gain from it.

Since it depends on the free flow of goods into other economies, Japan is increasingly dismantling the old economic barriers, keeping only those vital to its domestic politics. Because standards definition can be defended as an exercise of the "police power" of the state in its duty to protect the populace from health or safety hazards or inferior goods, it will increasingly be the major mode of domestic protectionism. Thus, both internationally and domestically, Japan remains one of the countries *most aware* of product standards and most sophisticated about them.

8 Standards as Boundaries

The Abortive Efforts of Soviet Europe

The Eastern Bloc and Standards

THE FAILED SOVIET BLOC CAN BE VIEWED AS an attempt to create a separate and interlocked standards zone, guarded symbolically on the West by the Berlin Wall. At the same time, the economic collapse of the Leninist-Stalinist system marked a failure to solve the problem of ensuring standards of quality in a nonmarket order.[1]

All empires radiate standards and furnish models within their zone of influence.[2] Russia itself was deeply influenced by French law and culture even though it rejected Napoleon militarily. It introduced the concierge system as a means of control, made French elegance—including Fabergé eggs—a standard of beauty and ballet a standard for culture, and even adopted French as the court language. Later, Russia became the model imposed upon the Eastern bloc, by force if necessary.

Given the avowed purpose of creating a socialist society, the Russian model of economics was the obvious blueprint for a presumptively revolutionary society. Because of the heavy-handed Russian political tutelage behind the scenes and the entanglement of a dictatorial political system that enabled a command economy, the Russian model was quickly established everywhere. Since postwar reconstruction was often extensive (in many parts of Eastern Europe, it was total), the new societies could rebuild and imitate the Soviet

Union profoundly. Only when there was deep-rooted resistance did the local Communists gain permission to incorporate more indigenous patterns. Perhaps because Poland was so obviously controlled by the USSR geographically, resistance was met with concessions, as it was in Hungary and Romania. Austria was inexplicably and peacefully permitted to move outside the sphere of influence while Yugoslavia seized that right. East Germany and Czechoslovakia, on the other hand, were ruthlessly repressed and strictly regimented. Geopolitics and the instruments available to the Russians are the usual explanations for these deviations, especially since variations occurred under Stalin as well as under each of his successors.

As with many more fundamental aspects of the Soviet system, the original postrevolutionary impetus for standards was quite different from the pattern that ensued. Lenin was an enthusiastic believer in standardization, maintaining it was a major building block of planning and that socialism required "uniform norms in the production and distribution of goods."[3] He personally attended to details of administration of standards and had in his library a shorthand report covering a 1922 conference on the subject held in Moscow. Notes to subordinates indicate his interest at a very detailed level.[4] Among key figures involved in standardization efforts were Lunacharski and Felix Dzerzhinskii, who established a reputation for effectiveness in founding the dreaded Cheka, which took over the leadership of official standards institutions in 1926.[5] This is regarded as the date of establishment of the Russian OST standardizing system.[6] Until that time, the struggle for control of the country dominated all other concerns. But even subsequently, the interest in standards was not firmly rooted in the society or the system of control.

During the Five-Year Plans characteristic of Stalin's years, standardization was in fact regarded only as a subsidiary tool. The emphasis on quantity drove out concerns for quality. Even where industries were upgraded, it was less important that consistent quality be achieved than that production peak. Under the Five-Year regimes, failure to achieve quotas could result in severe penalties, even death, for the managers. Complaints about quality months later could be treated as quibbles. David Granick reports it was only in 1938 that the Commission of Heavy Industry issued a directive that plants would henceforth be judged not merely on quantity of production but also on quality of output and per unit costs. As he notes, this was an implicit statement that until that time only absolute production was valued.[7] The attitude that only production of goods is significant, and that quality or distribution problems are trivial, persists to this day in Russia and most of the Eastern bloc. It is in a sense an impediment surviving from Marxist theory.

The standardization function was not merely subordinated to planning and buried in low-level offices. The function was passed around among newly created offices with various names and functions—all with limited authority—from 1930 to 1936 and again after 1940. An All-Union Standardization Committee gave some focus, but essentially, the OST program was kept subordinate to GOSPLAN units. At times, various other units set rival standards. The All-Union Committee was criticized repeatedly (especially in 1932) for failure to deal effectively with significant issues of standards and quality, in spite of its obviously limited authority.

While Lenin was interested in standardization, rationalization, and scientific management as potential theoretical building blocks for a socialist society, the emphasis under Stalin was on Stakhanovite extraction of additional labor and the full integration of industrial planning and political control. (This had been developing under Lenin as well.) While critiques of "low quality and faulty goods" were quite common, authority to deal with the problem was not given to standardizers and, on the whole, planners emphasized quality only when they had special goals—especially in heavy production tools and materials, and defense military goods. Certainly, foreign standards and foreign trade were not viewed as major concerns in building industry, since foreign involvement was carefully minimized from the top, on an "as needed" basis.

Xenophobia dominated standards even more after World War II. The USSR's key objective was clearly political domination in the geographic sphere, and efficiency was not at a premium. This indeed was the thesis of Vladmir Sobell's study of COMECON generally, which he describes (in British social science Newspeak) as "an international protective system (IPS) created primarily for the purpose of stability maximisation." IPS is the opposite of what might be called the international trade system (ITS), created primarily for the purpose of maximizing efficiency.[8]

Given the desire to establish a bloc and to undergird it with a socialist economy, the key remaining decisions probably seemed inevitable for Eastern Europe. Stalin's rejection of the Marshall Plan, and of any other American or European involvement (e.g. nonmember participation rights in the EEC) was primarily a desire to keep the Western world out of its unenthusiastic satellites and maintain as tight a control as possible over them. This in turn entailed a decision not to engage widely in trade with the West and therefore necessitated sharply limiting imports to match limits on exports. Under normal conditions of trade, the perpetual shortage of *valuta* (hard currency) might well have promoted emphasis on exports. But since foreigners were viewed with suspicion and barely tolerated at best, and trade relations, no matter how advantageous, were grudging concessions to necessity, virtual autarky was the only recourse. Looking inward, the system of production created a unique, barterlike, convoluted means of international exchange within the Eastern bloc. They elaborately planned and discussed, but poorly implemented, internal quality and product standards to reinforce their mutual dependence and further stiffen the cold shoulder they wished to give to the West.

In so doing, they were clearly driven by other impulses that reinforced those controls; shortages weakened quality standards and national rivalries prevented intrabloc standard setting. As the analyst G. Bogomolov wrote at a time when great circumspection was still needed, the "comparative isolation" of the Soviet trading bloc's mechanisms from both the domestic economies of the constituent countries and from Western international system, was a product of "a special price and accounting system," which carefully regulated both participants and commodities.[9] Bogomolov noted cautiously that complete isolation was neither possible nor desirable, but advocated "improve[d] joint planning to develop the scientific basis for foreign economic policy," advancing the Russian position that mutuality, or bloc trading, rather than international trade instituted by individual countries was to be preferred. That is to say, the inconvertibility of Eastern bloc money by itself provided a tight and adequate control on the extent of foreign trade.[10]

Stalin's paranoia was reflected in his decision to go a step further and make the bloc work at "the formulation and consolidation of the new, parallel world market."[11] The costs were felt almost entirely within the Eastern bloc. It is conceivable that this and other such actions were intended to preserve a Big Brother role for the Soviet Union, with many smaller partners, but any gain in that direction seems to have been rather slight. The process was designed to force a turn to the East, but the inefficiencies were so great that they reinforced dreams and fantasies of the West.

Problems in standardization within the bloc were exacerbated by rival standards, supporting Sobell's view of COMECON as a "don't rock the boat" operation. The East German TGL standards system was as comprehensive as the Russian OST plan and, for many products, was widely used throughout the bloc. This confusion persisted when rival standards centers were established by COMECON, headquartered in Berlin and Moscow. But COMECON also had a loose plan to allow national standards as well. At no point were nations forced to accept standards. Indeed, the chairman of COMECON noted that most nations kept their standards up to the point of actually signing treaties for trade with countries based on accommodating conflicting standards.[12] Presumably, costs of retooling buttressed political rivalries and achieving uniformity became a distant and deferred goal.[13] Even as technocratic a leader as Kosygin was not able to overcome the claims of nationalism and political sparring.

Quite clearly, these summary statements imply a coherence of objectives and tactics that was not present over so long a period. Those countries that longed for Western contact and whose leadership felt independent enough to pursue such a course argued that there were specific economic gains that could be met through such tactics. Often an argument would be made through analogies with Lenin's NEP (or semicapitalist) plans, which Lenin had defended as taking "one step backwards, in order to take two steps forward." The USSR itself took inconsistent steps of its own, sometimes seeking foreign partners for various reasons. The periodic failures of Soviet agriculture in particular not only entailed the purchasing of grain (generally from Canada and the United States) but also forced selling in world markets to produce the hard currency to cover the heavy cost involved. Trading units within the bloc governments were often anxious to expand, and therefore operated fairly consistently as pressure groups for a policy of international trade.

The countries in the bloc all had major problems of rebuilding after the war and this need, like Stalinism, kept them keenly concentrated on internal affairs. There was, however, major restructuring taking place in their bilateral relations and interbloc trading, since the various countries had traditionally looked to Western, not Eastern, Europe as their center of culture and their major trading partner. East Germany was a rump carved from a Western nation. In 1938 UN figures indicate over 70 percent of the Eastern bloc's trade was with Western Europe, and 10 percent with Eastern European countries. By 1950 intrabloc trading was almost 69 percent, and by 1960 almost 73 percent, of all international exchange. There was an underlying strategy. By 1946, 78 percent of Poland's imports were from the USSR and 50 percent of its exports were to that country. Forty percent of Czechoslovakia's trade was with the Soviet Union.[14] In absolute terms, the strategy was less successful. Although East-West trade rose slightly in the 1960s, it leveled off at less than half the level of Western trade prior to the war, except for very transitory developments.

While Eastern politics and bloc autarky were clearly evident, trade with the West was discouraged both by practical obstacles (such as currency controls) and, in the early decades, by Western efforts. The West was intent on keeping the Soviet bloc contained and weak. In any event, trade with the East generally required pump priming and special credit arrangements.

When satellite countries sought such arrangements in later years, they were often quite successful, since the Western alliance began to appreciate the political advantages garnered from such exchanges. In a sense, Western trade meant Western influence; impulses for secession were kept alive in the countries traded with. Western trade was also often the vehicle for further economic reform, as Western ideas and goods flowed together. It has been suggested that such investments permitted espionage coups for the West as well, and this seems eminently logical, since the essence of the relationship was the flow of money through high officials. The Soviets balanced increased subsidization (as in Czechoslovakia) with relaxed political control (as in Hungary). Only in East Germany was taut control accompanied by an acceptably successful economy; in Poland, a reasonable balance continually evaded the Russians and their allies. Successive waves of Polish leaders came to power as popular reformers, only to end their terms with the public perceiving them as failed collaborationists.

The 1960s saw the end of truly autarkic Stalinism, but the surge of satellite countries toward Western relations evoked a Soviet response to strengthen COMECON and to focus on true regional (as opposed to predominantly bilateral) planning. This was a subtle political response, which, if it had proved successful, might have garnered new power for the USSR from a deteriorating economic system. Increased trade and higher quality standards constituted an attempt to avoid basic internal changes by easing external relations. Country specialization was seen to permit higher standards. The policy was belated and proved ineffectual.

Originally, COMECON was largely a clearinghouse for data and a pretext for rejecting the Marshall Plan. The effort to transform it into a true counterweight to the EEC was to flounder in the general inertia of the Brezhnev era.

The period of shared power by Kosygin and Brezhnev was probably the high point of standardization and other technocratic efforts. COMECON doubled Eastern bloc standards adopted in the period 1970–1975,[15] a good index of the general effort. This thrust was not followed by similar efforts. There is some evidence that what was gained through greater interaction was lost because the Soviet Union gave up bilateral flexibility and the system was not limber enough to adjust. Gone, too, was the sense that each satellite could be dealt with according to its idiosyncratic characteristics rather than as coequal partners bound by the same rules. At this stage, East German and Czech representatives may well have been more Stalinist than the Russians in bloc interactions, and their countries may well have insisted on imposing or retaining rigidities the Russians were more willing to scrap. The Romanians, fearing COMECON would be used against them, also helped keep it from achieving effective power.

The basic economic order for the bloc was set out in COMECON communiqués, written in the characteristic Stalinist orthospeak satirized so well by George Orwell and many of the Russian émigrés of the 1970s and 1980s. They read like Soviet documents on foreign policy, political philosophy, or the celebration of workers' holidays. Only the nouns have to be changed to apply the largely ritualistic self-aggrandizing claims to other areas.[16]

Essentially, the enlivened standardizing system asked the different partners to specialize in manufacture of different products, to produce agreed-upon quotas in those products annually, and to receive from other countries their quota of other supplies in return. The product assignments reflected traditional strengths of the different countries—heavy machinery from East Germany or glass from Czechoslovakia—as well as some concept of equalizing the burden.[17] The existence of a strong tradition of German standardization was part of that confusing compromise.

Marxist, nonmarket thinking was quite evident in that these basic assignments and individual allocations were apparently not based on world price or production cost, or on any other accounting principles. Once set in motion, they were renewed regularly (and renegotiated, especially after emergencies), but the logic behind them, if there ever was any, was lost in the politics of those relationships. Economists were unable to completely disentangle the advantages and costs involved at the time, and have had no more success in retrospect, partly because of the system's many complexities (including the fact that many of these quotas were not met). The consensus has been that the Russians were subsidizing their partners, a conclusion that the population of each of the satellites naturally rejects. If such a flow of advantage was real, it need not be regarded as compensation for loss of freedom. The costs of autarky were also much greater for the satellites with smaller economies and historical ties to Western Europe.

The system was clearly jerry-built, because it only pretended to ignore the clear motivations of the different countries. No nation wanted to be totally dependent on the production of another, so the benefits of specialization were undercut by defensive duplication, the very thing that was supposedly avoided. The numbers assigned were based on past production and projected changes, but especially on haggling. Neither the true capacity for production nor the individual country's need for a product was necessarily approximated in this complex game with no rules. Priority of production was, it appears, not coordinated significantly with the priority needs of the receiving countries. Thus, for example, Country A might emphasize steel production because workers in those plants were politically restive, but might skimp on its commitment to produce nuts and bolts. Country B might receive the steel needed to produce bicycle frames and parts, but would be unable to assemble them until Country A caught up on nuts and bolts. Country B could threaten to cut off Country A's quota of brake linings (vital to its auto industry) or seek reimbursement for its losses from the delay in selling bikes, but that would be using a cannon to shoot fleas. The system fostered fits and starts, shortages and surpluses. If country B was exasperated enough that Country A thought it might cut off supplies, preventive emphasis on producing nuts and bolts might result in a vast surplus, while the diversion of steel might lead to A's failure to deliver its quota of metal, cascading into yet other shortages, such as brake linings, and therefore holding up car production.

Much the same pattern was played out in the Soviet Union itself. The 1970s witnessed the ascendancy of the technicians, with Kosygin at the apex of their demands. Quality was officially given a place of honor, ending preoccupation with quantity, at least on paper. World standards were seen as a desirable goal, nominally ending the quest for autarky.

Already in 1954, the All-Union Committee of Standardization had been renamed the State Committee of Standards, Measures, and Measuring Instruments, and was once again placed under the prestigious authority of the Council of Ministers. In 1971 its title was enhanced to "State Committee of Standards of the Council of Ministers." More important, its chair was made an ex officio member of the council. Standardizers still lacked Party clout, however. These table-of-organization efforts produced little evidence of any important change in the actual exercise of power.

The most important effort at standardization was a 1965 ministerial decree establishing grades of excellence for type standards: "highest standards," "first category," and "second category." "Highest standard" goods were given monetary premiums based on the economic advantages supposedly created for buyers. "Second category" goods were obsolete and were to be phased out.

The "mark of quality" producers of the highest quality goods were implicitly defined as those achieving world market standards. To assist in this implicit goal, the State Committee of Science and Technology and the State Committee of Planning were co-opted in December 1979 and the Ministry of Trade in 1984 to assure more rigorous and more international categorization.[18] Continual calls for more rigor in various decrees (in 1982, 1984, and 1985, for example) suggested what we now know from direct documentation: the original incentives were (and were kept) inadequate. Soviet economist L. A. Kostin wrote in 1980 that "not all products that are awarded the seal of quality are competitive on the world market."[19] Indeed, "highest standards" goods were sometimes dropped from production as substandard.

More stringent inspection and the evolution of organizations resulted in a significant number of removals of the highest category rating. Furthermore, published Russian sources complained that some products were approved without data on world standards. About one in five new products qualified for the rating. Malcolm Hill and Richard McKay, who are more accepting of Soviet claims than most Western writers, nonetheless conclude that the atmosphere of quality and the emphasis on its practice were at its peak in the 1970s, declining subsequently. That coincides with political and other evidence.[20]

Drawing upon exchange rights developed in British-Soviet agreements, Hill and McKay attempted a comparison between Soviet and British standards for a number of products: lathes and other machines tools, electric motors, autos, trucks and components, refrigerators, and cameras. Their appraisal of cameras and refrigerators was supplemented by an inspection of imports to England and a survey of users.

On the whole, their portrait of Soviet technology is more positive than that of foreign and Russian analysts, or of Soviet consumers. Perhaps they appreciated the access to documents they were given by Soviet authorities; perhaps they wished to suggest some "novel" results. Certainly, they wished to be meticulously fair.

Yet only their tone differs from the authors from whom they wish to distinguish themselves. They call for a reappraisal of J. Grant's conclusion (for a congressional committee) that Soviet machinery is similar in design but usually less durable, flexible, and (often) less efficient than Western counterparts. Yet their argument seems to be consistent with Grant's conclusions.

Hill and McKay's examination of standards indicates that the USSR's published standards were in most respects roughly equivalent to the British, which, for most products, were in turn based on ISO standards. With respect to refrigerators and cameras, they argue that a good, cheap, durable product appropriate to the Soviet Union was produced and that price advantages made it quite attractive to some British users. They do not attempt to compare performance, evaluate whether the Russians were price dumping, or judge whether the evaluated exports were typical products. They suggest the obvious: since only a few Soviet products were exported, they probably were not typical. Eastern bloc automobiles were not world standard but, on the whole, machine tool specifications were. They suggest that inadequate bearings (not fully specified) might well have changed quality ratings even for those products seemingly world-class, and that in some respects Russian specifications were less precise than British, especially when the consequences were not predictable in engineering and scientific terms. These could explain world-class standards on paper and below par performance of the products in actual use.

Those conclusions are similar to those of Grant, Borlimov, Granick, and other well-known writers on Soviet industry, including Berry and Hill. It was not the design but the implementation that was decisively substandard. (It is perhaps a bit fanciful to compare the paper definitions and performance ratio on product standards to the magnificent constitutional guarantees of the Soviet system and its wretched performance in implementing those freedoms.)

Hill and McKay suggest that the notorious sleight of hand of Soviet managers in passing off inferior products was similar to accounting manipulation of the books in the West, but this is an unconvincing analogy. Inferior goods were commonplace in the Eastern bloc, even in areas with precise and identifiable standards, and a careful reading of Hill and McKay (especially of footnotes and parenthesized qualifications) reveals that they basically agree with this assessment. They simply suggest that "some of the criticism of Soviet industrial quality may have been overstated."[21] By criticizing twenty-year-old studies and dwelling on goals, not deeds, they provide a small "corrective," a more carefully phrased restatement.

Other sources, however, fully confirm the general picture of low quality in performance. Not only was grading suspect (as Hill and McKay admit, and as Zigurd L. Zile documents based on Soviet commentators), but also, as Zile concludes, the Soviet commentators were in agreement that the remedies were largely ineffectual in practice. The law exempted produce from any liability, for example, and even *Arbitrazh* were not usually sufficiently punitive to alter industrial behavior.[22] Prison sentences and the dismissal of managers were unenforceable and ultimately unenforced.

Standards of quality were acknowledged as important, but mostly got lip service in a system where assigned quotas were the focus and were not easily achieved. In the early Stalinist years, a factory's failure to meet quotas might result in death to the director, who would be condemned as a "wrecker" and an "objective traitor." Even in the later, gentler days of *Arbitrazh*, where payment was the recompense for not delivering on time or for delivering inferior goods, it remained wiser to produce in quantity and quibble over quality later. If the legendary solutions for improving numbers—producing only right-handed gloves to avoid complications in the assembly process, for example—were no longer as frequent or as outrageous as they had once been, the principle remained. Failure to produce was a cardinal sin, while quality was the icing on the cake.[23]

The inability to develop any effective standards of quality was clearly a discredit to the system. Since the ultimate consumer had little or no buying power in a system of perpetual shortages, there was little or no leverage in the system. Goods were sold generally "as is." Ratings, grades, and labels were not readily available for most everyday supplies. Defective products and busts of Lenin stayed on the shelves of otherwise largely empty department stores, some of them enormous. Consumer cynicism about quality was unfortunately justified by the reality. Most people could quite comfortably meet the cost of bare necessities (which were very heavily subsidized) and went around with surplus rubles, prepared to act instantly if nonbasics—meat or decent-looking clothes, for instance—suddenly came into view. But they recognized such purchases were risky and often contained hidden flaws.

Even large enterprises were disposed to accept deliveries, contest problems, and seek adjustments through *Arbitrazh,* the parallel legal system of bargaining implied by its name, which developed in Eastern bloc countries to deal with disagreement between state enterprises. After all, enterprises could have substandard products repaired to acceptable standards, and they stockpiled labor to permit just that. Compensatory payment had minor consequence, but refusal of goods (except as a ploy for settlement), however justified, entailed delay in a market system where substitutes were not easily available. Generally, refusal of goods was precipitated by not merely marginal but major or continual failure to meet agreed-upon quality standards. Even in the more flexible later years, enterprises were far from free to seek alternative sources of supply and therefore did not possess the chief weapon available to consumers to protect quality.[24]

The structure of Eastern bloc factories made it difficult to enforce quality standards. Managerial authority was sharply contested and limited by the leadership of the party unit, which could challenge any management move. Mere competence or on-the-job performance was of minor concern to the party. Workers generally acted on an implied contract: little was paid, so little was given. The factory was a center for barter and trade information. Workers found friends to punch in and out so they could do their errands and cope with the endless waiting lines on state time. Therefore, though investment in heavy line assembly production was high, the result was barely improved products and poor product control. In Poland, for example, output per worker actually declined with greater investment. Pride of work was the exception, not the norm. Even official propaganda hailed the Stakhanovite, the worker who put in extreme hours and exceeded the quota, not the craftsman or painstaking artisan.

The rise to power of a more technocratic and less ideological leadership in the 1960s and 1970s led to a new attitude toward foreign goods and quality standards. In part, this was a product of the Eastern bloc's desperate need for *valuta* for the kind of purchases it absolutely had to make in the West. In part, it was an acknowledgement of the problems low-quality production were causing. The impulse toward improving quality was genuine enough, but it touched upon basic facts of life in the system, including the pact between government and workers that little would be demanded.

Since quality standards were buffeted from above by market forces and constrained from below by the workers' minimal efforts, it was not surprising that the bloc's efforts to raise quality or coordinate standards were essentially perfunctory. COMECON's strongest statement on quality was a 1970 agreement[25] that enunciated a long-range effort which, even as a document, was vague and uncertain of its own ground. It was clearly parallel to Kosygin's speech of March 30, 1970, to the Twenty-Third Party Conference in Russia, calling for trade with the West. This led to the Helsinki Conferences, which were to deal with an opening to the West; their ultimate influence, however, proved to be the seemingly routine words about freedom of ideas agreed to by the Eastern bloc negotiators, on the assumption they were merely paying lip service to the ideals. Ultimately, international trade did not develop, due to lack of quality, and the lack of trade doomed the real push for quality.

Nevertheless, the 1970 document was important for its clear change of attitude toward the goal of autarky and its weakening of the Stalinist resolve to face inward. The document is quite explicit in its recognition of weak standards in the East, and of the necessity for a major effort to move to world standards. Given the "equal powers" tone of most Soviet and Eastern bloc stands, this was a wrenching, difficult, and atypical pronouncement, no doubt facilitated by the fact that it was written primarily by technocrats for technocrats. It is nonetheless important to see how significant the quality problem was perceived to be there, and to understand the argument technicians made between the lines, that separatism was itself an aggravation of the problem.

The 1970 document provided for a ten-year effort:

Attaching great importance to standardization, COMECON members have agreed upon the following . . .

1. To implement the integrated standardization in 1971–80 of the most important types of products from raw materials to finished products . . . as well as the typization and unification of the most important types of machines, units and parts . . .

2. To work out in 1971–75 recommendations relating to standardization with a restricted number of main indicators in order to adjust national standards on a product that is the subject of . . . exchange between COMECON member countries for which there are no recommendations relating to standardization. And periodic verification and revision of COMECON recommendations on standardization with the aim of raising their technical level to the world level shall be carried.

3. To work out from 1973, technical normative COMECON documents on stan-

dardization defining technical characteristics and quality indicators to be produced and which are the subject of mutual deliveries between COMECON member countries . . .

4. In 1971–75 to work out and introduce a system of formative documentation an optimal nomenclature, the content and form of documents . . .

5. Before 1976, to create a uniform system of tolerances and fits . . . in conjunction with the recommendations of the International Standards Organization (ISO) ensuring the gradual introduction of this system prior to 1980.[26]

Lest this set of tasks seem simple, the comparatively late document also set as *goals* what some might have thought were prior achievements: uniform measurements, mutual collation of standards, and a joint research program for standards.

It is interesting how much the program inadvertently reveals. International quality and world quality standards were, even in aspiration, a decade away. As a goal, these were the most remote and the least likely to be achieved. The first "goal" was stated in typical Sovietese, and was a comprehensive and impossible dream that, in essence, logically included almost everything else. No machinery or real process beyond the date goals were specified, indicating that little in reality was probably expected. Furthermore, since over a quarter century COMECON had failed to develop a system of collecting and collating documents, it was almost laughable to think that, without a drastic change in level of effort and type of commitment, real cooperation in joint standards would occur.

The bloc was insistent on its fundamental self-sufficiency and its regional integration. The major instrument that could have directed the economy inward, as the Berlin Wall did figuratively and literally, was political control of imports. For example, the Soviet Union would not allow import of medicines not produced in the Eastern bloc, based on the simple assertion that the people's republics by definition produced every commodity needed for life. To be sure, this general policy also reduced outlay of scarce hard currency, but it was also consistent with an autarkic mentality for its own sake. Even tourism in the Eastern bloc took place in regimented groups, to maximize control rather than income. The need for hard currency in easy packages was carefully subordinated to other concerns.

Bloc leaders understood well that bloc standardization could actually contribute toward isolating the community and at the same time increase internal efficiency. Leninist thinking about production was rooted in much the same simplistic technocratic assumption that the standardization movement had begun with, but, like Lenin, technocrats continued to monitor world standards. COMECON declarations had little propaganda value and could hardly be expected to rouse the masses to a frenzy of populist approval. These declarations were written by people who believed in the goals. The voiced ISO aspirations represented no threat to a program of internalization, since ISO standards could be adopted, if so desired, solely for a limited group of products that planners decided were appropriate to offer abroad for hard currency.

In short, the program proffered in this 1970 document should have been a winner. Yet internal analysis shows its progenitors were ruefully aware it was probably a nonstarter. Why was it largely dead on arrival?

In fact, the basic system of national specialization did not work well. Each country duplicated the others' lines of products to the degree possible, since they knew or feared that in a pinch the needs of the producing country were likely to prevail over commitments. Had specialization truly occurred, there would have been a dominant standard for each product line. Problems would have arisen if, for example, German-produced radios required two-prong outlets and Czech refrigerators three, but a limited number of problems could have been presented to the standardizers for resolution. However, since most nations tried to develop their own refrigerators, cooling systems, radios etc., a profusion of product standards existed. The large number of models, each with low numbers produced in each locality, meant capital investment for any blocwide redesign involved a high percentage cost.

There were even more aggravating problems. Given low quality and uncertain delivery of products, purchasing agencies often succumbed to the lure of nonbloc bargains. Western countries often found ways to deliver manufactured products without requiring much hard currency, in exchange for raw materials, for example. During the Gierek era in Poland, the United States pumped in funds, hoping to elevate the economy and maintain Poland's nationalist struggle against Russification. Hard currency, or even credit, could be used to buy Western or nonbloc goods at low prices. Such goods were supplemented by bargains secured by the consolidated purchasing power in each national agency, a convenient and noncontroversial way for nonbloc nations to "dump" unsold goods. These were, however, often one-shot deals, which compounded the problems of an economy plagued by zigs and zags. Often the outside purchase was the dominant available form for a limited period of time and then was no longer purchasable. Parts and repair facilities were scarce or nonexistent.

Generally, those in charge of national purchasing were not planners and were either unaware of considerations of standardization or were indifferent to them. The fact that a country might have available goods based on its own standards, on those of the dominant bloc producers, or on those of one or more of the nonbloc producers made uniformity unlikely. This had high costs. Perhaps because, as Schumpeter argues, socialist economies privilege the present and ignore the future, even the "dominant" country's producers concentrated on the maximum possible purchase of new units, and stocking of spare products was notoriously inadequate. One-shot foreign goods made spare part maintenance rare, and cannibalization or makeshift arrangements were relied upon.

This maze of multiple standards was daunting, and mastering the problem meant controlling not just the community's planning process—which was never allowed much real authority by the Russians—but also independent buyers and planners. The whip hand remained in Moscow and COMECON simply could not command enough respect to change the impulse of the different countries to provide products for their own self-sufficiency or to buy abroad when a good deal came along. Just as quality standards were pious goals that did not fit the realities of underproduction, the pursuit of bloc standards ground to a halt in the face of the impulses toward nationalist advantage, which Moscow thought too basic to thwart and insufficiently threatening to cure.

Is the Failure of Eastern Europe Conclusive?

It is tempting to suggest that the failure of the Eastern bloc to develop a system of comprehensive divergent standards argues for the impossibility or at least improbability of such efforts in the future. A rigid use of force, after all, kept the population hemmed in for decades, yet those policies deliberately resulted in exile and defection of the bloc's finest creative people. The system of monetary controls allowed exchange of goods and services to function even though some of the limitations were counterproductive or even stupid. But separatism in standards broke down without ever getting off the ground.

It is important to remember, however, that the basic system of quality standards also failed to take hold, as did the program of distinctive interbloc standards. The failure to establish effective quality control was an economic disaster for individual countries and an interbloc political defeat. While these parallel failures occurred for slightly different reasons, the mechanisms that might have been installed to control the centers of opposition were only weakly supported. That is to say, the failure of the quality and autarkic standard efforts resulted in large measure from deficiencies in the Leninist-Stalinist model of economies and the deliberately contrived subordination of COMECON, rather than from the inexorable force of economic realities.

On the other hand, the fact that world standards are referred to (and not only in the 1970 document) suggests the obvious: to obtain the hard currency needed, if only for the occasional emergency purchases on the world market, world-class goods are required. But, of course, such trade generally requires world standards in other areas as well. A world-class product must have legs and must adapt easily to follow-up conditions—storage of spare parts, service, communication with the customer. These imply continual, not sporadic, efforts.

The weakness of autarky is often summed up in the formula, "You can't sell if you don't buy," but the reverse is also true: "You can't buy if you don't sell." An invisible fence of unique standards is difficult to construct, or even imagine. Isolating a country in Albanian style is a difficult project to imagine on any large scale. More relaxed forms of the model have been employed in Maoist China, North Korea, and Cuba. China has moved to end its xenophobia and the other two systems may have endured only because of decades of very heavy external subsidization. Whether a system so established can long persist when the subsidy is withdrawn remains to be tested by time.

In short, while the difficulties attendant upon such a system are apparent, disaster does not immediately confront those who attempt such systems. It is logical to expect decline, much as companies that excessively constrain choices of their customers ("the Gillette strategy") find that potential clients are generally wary and prefer more flexible arrangements. The strategy is ultimately self-defeating. The analogy between a society and a company is not far-fetched, and may even be comforting, but one has less say in choosing one's country than in selecting a razor, and throwing away a razor because the blades are too expensive is not nearly so difficult as starting life afresh in a new culture. Hence, the analogy should be used with great caution.

Whose Failure? Inadequacies of Marxism or of Autarky?

To what extent is the Eastern bloc's failure to achieve separatist standards a product of the Marxist model and to what extent is it a sign of the growing difficulty to "go it alone" in the "new world economic order"? (That term was current over a decade before President Bush's handlers attempted to hijack it, by transforming it into a "new world political order." Clearly, the earlier term is more appropriate, though still grandiose, since even the economic order is more a trend than a reality.)

It is especially difficult to answer that question because, as we have seen, the establishment of separate standards was just one of many motives for Eastern bloc planners. Not only did their resolve waver, but at times they actually promoted world standards in production. What was put to the test, therefore, was the execution (which proved to be incoherent), not the strategy itself.

The artificial introduction of new and more isolating measures carries with it increasing costs in the modern world. Albania and North Korea show that resolve permits a regime to be sustained in spite of those high costs, but entails a high probability of internal decay if the course of separatism is blindly pursued. Such a course has reasonable payoffs short term, but poor prospects "in the long run." The adoption of unusual standards is an extra cost, and often fails precisely because it does what it is usually intended to do—keeps domestic products in and foreign goods out.

As both the American and Japanese examples indicate, maintenance of existing differences is not fatal to trade or inevitably costly. Standards differences can be overcome by manufacturing different product lines or by supplying adapters and the like.

The Eastern European example, however, makes clear that differences in quality standards are likely to prove decisive even when price is adjusted downward. There is a niche for a simpler or more primitive product, but that niche tends to be small for most goods. Style and design differences can be adjusted for, and, if the costs can be contained, such products can remain competitive. This is less simple than it appears, since the adaptive process must not be cumbersome, repairs and adjustments cannot be mysterious, parts must be available and a whole backup system must be in place. But quality unreliability or failure to maintain consistency is even more debilitating and more likely to destroy partnership relationships.

The transformation of Eastern Europe into a trading bloc was initially established and maintained by military *and* political measures, not consumerist inducements. Fiat and force were at its root. It was maintained on a day-to-day basis by an arcane barter system that permitted exchange within the means available, making the cost of goods obscure. The development of localized standards was a buttress, not a creator, of separatism, and therefore never a high priority. When, intermittently, attention was shifted to world trade and world standards, COMECON suffered and stalled.

Reliability probably improved over time, just as productivity improved slightly overall with intensive investment. But just as the yield was nowhere near what it should have been given the level of capital invested, quality did not keep pace with evolving world standards. The Eastern bloc lost ground in the attractiveness of its goods to the West and ultimately to itself. Furthermore, by neglecting the product infrastructure—training, repair services, inventory of spare parts—it sacrificed the advantage of product compatibility and the simplicity of maintaining old machinery without retraining staff.

Once the bloc was created, decent attention to quality might well have made its day-to-day affairs viable. If worldwide quality standards had been approached, the bloc might have been competitive on the world market as well, especially if it were willing to bear the costs of adapting separatist standards to world standards.

The Imperatives of the Modern World

The characteristic movement of this century has been, in Rupert Emerson's felicitous and wise title, "From Empire to Nation." One might think this movement produces more units of governance but fewer discrepancies in behavior among them than in the past. Obviously, that is not easily demonstrated and far from proven. Essentially, the argument would be that the smaller the nation and the easier the emigration of its people, the more nearly policies will converge, under the pressure of competitive alternatives.

The international economic order lays the groundwork for convergence by setting up standards and metastandards. The precise requirements are few, but the general outline of a process does push toward constraining choices and diminishing differences.

So, of course, do the multinationals. By and large, they benefit the most from interchangeability. They seek world standards that permit the fungibility of goods, allow executives to fathom processes in countries they need never visit, and make possible a transfer of skills from place to place.

It is dangerous to simply extrapolate from the past, but still more dangerous to ignore its direction. If country lines continue to be less and less significant and large regional powers with economic hegemony emerge less readily, the development of a set of worldwide standards seems more likely than any other outcome. The major properties and productive forces of the future—the electronic impulses that already transcend geographic controls—entail considerable worldwide coordination. They will be difficult for an autarkic system to constrain without severe, obvious, and contentious costs to its citizenry. Standardizers are likely to be prophets of the future, but the most significant "standards" will be of impulses, ideas, and concepts, which will no more resemble "standards" as conceived in 1890 than the atom studies by today's physicists resemble those conceived by the Greek philosophers.

Part IV

Becoming and Evolving
The Future of Standards

9

The Evolution of Standards and the Processes of Formalization

THE DEVELOPMENT OF STANDARDS IS A PROCESS, an increasing approximation to formal legalization. That becomes clear when what was once a design feature or an inventor's whim is repeated (or ignored) only at the risk of evoking the long arm of the law. It is equally clear when, though such punishment is not involved, a feature becomes as firmly incorporated as if it were law. To a student of law, standards are instructive models of the nature, potentiality, and limits of law. Since they leave physical traces, product standards can be followed, observed, and tracked with considerably less ambiguity than implementation of and compliance to most other forms of law. It is a visible and simplified real-life model of the essence and path of law.

As such, standardization has elicited many of the usual explanations for a law's emergence, though perhaps in somewhat simplified form. The *technocratic* explanation of standards is that there is an optimal—or near optimal— form for physical products.[1] Careful, objective study by qualified experts will tease out that form and present it as a verifiable norm. The essence of standards is some neutral, almost definitional finding that stems from the nature of the product itself. Expertise ultimately defines the nature of the goods and what they require.

The main rival of this explanation is a diffusion model. An innovator (inventor, adopter, usurper, opportunist) selects a useful or expedient form from among many options or alternatives. That form is widely copied, partly because it is efficient, partly because mankind is disposed to imitation; future authenticity is judged by success in duplicating the first effort. Although modifications that are decisively more desirable may come to be accepted, some arbitrary configuration is ultimately settled upon. In this interpretation, standards are seen as contingent, loose approximations of the optimal, as much a product of accidental innovation as helpful protection for the purchaser or user.

A related but opposite notion is the restrictive view of standards. In this interpretation, the purpose of the standard is to accord special advantage to someone—the inventor, a developer, or a group—by restricting production or distribution or by requiring others to produce or distribute in a nonoptimal manner. Standards are shell games, licenses to extract advantage. The fiat interpretation suggests that the arbitrary nature of standards is even greater. Legislated norms can create usage as much or more than usage creates norms. Societal design and its needs and claims (safety, harmony with other components of the culture, autarky) dominate the material properties of the object, which are much more malleable and socially determined than people believe.

The bargaining-information model suggests that standards are arrived at for the mutual benefit of the producer and the purchaser, and therefore are best processed in a way that conveys the maximum of information and utility for each side. In a sense, social regulation for safety and health is an intrusion on that process, but information on vital matters is quite clearly a major objective of standards and so develops closely with their usage.

In this chapter, I make the not surprising claim that no single explanation is adequate to account for all standards. Each perspective helps develop an informed approach to different issues.

The Technocratic Explanation

In the technocratic view, standards are immanent, not so much developed as found. It is an approach akin to "natural law" in jurisprudence and draws upon the older tradition of Western culture, which thought that nature's regularities and social regulation were one, that "the law of gravity" was the same type of law as the "laws of marriage and divorce." Yet the fully technocratic point of view of standards is normally espoused by science zealots who would regard natural law as nonsense.

At its extreme, a truly immanent standard obviously needs no formalization. The wing shape for airplanes need not be prescribed, since without the benefit of the shape, which permits the essential lift, the plane simply will not fly. Nonetheless, strong regulation and specification of the composition of the wing and its support system is in order because of the consequences for rupture once the plane is in the air. A plane out of control is in turn dangerous to others in the air or on the ground. The engineering or technocratic aspect defines risks involved, but even here, the safety factor is also a social decision. We make bridges twice as safe as theoretically needed, even increasing that standard formula by a factor of three or more under special circumstances. The same is true of airplane wings. The expert can provide theoretical safety calculations, but the balance between safety factors and cost remains in part a social decision.

Experts may be willing to calculate a reasonable optimal point based upon experience, and may even report that, beyond a certain point, design or component construction is useless, counterproductive, or not cost-efficient. As with atomic energy, however, those pen-and-paper calculations may ultimately prove misguided. Factors that are conceived as independent often turn out to be interrelated, and are therefore much more likely to occur together. Sometimes, a society may even wish for *less* safety than expertise suggests is desirable.

The naturally determined component of some standards is useful in circumscribing debate. On many matters, however, the technical and social are intertwined. Expert recommendations usually extend their privileged knowledge into domains where their judgment ends and intuition or guesswork takes over. Their assumption of authority, however, often spares society anguish and avoids the substitution of decision makers with even less claim to knowledge, experience, or informed intuition.

The Diffusion Model

Most standards have developed from progenitor inventions, though sometimes there are multiple origins. Product names often become part of the language. Coke, Victrola, Holerith cards, Bessemer Steel, and Babbidge Machine are only some of the generic terms designating families of products created in the image of the prototype. In industry after industry, country after country, one enterprise or person sets the standard and the others follow. Schools of art, genres of production, incorporation of specific mechanical contrivances and aids, rods and levers and gears, tubes and transistors, all set patterns and norms for others, whether through apprenticeship, observation, licensure, or reverse engineering.

A product is seldom "inevitably" in a precise form or shape, but the invented form is copied. This accounts for the variation in products in different societies, which often spring from a different prototype built on the same principles. (Most modern inventions like television have multiple originators, and often many countries claim that one of their own started it all. Even calculus was developed independently by two mathematicians using different notations.) Diffusion is also aleatory, so that a product accepted in one place may be for a time unknown in another.

There is, diffusionists insist, a surprising persistence of accidental qualities. Railroad gauges are believed to have been styled on the location of wheels in horse carriages, and certainly, the automobile's design is still recognizably that of a horseless carriage. Of course, the functions of these different contrivances are also remarkably alike (and therefore "naturally" similar), but in the abstract, greater diversity might have been expected. Clothing is a remarkable tribute to useless persistence of old touches now seen as decorative or ornamental: buttonholes with no counterpart button, buttons without holes (once used to train children not to wipe their noses on their sleeves), fancy little pockets to keep kinds of watches that not one person in a million owns these days, all suggest the remarkable influence of past goods on present-day sensibilities.

Innovation of style as well as function then becomes possible. The new style may serve as a prototype. Indeed, the original attribution may be assigned to a populizer who "knocks off" the innovation, rather than to the genuine originator.

The diffusion model, of course, demystifies standards and suggests they are not God-given, as in some sense the technocratic concept implies.

The diffusion model recognizes that standardization may negatively fix a product, either through usage or prescription. Inferior products may continue to dominate simply because new products are hard to introduce or because a service industry has developed around them and would be difficult to duplicate. Timing may result in a form of product becoming fixed and difficult to dislodge—cassette players, for example. We have noted the effect of social mores on the position of the rider in bicycling. A very clear example of U.S. limits is the shape of electric sealed-beam headlights for cars. While European and Japanese manufacturers produced better lighting in the 1970s, this was not legally feasible in the United States. Still, when auto manufacturers were freed from the restriction in the 1980s, manufacturers remained more interested in innovation in shapes for styling than in power and lighting.[2]

Restrictiveness

The restrictive model goes a step further. The origin of standards does not lie solely in the accidental history of their creation. Standards are a way of freezing technology because the original producer does not wish to see the initial capital investment diminished in value by others who introduce simpler processes. As we have already noted, many economists and most cynics suggest that old firms (and established countries) are profoundly, even principally, interested in coercive standards to "help consumers" by trying to lock their own technology into a process. Their capital investment is a wasting asset and, by forcing others to duplicate it, they are subject only to normal depreciation, avoiding the sharp decline coming from the introduction of cheaper or more efficient production methods.

It is not only older firms that are suspected of such disguised protectionism. It is also alleged that "developed" countries are eager to impose greater restrictions on up-and-coming countries.[3] If others are forced to overinvest in methods of production, they may conclude that profit will not be forthcoming and may abandon their competitive efforts. If they do go ahead, it will be on a level playing field, when they might have had an advantage from more efficient and newer technology.

Developing nations and upstart companies in the United States lend support to the view that the "green movement" is often supported by entrenched industries who engage in a form of restrictiveness by adding higher costs for new enterprises. This increases entry costs as effectively as tighter production standards would do, since older industries are often "grandfathered" in or given time to phase in new technology. On the whole, these suspicions, though logically argued and cogently predicted, have not been demonstrated in any study of a complete regulatory regime or in a cross-sectional study of older and aspiring firms in an industry.[4] Quite obviously, there are many discrete examples of such protectionism, as in the building industry, where many home regulations are designed to protect archaic technology or eclipsed craft techniques. But even at its most conspicuous, the package of standards required, taken as a whole, has not been demonstrated undesirable or even particularly costly. (A good indication is that prefab production of homes has not been found particularly cheaper, nor has it found a strong niche in the industry.)

Of course, there is a clearly intentional restrictiveness built into copyright and trademark regulations. These are monopolies granted on the theory that one must encourage creativity by giving more than a "first strike" advantage to creators, since they are unlikely to recoup their investment or gain a decent return without such extended opportunity. Songwriters, to take a graphic example, would not be able to gain financially merely from the very first performance of their songs. Similarly, drug companies would find most of their medicines duplicated through "reverse engineering" techniques, well before the costs of research were recouped. Imitators who did not have to spend the sums invested in abortive and successful drugs could easily undersell the originator. While there is dispute about the optimal time span of such government-granted monopolies, the amount such companies should be allowed to charge, and the amount of aid the government should give to such research, few contest the basic premise that on the whole, societies are better off with these restrictions than without them.

The argument that patents are good because they encourage new developments is largely a matter of faith. It also cannot be demonstrated that the net effect of restrictiveness is positive. Fritz Machlup argued the case nearly three decades ago, and economic research has not improved on his conclusion very much; a sort of sociology of the economics of invention has developed, but it defines the conditions of invention rather than assessing patent gains and losses. Still, common sense and expert opinion are inclined to believe there is a need to reward discovery to encourage individuals and companies to pursue new products.[5]

Interestingly, this casts some doubt on the premise that protecting "older industry" through standards is inefficient per se. Often the difference between patentable invention and the "ingenious" adaptation of a process to specified conditions is scant. Since grossly archaic standards have a narrow "half-life," they may operate much like patents to indeed protect the basic investment and thereby encourage further and new capital risk taking. Thus, cynics might be right about the motive, yet wrong about social advantage; this may explain why it is so hard to demonstrate their eminently logical case.

Fiat

All these analyses, except the technocratic, suggest that governments (or private organizations) have considerable leeway in what are less than foreordained processes. Some analysts and social activists, however, see standards not just as recipes but as a positive, socially purposeful program that can represent aspirations and goals. Government's reach can also exceed its grasp if it tries for nobler goals through standardization.

A highly successful example of this type of regulation came decades ago when legislation passed to limit the fat content of chopped meat to 10 percent, with responsibility for enforcement delegated to the Department of Agriculture. At that time, there was no known measure of fat content, and highly experienced chefs could not estimate the presence of fat any better than casual customers. Fat was removed during cooking, but could not be measured precisely before the meat was cooked. It was almost whimsical for the federal government to regulate what it could not enforce.[6]

The result of the legislation was the development, almost on the eve of its enforcement date, of a quick-sampling technique involving the cooking of the obtained sample. As simple as that was, it was a major breakthrough for American diets, the control of fat content in the form of meat most used in American homes and restaurants. The task of finding a quick and cheap testing device had seemed achievable to the legislators in principle and was in fact achieved.

Stephen Breyer suggests this type of effort be called a "technology forcing" regulation. He also notes that, early on, OSHA demonstrated the problem it entails. In the case of modifying bumpers for greater safety, OSHA prescribed a change, based on a very sketchy study, that solved the problem, and the organization even correctly estimated the increased cost. But with respect to brakes, it bet on a faulty design that was deleterious rather than desirable.[7]

The most interesting aspect of the fat content story is how atypical it is. When government has set utopian and unmeasurable standards in the hope that completely new instruments will be developed, it has usually waited indefinitely. When it has required the undoable in the expectation that life would generate an orderly solution, it has often created something of a mess. Much EPA legislation originally instructed the agency to create a technology to measure air pollution by gases and droplets and to set reasonable levels of human tolerance.[8] Not only has that not occurred, it seems more probable than not that the thrust of the legislation, and the EPA staff recruited to deal with these goals, has diverted research from what may well be the most serious air threat—soot.[9] "Environmental Impact Studies" do not seem to measure dangers to the environment and have served as legal handles to end projects that judges do not like or that have become very controversial. By adding costs, they discourage all major construction and industrial moves, good or bad.[10]

Even more discouraging is the example of artificial dialysis machines. The premise of a 1973 amendment to the Social Security Act was that technology was on the way for individual home machines (based on a modification of dry-cleaning machines). By a provision assuring all those with kidney problems a right to dialysis, it was expected that a market for such machines would be created through government underwriting of availability. The technology failed and the result was excess demand and a need to create a rationing system for use of available machines. There was suddenly community assessment of an individual's right to live.[11] While this system of rationing of a truly vital good was not necessarily inferior to rationing by price and access to doctors (it might well have been instituted in short order anyway, with the growth of health insurance plans), it was not what Congress intended at all. Only in the 1990s did new optimism develop for another type of simple home machine, which had been confidently expected decades earlier.

Yet while government cannot routinely command creativity, there are many other policies government can easily link to standards that are enforceable. A government might, for example, regulate child labor by granting certification for other standards. In a sense, the Roosevelt administration's National Recovery Act involved this. To get "Blue Eagle" clearance for interstate commerce purposes, manufacturers had to comply with an industrywide code that typically embraced union recognition, wage and hour regulations, child labor, and whatever else was included interstially with specifications regarding quality and grading.

When these goals are marginal to the purposes of standardization and in themselves uncontroversial or at least nonincendiary, governments may feel they are efficiently solving a second issue with less cost than if it were dealt with separately. Paper plates may reasonably be required to be biodegradable or made from renewable forest trees as part of product standards. But when the connection is tenuous or in itself contested, the linkage may undercut the rationale for basic standards themselves. The attraction of the technocratic rationale for standards is precisely that it provides a "natural and objective" cover for marginal policies that often escape the level of scrutiny that bald ukases and separate actions attract.

One must also recognize, however, that "core" technocratic decisions may also entail arbitrary elements. In the absence of information, when decision makers must choose whether to route traffic right or left, for example, the only imperative is to require a consistent policy. As indicated earlier, we now have evidence that the favored choice increases accidents. The intuition of experts is probably more discerning than that of nonexperts, but intuition is a very fallible source of decision. It is in reality often a polite name for slightly informed fiat.

Standards as Communicated Bargaining

If one of the main purposes of standards is to convey a maximum of comprehensible information, then the amount conveyed can be regarded as a compromise derived from a process in which consumers and sellers participate to reveal what is vital without revealing everything. Consumerism tends to favor full and complete disclosure, even at the risk of factual overload for most persons. Its support for standards in the early years was a product of the assumption that standard setting was such a process of disclosure. Manufacturers, preferring brand names and self-validation, will agree to standardization if it is the least offensive necessity or if other gains, such as insurance protection, are made in return.

Such compromised agreement between sides with different purposes involves a message that is understood by both buyer and seller. It is, of course, possible to communicate in terms imposed entirely by a third party. Still, a mutual understanding is often of maximum effectiveness. The weakness of one-way control by either side is that it may be misperceived and viewed with suspicion and cynicism. If, on the other hand, the purpose of standard setting is to reduce competition or camouflage a lack of regulation under the guise of control, then exclusion of the other side is a preeminently logical strategy.

Since it is abundantly clear that standard setting is often a closed or highly restricted process, and that producers are almost never unrepresented, it follows that the communication bargaining view of standardization is either incorrect in its essence or an overidealization in one of its aspects. Unlike other approaches, one can readily measure its basic operations and see that it is wrong, inasmuch as participation by consumers is restricted. Obviously, not only is consumer interaction not stressed, it is not even wanted in many instances. Of course, once standards are set, claims may be made regarding their advantage for consumers, but when consumers' counsel was clearly not sought or resisted, producers' intentions to inform are easily discounted. Furthermore, the producer of goods requiring interactive and repetitive selling has an interest in consumer interaction, while a "one-shot" seller or one producing inferior goods has a stake in minimized communication.

An Overview of Standardization: The Range of Social Choice

Clearly, fiat is not the dominating aspect of standardization. To be sure, the French have regulated (and largely defined for other countries as well) the true nature of a "croissant," including its shortening, size, and shape, and have also successfully mandated the weight of other types of bread. Most countries have other standard sizes and weights. But it is simply too easy to vary loaf size in different times and places while meeting most of these standards, which, after all, are minimal and imprecise. The shrewdness of the French was no doubt derived from experience, presenting sizes bakers were already making and that customers were finding convenient. Ten kilo loaves would hardly have been acceptable. Fifty kilo loaves would not have fit into the ovens. Croissants made of cornmeal might have ended all interest in the product, but acceptable croissants could have been made a trifle larger and vegetable oil permitted in Paris as it is elsewhere. The basic design of a product, its very essence, is called its "patent" in some languages: it is quite fixed or it simply would not work. The location of the motor in a car body may be fixed (or the options may be specified), and the mountings may also be required for safety reasons. Those specifications are as likely to be based on experience as on engineering principles. Since "experience" is a sampling of the past, it adds other chance elements to the variability of inventors' original designs. Other mountings, not necessarily thought of or tried, might work just as well or even better.

Standardization fixed by nature versus standardization by fiat thus seems to be something of a continual underlying variable. At one extreme, there might be only one feasible way. In those instances, no standard (basic wing design, for instance) need be promulgated, no law passed. ("Everyone is required to breathe" is not a necessary regulation.) The moment two or more rival feasible modes exist, standards may be promulgated. If poor execution of the design will result in superficial success but guarantee ultimate failure, standardization may occur or be imposed to ensure safety (wings must not be fragile), to protect against fraud (suits must not be made of shoddy material), to promote efficiency (construction wood must be well defined), to establish convenient sizes, or to maintain appropriate inventory.

Thus, in the beginning, standards may be entirely rigid, where the purpose is to provide the producer with a recipe, blueprint, or correct prescription of a good, and may then fan out to envelop ever increasing social options or chance elements in the design. The three elements here—the natural range of workable options, accidental imposition of design for experimental reasons, and the conscious social preference of options, are generally confused, especially by societies suspicious of innovation. People in traditional societies will ape the past, even going through needless production steps the way their master trained them, because they do not separate creating the object from its function and original design. To change it would risk losing its functional efficiency, but also some mystical property that might have served in a nonrational way to preserve its value. Ultimately, societies might even invoke the wrath of gods and ancestors.

The importation of social choice and purpose—"it will be made of paper rather than plastic to preserve oil for fuel"—is in most societies a later mode of imposition. There is ample evidence that wise leaders made such practical choices, often in Machiavellian manner, by invoking tradition and divine or occult forces as justification.

When Choice Seems Open-Ended

The wide domain of choice raises the question of whether standards are optional or necessary. Also, are they are created for the benefit of producers, consumers, the public, or government? The short answer seems to be "yes."

It is not clear why people so glibly assume that a set of behaviors that is apparently and overtly neutral should always be employed for the benefit of one group and eschewed by all others. If a product's standardization confers benefits to an originator, it is, after all, likely that those benefits will be sought. If competition is reduced (by keeping entry costs high, for instance), royalty payments for patents and monopolies required, or risk of obsolescence minimized (by specifying the production process, for example), why would not most originators accept and seek such policies? Most would pursue those insurance policies at least as vigorously as they would improvements in their products.

Yet buyers are seldom as hopelessly overwhelmed as, say, Soviet consumers. Eastern bloc purchasers had little buying clout and even less political clout, somewhat like a medieval serf whose major weapon was a choice between enthusiastic or sullen obedience. Popular support was of some, but limited, value to Kremlin leaders, who chiefly represented production needs, and only secondarily regulative forces; hence the almost complete neglect of the environment.[12] In a monopoly situation of chronic shortage, mere consumers could largely be ignored, especially since the most influential individual consumers—the political, organizational, and cultural elites—could buy in quite another, more privileged market. Most products were prepared for other government units, and these had their own standards.

The consumer interest in most societies is seldom so weak, though it is generally at a disadvantage. For starters, it is difficult to create standards without drawing on the expertise of the producer. Enforcement is more often dependent on producers' actions than on those of customers. For these and other cogent reasons, regulators can seldom ignore producers, but may minimize consumer power and influence.

Socializing or socialist regimes may be willing to formulate unrealistic economic proposals that penalize producers. Thus, the Allende regime's program in Chile seemed precisely designed to doom some capitalist enterprises, and the early Mitterand years in France, by diminishing profitability, seemed to lay the groundwork for limited collectivization. But Allende's effort was thwarted by the military and Mitterand's by the flight of capital. These examples are highly unusual, especially when compared to the more frequent occurrence, when standards are essentially a monopoly of prevailing industrial firms, subject only to a possible veto by (or occasional bargaining with) a sympathetic public regulator. Often, too, the government unit involved is an agency enmeshed in some business relationships that make it as much the industry's representative as the public's.

Clearly, however, there are spheres where public concern predominates, notably safety and health. The tenor of standards—rigorous or weak—suggests both the strength of a regime and the relative bargaining power of providers and the general public. Most systems tacitly assume that their own viability rests on delivery of at least a modicum of such protection (as well as physical safety). Standards of food and drink, fire safety, and health will reflect the economic status and general degree of equality of the community more than anything else. Since extreme conditions like disease and fire are not easily confined to consumers, but also threaten producers, there is some case there for an objective "public interest" maximizing social objectives.

Additionally, standards are often formulated to ease the task of bureaucrats. We have noted that design standards, that is, prescribed production standards, are usually preferred by regulators over more complex performance standards.[13] The easily classified is usually preferred to the difficult to ascertain. This aspect of bureaucracy is the subject of anecdote and novels, sociological jargon and citizens' scurrilities. Bureaucrats—like others—may insist on standards to perpetuate jobs and increase their jurisdictions. "Red tape" is a universal phenomenon, though spread differentially, the elaboration of formal rules designed for the protection, ease, employment, and aggrandizement of the petty officeholder.

Thus, each type of player has its leverage, its reasons for backing standards, and its moments when its influence ebbs and flows. Producers not only have the "first strike" capacity of setting out the basic module and the social power that goes with wealth and productivity, they are also a principal font of information and a vehicle of enforcement. Consumers are ultimately the purchasers and, when all is said and done, constitute the bulk of society. "God must have loved the poor, he made so many of them." And indeed, consumers include the rich as well. Governments have power and the means of formalization, and bureaucrats have the last word, often under unreviewable circumstance. Cui bono? It all depends.

Accidental Standards

The argument for imitation of original products and the persistence of initial standards is actually an argument for the persistence and replication of errors made at some stage of development. The familiar has staying power, even at the expense of a slight improvement. Revision means scrapping capital investment, reeducating the public, transferring "goodwill" and familiarity to the new bottle or brand name.

Rationalists would suggest that standards errors that are too costly always get redone "in the long run." These analysts are at a loss to explain why people die in famines in India while watching cows run through their homes. Obviously, change occurs, usually in the direction of efficiency. But it is difficult to explain the survival value of the system of English spelling or the ridiculous system of measures and weights Anglo-Saxons have perpetrated on their societies. The number of inches in a foot meshes poorly with the number of feet in a yard, or feet in a mile. A pound of feathers weighs more than a pound of gold, because we have preserved competing systems of weight for different products. Our system of spelling is not phonetic and wastes secretarial time; its main advantage is that it allows grade school students to achieve national championship status in what should be a decaying art form of useless obeisance to our ancestors. Yet purists assail us for moving too fast, not too slowly.

Rationalists will argue that resistance to the metric system is not particularly inefficient. Our market is sufficiently strong that it is more economical to convert the small proportion of externally shipped output to the metric system while retaining the domestic measures.[14] This is plausible, but it must be acknowledged that there remains a residue of remoteness that carries on in other ways and subtly keeps our export level low. The metric system is in most respects simpler for domestic purposes as well.

The sentimental attachment is not just to any past, but to one's own imputed past. In the arena of language, there is a sense of identity, second only to religion, that pulls people together. Arabic is such a language, a classic structure unifying even those peoples whose vernacular forms of it are barely comprehensible to one another. The painstaking construction of modern-day Hebrew from a language in suspended animation for thousands of years required concocting terms overnight for electricity, pipes, income tax, and various forms of modern machinery. This was correctly seen as a step in nation building that rivalled a declaration of independence, and was obviously more needed than a constitution.

Other more mundane artifacts do not seem to have the same survival value, but there is a cultural inertia, which Hume celebrated and most social analysts underestimate. Economists usually point out that new products with profound advantages—technology, birth control—often get adopted even when superficially repugnant to a society. Anthropologists tend to emphasize the persistence of rejection, and the usually slow pace of acceptance of such products.

Once a standard is accepted in a society, it generates a system around which the product is organized. The United States moved quickly to embrace electricity. Edison was a strong organizer and good businessman; the Edison name is not mere ceremony in electric companies, but a sign of original and continuing family involvement. Still, the United States made choices that were not as efficient as the ultimate European higher voltage transmission.[15] Since other factors dominate efficient cost, scrapping plants or installing a vast system of adapters has never been contemplated.

A conventional explanation for the decline of Britain and of America's "rust belt" has been that they are imprisoned by their past and their inability to transcend obsolescence.[16] At the same time, Japan's relative status (but not its net trade surplus) is diminished by the adaptation of its techniques by upstarts such as South Korea, Singapore, Formosa, and even mainland China.

But those very elements—infrastructure and well-developed skills—are precisely the factors called for by students of innovation and entrepreneurship. It was not the manufacturing tabula rasa of postwar Japan that was its ace in the hole, for on those grounds the middle of the Sahara would score the most points.[17] It was the human resources and social system that could pull together and bring about prosperity.

Obviously, accidental inefficiencies as well as intentionally biased aspects creep into standards. Those "errors" will generally persist unless the advantages of change become clearly apparent. Since the costs of change are often diverse and not easily enumerated, however, and since veto groups are not easily convinced, the status quo almost always gets a good run for its money.

The Domains of Standardization

In general, standardization tends to occur in clumps. Some areas are ripe for the process, others resist. Food and drugs are closely regulated, particularly against innovations. The protection of health is a core government function that generally yields regimes more advantages than risks.

The clothing industry is surprisingly dotted with standards. Many are unofficially designed to validate advantages not overtly visible—Sanforizing to prevent shrinking, nature of fabric, skill of tailoring—assuring or at least asserting quality. This may be a relic of the guild or craft tradition, but it also an extension of the trust necessarily accorded one's tailor, whose inseams and linings cannot be easily evaluated. Clothing labels also disclose fabric content because of the need for appropriate handling and cleaning.

Chemicals and volatile objects are of course regulated carefully and standardized so that interactions will be predictable. Firecrackers and dynamite should produce controlled explosions, acids should remove surfaces, not eat away the entire object or damage eyesight. Again, there is a mutuality of interest that leads to standardization and controls. Pharmacies fall into this domain, since the items they sell are digested or applied to human beings, and dosage must be controlled carefully.

By and large, home utensils are seldom regulated to any great extent. In rare instances, there is a prescription for safety. There may also be special demarcation of nation, sect, or caste in designs. Special styles may be required or forbidden. Furniture is only prescribed by limited regulations regarding materials. Generally, only chairs have distinctive style protection (patents), though some desks and tables do as well. Yet, in spite of this, utensils and furniture are among the most distinctive features of any society. Although they are also among the most widespread and modish items, societies have deep, conservative notions about home furnishings. Residences are usually quite recognizably like those of parents and peers in the society. Social pressure preserves a general style, though the sense of personal freedom regarding such a close extension of self results in somewhat more freedom for those who seek it in this domain than in others. Of course, governments and manufacturers can exert considerable control through availability of styles and materials, but again, the fact that individual artisans or ingenious improvisors abound limits restrictiveness.

It is, of course, complex manufactured goods that are usually regulated and that cry out for regulation. Taking place at a fixed locale, typically by processes not easily altered, manufacturing can be observed and regulated with reasonable predictability by monitors. Typically, when much of a product is not visibly available for inspection or will not yield its secrets to nonadepts, some process of inspection and quality control is extremely valuable. Sometimes, it is essential. In that sense, a manufactured good is like a house, a complex mechanism with engineering problems and hidden aspects, which an expert can deduce from overt clues. This allows a buyer to have some confidence that preexisting problems will not suddenly make themselves known at disastrous cost.

Industrial products that are themselves productive instruments, like robots or machine tools, are even purer examples of the need to control and evaluate. Since they are subject to near continuous use, their breakdown is not just a nuisance but a severe tax on an enterprise. Guarantees, repairs, or free service calls are not adequate recompense for problems breakdowns create, not merely in lowered production but also in the threat to promised delivery schedules and an enterprise's reputation for meeting commitments. Cost accounting methods that reveal the cost of such delays also emphasize the need for dependable products and the cost of unreliable components.

The need for repair parts is a major component of the intricacies of standardization versus progress. One method, an extreme form of "simplification," is to minimize changes to actually prevent technological progress. There are few enterprises for which this is a reasonable strategy. The problem of backlogged parts thus becomes a major issue in standardization, and the maintenance of a reasonable supply of spare parts, as models and innovations multiply, can become a sorcerer's apprentice problem.

As on many other issues, Alfred Marshall displayed great wisdom and prescience on this matter. Simplification and standardization, he suggests, are most appropriate and valuable with respect to components and modules.[18] Such simplification has profound effects on warehousing, interchangeability, and the ability of the repairer to handle matters. But it retards new developments only at a fractional rate of attempts to standardize the final product. That can develop and change through new combinations of old modules or addition of new modules with the old. Of course, modules may also evolve, from vacuum tubes to transistors to chips for example. But this leads to "generational" problems rather than day-to-day ones.

Sometimes, though, standardization of the total product works. France has done better with a standard design for atomic electric generators than the United States, which allowed a thousand plans to bloom. But, had the French adopted a plan which in practice worked poorly, they would have suffered geometrically as a penalty for the decision.

In any event, replacement parts are always a problem. One method is for each major user to maintain a supply of parts for each particular model. This is a high-cost solution, particularly since total per part costs are in general considerably higher than the value of the finished product.

The Japanese "just in time" system is a good example of the prevailing parts strategy. They maintain a supply of parts in accordance with game theory models, allowing for reasonable delivery to producers within a time frame considered to be sufficient, generally twenty-four to forty-eight hours. (This, incidentally, provides the framework for a magnificent system of courier service throughout Japan.)[19]

Original manufacturer's parts are generally not available forever. A reduced-cost, used-part supply system competes with a computer register of available new parts. Cannibalizing of used parts becomes more prominent as a model ages and is no longer compatible with new replacement parts.

Of course, the organization of an information system is vital to this concept and is neither easy nor automatic. In the early years of a product, it is often profitable for manufacturers to maintain a good inventory and to have their own distribution system. Ordinary consumer products can be serviced through factory-based mailings for example, while major producers might receive regionalized help and be directly serviced. After a time, supplies may be sold to a major parts distributor, whose lower cost margins permit profitability even though demand shrinks. This may be linked to, or in competition with, a parallel cannibalizing market. Japan's system, linked to a minimal supply inventory, generates overnight package delivery at much lower cost per item than in the United States, but basically the system works roughly the same way.

Of course, not all items justify the expense of computer linkage and the organized listing of parts. Electronics advances are rapid and obsolescent equipment may be of value to most users only as long as it operates. This will reduce willingness to pay the cost required for maintaining a parts system. Dealing randomly with junk dealers, or finding a "Mr. Fixit" who can improvise or ferret out parts, may become the only method of operation.

The continued emphasis on modular construction facilitates such a system; standardizers regard modules as simply a specific form of the general logic. To be able to use motors, pumps, or chips from totally different products to meet a need is a supplier's dream. But even modular replacement in 1991–1994 cars is a help, resembling the advantages of standard sizing of wood boards.

This is not a trivial part of the standardization process, but an important and even vital aspect, as the discussion on Eastern Europe indicated. Jerry-built repairs are as good as the skills of Jerry the mechanic. Standardized parts allow the use of basic machinery with a journeyman's help and are therefore key aspects of diffusion of production systems. An army, it is said, marches on its stomach; a production system (and its products) advances with the availability of component backups.

Beyond a minimal effort to require supply parts for a limited time, efforts to regulate (as opposed to encouraging maintenance of such supplies) seem misguided. Except in the case of some rare products like airplanes, regulation is both difficult to police and ultimately stultifying.

The Mapping and Spread of Standards

Standards, whether diffused or imposed, tend to move out from core products and core areas along paths laid by cultural and political domination. Clearly, superior products move quickly; those merely expressing styles or prestige in their use are usually slower, but attitudes toward the dominating culture will affect their acceptance (see table 9.1).

These patterns of diffusion can be quite fixed. To this day, Iran, India, and China are the principal creators of Persian rugs, handmade from traditional patterns with traditional materials and number of knots. The reach of the moguls across the centuries is unmistakable, as is the influence of cookery derived from the moguls across a broader expanse of territory.

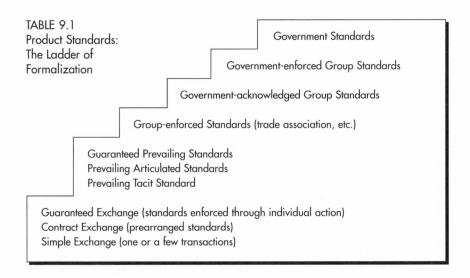

TABLE 9.1
Product Standards:
The Ladder of
Formalization

Government Standards

Government-enforced Group Standards

Government-acknowledged Group Standards

Group-enforced Standards (trade association, etc.)

Guaranteed Prevailing Standards
Prevailing Articulated Standards
Prevailing Tacit Standard

Guaranteed Exchange (standards enforced through individual action)
Contract Exchange (prearranged standards)
Simple Exchange (one or a few transactions)

Probably the greatest example of spheres of influence that established standards for periods far beyond their own hegemony is Rome. The Romans laid down the infrastructure that undergirds European society to this day: law and political structures at the interpersonal level, and roads, aqueducts, civic buildings, and bridges at the technical level. Furthermore, they borrowed, adapted, transmitted, and fixed basic cultural and religious values from the Greeks and Jews. In modern times, the French exercised some of that same sway over Europe and South America. The British were remarkably effective in transforming society in India and Hong Kong, and their settlements in Australia, New Zealand, and most of Canada. In our own time, American leadership has been the model not only for consumerist society (with American tastes and products dominant) but also for business restructuring, modeled on the skills and opportunities afforded by the computer. Japan may rival or lead America in the robotics of assembly line computer control, but in organizational and office reform they are not competitors at all.[20]

Within these spheres, effective product dominance can be achieved through product desirability. British dominance over textiles was a constant of the nineteenth century, but that did not prevent the superior German chemical industry from making inroads in dye and other fabric finishers in Britain itself in the early twentieth century. The post–World War II prominence of Americans in the fabric industry was a result of their control over the production of synthetic fiber, not a privilege of hegemony. German and American influence in airplane design and production fluctuated according to design skills and control of capital investment, and was not a measure of political dominance.

Styles and symbols are much more arbitrary and more likely to be adopted for reasons of power and prestige. The first flush of Soviet dominance in Eastern Europe brought to the fore a cadre of Marxist thinkers who vigorously reinterpreted many fields. As Russian legitimacy waned, so did concern with Marxism. But East German radio and television sets were appreciated by anti-Marxist thinkers as well as Marxists. The domain of influence of a society is broad, but is seldom of a piece, seldom operates consistently in all aspects of its sphere of influence. It is a force of varying intensity and depends on the receptivity of the influenced nation as well as the thrust and drive of the influencing nation.

10 A World of Increasing Sameness?

THE WORLD, WE ARE TOLD, GROWS NOT MERELY smaller, but more drab. Distinctive features like the rain forest (aka jungle) and even true solitude are endangered. Cities grow more alike, festooned with interchangeable skyscrapers and neon signs. Articles of dress and everyday use, once varied, are increasingly and monotonously the same. If we wish to experience true difference in a shrinking world, we must hurry, before 747s, Chunnels, and growing common product norms homogenize and soften it even further.

Standardization drives out differences and the advantages of standardization take a toll on the exotic and the exceptional. The world grows more alike because humanity has always been quick to imitate those products and patterns that enhance day-to-day existence. A more tightly bound world, in which overnight travelers bring back exotic products, televised holographs provide models of new inventions instantly, and enterprises can be organized by fax or E-mail, is a world in which diffusion is not merely faster but also infinitely easier. The efficiencies of standardization and mass production of luxuries (even if they are somewhat inferior to the prototype) make life at every point on the planet more nearly alike.

At the same time, there are limits to standardization: cultural and national interests have powers that can be expected to brake the impulse. Ballpoint pens and digital wristwatches are generally of universal use, and jeans are the uniform of modernity everywhere, but cooking utensils still reflect distinctive patterns that have evolved from local conditions and culture and are likely to continue to do so. These items facilitate as well as reflect eating patterns. Air conditioning does not seem destined to end the firmly rooted and logical mid-day summer siesta in Mediterranean and other hot climates. Sameness in a genre of basic commodities does not entail sameness in every aspect. Even in this era of global uniforms, pickpockets can generally spot a tourist by dress alone. Subtle appearance of color, style, and cut remain, and a teenager has no difficulty differentiating men's and women's jeans, even when displayed for sale flat on a shelf.

If difference clearly has the capacity to survive, an intriguing question arises: can (and should) it be promoted for its own sake? Should societies max-imize their uniqueness or (an even more basic question), do they have the capacity to do so, to slow down global homogenization? Is cultural or artifac-tual autarky any more viable a strategy than economic autarky? Is product dif-ferentiation of the things of everyday life a contribution to national or societal unity, or simply an empty form of Babbittry destined to disappear? Is it more like cheering for the Dodgers or a soccer team in Europe, or is it a deep cul-tural and life-shaping event, like a British teenager resonating to Gaunt's speech in *Richard II* or a Finnish student to the strains of *Finlandia?*

Strict standards of cultural conformity are usually intended to create boundaries. Those who make such rules are usually "sectarians" or "purists," who would prefer to establish total, controlled, and precise standards of behav-ior in all aspects of life.[1] As a practical matter, they may not always seek to do so, or they may be thwarted in this matter.

Tight control over technology requires a reasonably precise standard of the permissible and the forbidden, usually in the name of faith or culture. This core of values—which may seem loose, permeable, and even inconsistent to an outsider—must be tight, real standards to the insider. Still, a dress code or lan-guage, food, and product standards may circle the wagons in defense of a sys-tem, but they do not define what is being defended. Religion and nationalism are generally the value systems at stake and religion has tended to be the more powerful.

We cannot replay history or create experiments to replicate it; real history is embedded in so many contingencies that plausible alternative situations are usually easy to construct, refuting the bland claim that what happened was inevitable. The key variable can be religion or language, or sometimes simply experience. Ernest Gellner pregnantly points out that literally thousands of potential "nationalities" exist, but relatively few sprout, indicating that the obvious necessary conditions are supplemented by complex and exigent conditions needed for success.[2]

Technical Standards and Boundaries

All social systems can be conceptualized as value systems with boundary maintenance and standards of conduct as their parameters. How do product standards intrude upon this picture? The answer is quite simple, as the history of EC suggests. In the modern world, nontariff barriers—primarily import-export barriers—constitute more effective impediments to trade than do taxes or subsidies.

Indeed, the most effective nontax barrier is not a prohibition at all, but physical rejection. If differential electric current renders a product unusable (as with older computers), formal prohibition is unnecessary. Thus, the introduction of products based on separate standards may create strong and perhaps defining standards.

The consequences of autarkic standards logically encompass those that keep outside influences out and those that keep inside practices in. The conventional motivation is generally trade advantage, but the process may also be contrived to separate societies. Of course, both motivations may be at work.

The development of incompatible standards cuts across all logical categories. Those countries with unique time zones, for example, confound everyone within them who has to deal with the outside world. But even mental adjustments of half an hour, an hour and a half, or ten and a half hours can be made by those who deal extensively with such outlier anomalies.

Obviously, however, some anomalies are more difficult to cope with than others. The ratio of adjustment cost to underlying transaction cost will determine whether people strive to overcome the anomaly or decide it is not worth the effort.[3] Using a transformer is one possibility, but simply buying a duplicate local electric product is another. The most graphic example of isolating and incompatible standards is railroad gauges. The almost totally arbitrary width of tracks is an effective limit on the flow of traffic and brings trains to a screeching halt at many a border. For a century and a half, transportation experts have worked to standardize such gauges, with some results but not total victory.

The main problem is capital investment. Replacing rolling stock all at once rather than as it becomes obsolete is expensive, as is reconstructing a complete track system while maintaining the existing one. Building a brand-new railroad on top of the old is not done lightly, though it usually can be done in stages. In addition, there are special problems. Mountain passes or tunnels may require total reengineering for wider tracks, for example. Many of the persisting deviations are trivial, self-contained complexities that are likely to shrivel or disappear, but sometimes they present genuine physical obstacles, as in the case of the Chunnel. A smooth direct operation of trains from continental Europe to destinations in England and vice versa would take full advantage of this technological major achievement of recent decades. That free flow is prevented by Britain's deviant narrow gauge. Transshipping is therefore necessary at the English shore as in the days of the ferry, making the improvement of train service marginal, at least at first.[4]

If we think of the Chunnel as a deliberately contrived experiment that eliminates rather than creates a barrier, we can find the example instructive. Trucks would appear to benefit the most from portal-to-portal free flow, while railroad traffic (both freight and passengers) will have to be disembarked and transshipped. There will be pressure to find a more convenient solution. *Talgo*-type trains (with adjustable wheels) might be adequate; more likely, a limited track system with continual gauges will be built to bring the trains to a more logical transshipping point. Alternatively, a good system of rail-to-truck retransport, probably in England, could resolve the issue. If so, a passenger service upgrade will require some realignment of train flow so that some passengers do not have to travel to a central point and then double back.

Yet when things are fully ironed out, many observers believe, the consequences will far outstrip the unifying political contrivance of Maastricht. The myriad changes likely—ready access to continental roads and Spanish holidays without airline travel, a door-to-door supply of industrial goods, steady jobs for IRA terrorists in Paris and terrorism on the weekend—are as varied as they are unpredictable.

Karl Deutsch's communications approach suggests that, to measure integration, one must look not to legalities but to human transactions: phone calls, business deals, tourism, intermarriage.[5] That approach is captured well in a *New York Times* suggestion of a simple index: "To track unity in Europe, watch its fast trains." As the author of the item argues, this literally tracks technological development, political will, and cooperation, as well as public usage and travel.[6]

To what degree can the opposite—the creation of isolation and difference—be engineered? History suggests that such efforts need a great deal of luck to succeed, and usually the cooperation and ineptitude of opponents. When built on existing fault lines of community affiliations, conscious human effort may be the catalyst but is seldom the cause.

Products are a superficial manifestation of culture and therefore reflect it more than mold it. Nonetheless, they help create a milieu, and on a practical level, people make choices on such matters. A Frenchman rejecting jeans and McDonald's may be rational and not un-American; or he may be anti-internationalist, but may still like personal computers, running shoes, and "non-stop" stores and restaurants. Peasant crockery can be used in a microwave and *grandmère's* recipes revised to contain less fat. But a Japanese house with electricity and modern plumbing is already an altered structure. A Buddhist fundamentalist as well as a Gucci-label baseball fan who aspires to be a Western-style salary man may live there. It is *possible* to eat only one olive from the jar, but the next comes easier and is therefore more likely to be consumed.

Sumptuary laws are attempts to prevent the first olive, or the first bite from the fruit of the tree of knowledge, from being taken. In effect, they say, "We are drawing a line, not because what you propose to use and consume is so bad in itself, but because you will be moving on the wrong path, and this step will lead to further disintegration." The Amish prohibition on bright colors reminds them to avoid the allure of all luxurious things of the world. The colorful images of television and movies might suffuse their minds, distract them from essentials, make them chase after goals that will make them un-Amish and will encourage ungodliness. The breakdown of barriers begins with a small incursion.

Sumptuary laws are seldom passed for economic reasons, though they may correct trade imbalances. This is probably because obedience to such measures could not easily be maintained on economic grounds. If I can afford a television set and prefer it to a new suit, why can't I buy it? A moralistic answer must be provided, usually by depicting foreign devils and the evils of luxury, and by maintaining the boundaries of society. At the least, a domestic substitute (even if inferior) for the forbidden product would be called for, if economic justifications were used exclusively.

Protection of local products is of course the most common form of sanction, and it can be achieved in multiple ways for multiple purposes. Economic well-being is at least superficially enhanced and foreign involvement minimized. Discrepant standards are usually the most effective and least obtrusive means for such protection, and should therefore be favored by Machiavellian leaders. It is, however, difficult to contrive effective artificial mechanical controls.

Some efforts to achieve greater boundary control include excessive centralization of communication lines and even of transportation. This is highly inefficient for a society, particularly if mechanical improvements are ruled out for political reasons. Use of computers is often restricted by authoritarian regimes because they facilitate both internal and external communications, but that policy heavily penalizes the industrial system. Use of dedicated computer systems to facilitate monitoring, for example, would appear feasible, but is easily overtaken by inventive efforts that allow users to bypass controls. Freezing technology at the time of control is also usually involved, ultimately exacting heavy costs.

Restriction of outside products is most effective when later innovations reinforce the initial prohibition. If smuggling a car into a country is all that is involved, cars can be superficially altered; or the police may ignore the illegal intruder. But if you cannot get the right gas or spare parts on a day-to-day basis, enforcement is almost automatic. Having to buy a transformer—or set of transformers—may be more of a deterrent than paying a heavy tariff, particularly if the product performs less efficiently with a transformer, as is often the case. The ultimate solution would be a standard supply system that corrodes and destroys alien products, or even enables such discrepant imports to damage the user's basic support system. ATT used to hint darkly that non-ATT equipment could cause damage to the wires, and that the consumer would be forced to pay for such bootlegged products. It seems to have been a total deception on the part of the company.

Prohibition is not interdiction. A friend recalled her fascinating experience lecturing in Saudi Arabia. She was invited to a dinner party in her honor by one of the many princesses of the royal family. The women at this all-female affair arrived totally enshrouded in traditional robes but doffed them to reveal expensive Paris gowns underneath. Puritan prayer books and bibles that are jewel-studded underneath a plain cover were once similar outlets for forbidden luxury. The rich collectors of stolen art that can never be publicly acknowledged suggests that illegality may even have glamour.

Style and design clashes are a less effective deterrent to foreign products, but can also be useful. People may raise their eyebrows when they see others wearing shorts or certain colors or cuts of clothes. This can have a derivative effect, like discouraging the use of the type of hats normally worn with the downgraded shorts, though that hat was not originally frowned upon. Plumbing connections for an illicit unit may be difficult. Even though the unit itself is self-contained, it may not tie in with other units that feed into the exhaust system.

The lack of official approval (even absent a prohibition) may affect insurance or rental agreements or other such matters. Even if the potential purchaser is personally satisfied, she may hesitate because someone else down the line of resale might not be. The principle that accounts for the standardized mediocrity of most office buildings—built for resale—applies here as well.

Another danger of restriction is that it can impart the glamour of the forbidden or the attraction of the novel. Prohibition made drinking a cheap (and relatively risk-free) venture into the "dangerous" and the "illicit." In order to have the only IBM-compatible computer in Bulgaria, a company might choose to pay a premium for adapters, particularly if the owner is a buff who is willing to fiddle around with it.

The process is reversed to prevent seepage out to the rest of the world, but its purposes are similar. A sect controlling the minds of its members may wish to restrict information about the real values of the society. Too much talk to foreigners may be discouraged. The most common such effort is to protect production secrets through isolation and censorship. Thus silk production methods were state secrets in ancient China. To this day, the handful of New York City bakers who have an oligopoly on the production of bialys (an old-country cousin of the bagel) will not divulge their methods to others. Coca-Cola's original recipe is a trade secret, as are many food products or recipes. Societies may try to protect revenue by restricting information on how to give glass a certain color, or how to produce a particularly strong but light plastic. A monastery may guard its relics, but especially restricts the recipe for a highly prized cognac.

It is particularly hard to control access to manufacturing goods since the finished products are easily subject to what is sometimes referred to as "reverse designing" or "reverse engineering," where a purchased model is disassembled and analyzed. Most products give up their secrets quickly to knowledgeable persons—engineering experts, chemists, and the like—but as many models as are necessary can be purchased and analyzed if the secret is not obvious. What is not physically discernible can be imagined or an alternative designed creatively. Of course, outright industrial espionage can be resorted to, but this is seldom really necessary. (As with national espionage, commercial espionage is generally more concerned with sales and pricing strategies than with physical components.) Nonetheless, economically based interdiction does occur. Export of computers from the United States to the Eastern bloc was forbidden or discouraged, largely for strategic reasons, but competitive notions and commercial rivalry figured in the discussions as well. "Why give the tools for destruction?" was the basic claim; "Why give the tools for industrial regeneration?" was a secondary and more potent argument.

Why National Standards Will Grow in Number But Have Less Bite

In an era of increasing ethnicity, nations attempt to assert themselves through their unique identity. The growth of the nation-state and standardization have gone together in a chicken-and-egg process of historical importance. Certain characteristic marks of nationhood are not merely exercises of sovereignty but necessary standard choices made by such units.

Many of these choices are cultural—official language or languages, basic elements of ethical outlook—while some are physical—coinage, road building. Still others are product standards in the true sense of the word, enacted to create boundaries or to regulate, or for any of the other reasons adumbrated above.

The majority of existing nations have been established since World War II. While continued attention is directed toward globalization and unification, disintegration of old empires and ethnic claims to separation have been more numerous than the slower—perhaps ultimately more significant—processes of integration.

While it was possible in the past for cultural separatism and ethnic identity to proceed in parallel and sequentially, nations no longer have centuries-long periods of gestation and the luxury of a gradual selection of standards that contribute to identity. Legislation substitutes for history. Languages are "adopted" by fiat, and cultural and product standards are legislated. Precisely because the basic cultural choices are artificial and precarious, nationhood is asserted through prohibitions and requirements that are formal and, it is hoped, identity-forming, rather than taken for granted or given recognition to prevent decay of identity. These political imperatives join the cultural and technological factors that move individual nations toward defined sameness by producing larger numbers of standards that are more precise but less meaningful. To compete in transnational markets it may well be necessary to define local arrangements in accordance with optional international requirements, rather than leave them to the individual producer, as the Japanese have so clearly demonstrated.

At the same time, a nation's individual emphasis takes shape through regulations designed to cope with growing globalization. We noted that the growth of ingenious nontariff barriers was one by-product of the old EEC efforts to eliminate barriers by striking down tariffs and other obviously discriminatory measures. In 1995 the *Economist* reported on a survey by a European business lobby, on what it called "regulatory inflation," indicating vast recent increases in national legislation, even as the rate of EU legislation has declined. Britain's new legislation involved a 600 percent increase in pages of legislation between 1980 and 1991, while the EU regulations declined by over two-thirds. It is highly likely that standards were overrepresented in this new legislation, as European national systems coped with the largely completed "single market."[7]

Standards can also be expected to proliferate as a result of factors associated with the growth of globalization. When performance needs become relatively known and established for a product, that information is likely to be reduced to a standard. When impersonal business relations prevail, standardization becomes increasingly necessary. This first condition—increasing knowledge and specification of performance levels—is characteristic of a growing technological community, where information is quickly transmitted. Even Japan is modifying its emphasis on unique suppliers for individualized products.[8]

Characteristically, component interchangeability and standardization—which Alfred Marshall presciently understood as a component's finest form—prevails. Components are brought together from all over the world, and are assembled in all kinds of locations. The raw materials, components, and processes have to be well defined and prescribed to permit known products with expected performance levels to be entrained.

Two things may limit the expected increase in standards. Much of the proliferation is of already operative norms under new political sponsorship. Some is also technology driven or market driven, so that the numbers do not reflect much real impact or the ability of a society to shape itself. Much of this, too, implies fairly stable technology. New technology overtakes standardization and undoes it, or moves too fast to permit standardization in the first place.

The Globalization of Standards

Within the burgeoning standards field, the growth of international standards is especially noteworthy. Some is quasi-juridical, but most occurs as a fact of economic development.

A complex of organizations now unites standards organizations and other technocratic and economic entities into loose affiliation bound by agreed-upon principles. The WTO, GATT's successor, is the most far-reaching of these, but there are both regional analogues and more specialized agencies having sectoral and product domains.

In the case of WTO, disagreements are to be adjudicated in a procedure that is easier to follow than it was under GATT. Some see this as an exercise of governance, but that seems far-fetched. While WTO is seen as a more day-to-day structure than GATT's periodic "rounds" of negotiation and renegotiation, the source of new agreements is the partner nations. Agreements are essentially contracts, with arbitration and (unlike private contracts) continuing interpretation.

As far as standards are considered, WTO's chief importance is in prescribing procedures for standard setting and defining the modalities of standards (as, for example, the preference for performance standards), not in drafting actual standards. Complaints of violation of these terms can have considerable impact, however. We have noted that the principles of transparency have altered a good deal of Japan's administrative practice, even though they have not been very effective in crucial areas. This general picture has not been studied in other aspiring industrial nations, but it seems likely that it is the prevailing pattern. Acceptance of the norm of transparency has great power, except when powerful local interests are involved.

The growth of ISO and regional and sectoral standard setters is remarkable, but it is a clear concomitant of a "new economic order." New industrializers illustrate Japan's claim that, to enter new markets, competency and quality control must be demonstrated. Accepting, implementing, and conspicuously supporting worldwide standards is the simplest, most effective, and most rational card of admission to the world of producers.

Since rationalized assemblage of components produced to take advantage of competitive advantage is increasingly the mode of production, raw materials and components must be made to meet world standards as well. From the standpoint of the final assembler, the component manufacturers, and the raw material supplier, worldwide specifications are most efficient. This minimizes the leverage of monopsony and allows the final assembler to proceed when suppliers fail as well. Standards multiply because standardization makes sense.

Within some areas, such as electronics and telecommunication, international standardization is more than rational; it is actually compulsory. Not only must there be encipherment and reading in these areas, requiring agreed-upon codes, but failure to control signals or means of communication may result in sound interference or other disruption. While this is the clearest case of technological imperatives for standards, others instances raise similar issues.[9]

The Growing Flexibility of Standards: Toward Nonstandardization

The burgeoning of standards at both the national and international level should not blind one to their limited use. Only a small percentage of products, even in a country like Japan, are manufactured in full pursuance of international standards. MITI experts estimated it at 3 percent a few years ago. Production in accordance with national standards is even more difficult to estimate. Perhaps more pervasive are products in which some elements are constructed in accordance with international or national standards.

Of course, if only certain aspects of a product are standardized, there remains room for individualized and cultural variation. Lamps need to conform to requirements of safety or combustibility, but can vary by size, shape, styling, material (with some exceptions), and color. Nothing prevents the Greeks from preferring blue tablecloths and the French white. Individual manufacturers can maximize lamp safety or skimp on safety in favor of interesting shapes. Standards are in this sense a floor, but neither a ceiling nor the side walls.

The picture of standards as rigid restraints tended to be accurate in the past, but more as the result of an intersection between standards constraints and mass production restraints. A prototype was approved within the parameters of acceptable standards. That prototype was then created, generally on an assembly line, and changes in prototypes required expensive redesign of the whole process. Elements of assembly convenience were balanced against consumer preferences. Customers could have "any color as long as it was black," not only for ease of painting, but because black paint dried faster and one-color drying time could be controlled more easily.

The Chaplinesque assembly line depicted in *Modern Times* is in eclipse. Computers, robots, and subtler machine tools allow for a more complex, flexible manufacture that accommodates customers. Just as New Balance vaunts its shoes as "available in widths, the same as feet," modern producers can within limits produce variations in their products. Feet come in continuous width variations; shoes are still cut in artificial lengths and widths. But that could change.

The costs of "flexible production" are greater. Machinery must be accommodating, raw materials or components accommodated, or inventory costs increased. Similarly, shipment fees and final product inventory costs are increased and management costs incurred.[10]

Those costs can be monitored and controlled; for many products, they are insignificant. Even when they are real, the advantages of reaching subpublics or niche groups unserved by mass production methods often outweigh the costs. Increasingly, manufacture is "flexible" rather than mass because a more useful product results with a minimal increase in cost.[11]

Segmented marketing produces a different type of standardized (but variegated) product and in turn requires more flexible standardization. This is less paradoxical than it might appear on the surface. For example, one of the most rigidly standardized areas of human endeavor in terms of materials and components is building construction, yet standards constrain but do not eliminate innovation in architecture.

There are a number of ways that standardization has become more flexible. In both Japan and the EC we noted the adoption of design types and the subsequent ease of approval of variants, either by government or authorized standardizers. Again, the ISO 9000 series, which is virtually the self-creation of a standard and a concomitant independent quality control process, points the way to remarkable possibilities for flexible standards meticulously enforced.

The specter of a gray, uniform, and styleless world of mass-produced sameness does not loom large today in the world of standards. By defining parameters for self-standardization in some areas, authorizing and policing standardizers and quality-control testers, and maintaining an intelligent eye on the machinery of standards, standard setters can ensure that the social product serves multiple social purposes. Standards may give us restraints imposed by necessity and protection against hidden product disabilities with minimal costs in variability or variety. Product standards can be as flexible as the products they constrain.

Appendixes

Notes

Index

Appendix 1

International Organizations Affecting Standards

International Organization for Standardization (ISO)

ISO is the leading international standards organization and publishes its work as International Standards. It also publishes standardizing guides and terms and work on certification. Its worldwide membership includes Eastern European, Asian, and African countries as well as industrial Western countries. It generates standards in all fields except electric and electronic engineering, which, by a 1976 agreement, is covered by the International Electronic Commissions (IEC). In recent years, ISO has pioneered its series, ISO 9000, which provides for self-developed standards or self-developed certification for a vast range of products, from computer software to complex industrial output. ANSI is the U.S. representative.

General Agreement on Tariffs and Trade (GATT) World Trade Organization (WTO)

GATT was a loose regime aimed at liberalizing trade through a set of involved international negotiations known as "rounds": the "Kennedy Round," "Tokyo Round," etc. It maintained a small structure to facilitate negotiations and enforce results, including a hearing process on alleged violations. It did not developed standards, but the GATT Agreement on Technical Barriers to Trade, which was a by-product of the Tokyo Round, established principles for national standards and is popularly known as the Standards Code. The best known of these standards is the "transparency" requirement. The Office of the U.S. Trade Representative is the American member. Under the 1993 agreements, GATT was superseded by a more structured international trade agency known as the World Trade Organization.

Organization for Economic Cooperation (OECD)

A nation membership association, OECD is a broad developer of world trade and offers aid to nations interested in development. It disseminates established standards through libraries and develops highly targeted standards on grading seed, fruits, and vegetables, and for testing chemicals and tractors. It also has guidelines for laboratory practice, multinationals, and protection of privacy.

The Transportation Standardizers

There are a number of international standardizers in the field of transport. They include: the International Civic Aviation Organizations (ICAO), a UN system organization housed in Montreal (it was created by the Chicago Convention of 1944 and enforces that convention); and the International Maritime Organization, a specialized agency within the UN. Both develop and publish standards and guidelines for their field, as does the International Union of Railways, a mixed government association membership group.

The International Union of Radio Science (URSI) is a communication organization not affiliated with the UN; it has approximately forty member countries.

The International Atomic Energy Commission (IAEA) is a UN agency with approximately one hundred and twenty-five members. It has extensive standard-setting, certification, and inspection activities. The U.S. delegation includes representation from the Department of Energy, EPA, and NIST.

There are numerous international structures in agriculture, building construction, environmental meteorology, and industrial machinery. In addition, there are specialized organizations dealing with lighthouses, hematology, jute, ground nuts, and demolition.

For a detailed listing, see Maureen Breitenberg, *Directory of International and Regional Organizations Conducting Standards-Related Activities,* U.S. Department of Commerce, NIST Special Publications 767 (Washington: Department of Commerce, 1989).

Appendix 2

A Profile of Standard Setters

Some of these leading organizations are well worth a short description.

ANSI (The American National Standards Institute)

The "peak association" in standards setting, ANSI has evolved, reconstituted, and renamed itself, distancing itself from its origins as an appendage to the National Bureau of Standards. It retains important vestigial connections as the presumptive national representative in international standard setting, in its ex officio representation by government in the organization, and in its considerable certifying powers of other organizations. ANSI has 250 organizational and societal constituent members, as well as 1,200 company members and a labyrinthine, semiautonomous committee structure.

In general, ANSI does not directly write standards itself, though some of its committees do. Rather, bodies are certified as standard setters by ANSI if they meet its requirements, which relate largely to the nature and representativeness of the certifier and the care of its procedures. Standards approved by an approved standardizer are then vetted through ANSI formalities, after which they are issued as ANSI standards. The process is arduous, and by and large published ANSI standards are the most respected in the world. ANSI helps insure this via a Board of Standards Review, which will hear challenges to procedures followed or to the objectivity of the standards.

Criticism of ANSI focuses on its lack of purpose and slowness, not on what it does. Critics think it sloughs off many of the most difficult tasks, but does what it undertakes very carefully.[1]

ASTM (The American Society for Testing Materials)

Originally formed in Philadelphia in 1898 as a chapter of an international organization, the ASTM separated from it in 1902. Its original interests involved products of regional concern: it tested heavy machinery in railroading and established standard definitions of raw and semifinished products such as metals, petroleum, coal, and timber. These have expanded with its membership, now over 33,000, and ASTM publishes extensive technical standards relating to uniformity, adequacy, and quality. ASTM was one of five founding constituents of the American Engineering Standards Committee, which evolved into ANSI, but the broad approach of each organization has resulted in a rivalry. Cheit reports that "the organizations trade allegations of 'turf grabbing,'" and notes that ASTM no longer submits its standards for ANSI certification. ASTM works through volunteer committees and its membership embraces a wide variety of "interested" as well as disinterested parties.[2]

Building Code and Fire Protection Agencies

A number of overlapping organizations deal with safety in construction of homes and buildings, performing a vital service to the society in a relatively decentralized and nonbureaucratic way. The major vehicle is the model building code, the most universal of which is the Uniform Building Code promulgated by the International Conference of Building Officials. More regional in scope, the Southern Building Code Congress International and the Building Officials and Code Administrators International have similar comprehensive model codes. These three organizations coordinate activities, especially product certification, through their own consortium, the Council of American Building Code Officials, established in 1972.[3]

These organizations undertake the Sisyphean task of sifting through standards of other organizations, systematizing them, and monitoring changing conditions, knowledge, and products. Their functions are what an idealized legislative committee would be expected to perform but would seldom have the technological skills to do. As the amicus brief of the State of Illinois in *Allied Tubing* indicated:

In highly technical and complex areas, for example, safety codes and building regulations, state and local governments rely heavily upon a variety of model codes and other standards developed by voluntary organizations. . . . State governments themselves lack the governmental resources to initiate, develop through public proceedings, adopt and defend comprehensive codes.

Development of such complex codes requires public hearings, which usually involve technical, scientific data and issues. Hearings are frequently time consuming, particularly when controversial matters may result in judicial challenges to adopted regulations. Furthermore, airing of the technical issues requires expert staff to conduct the hearings, analyze the evidence, weigh the sometimes conflicting data, prepare the appropriate code language and disseminate adequate information to those affected by the regulations in order to secure compliance.

As a practical matter most state and local governments lack the necessary resources to conduct their own investigations. For that reason and because the NFPA and other groups do a professional job in their own right, state legislatures depend on the NFPA and like code-making associations to become, in effect, their committees and scientific laboratories.[4]

There are also specialized code writers in the complex area of construction. For example, the International Association of Plumbing and Mechanical officials has a uniform plumbing code incorporated by reference in thirteen states, as well as fifty-six product and other installation standards.

The National Electric Code of the National Fire Protection Association[5] was described in the *Allied Tube* case as the most utilized standards code in the world. No comparative evidence was adduced for the claim, but at the time twenty-seven states incorporated by reference and nineteen utilized minor changes, while thousands of local jurisdictions also adopted it. It has over fifty thousand "voluntary" members of diverse background, including manufacturers and other interested parties. NFPA publishes proposed changes in the *Federal Register,* by arrangement with NIST.[6] NFPA was once the most overtly populist of the major standards organizations, actually setting standards in an open membership meeting. After the embarrassing packing of the general meeting in *Allied Tube,* when four hundred votes (out of thirty thousand members) hijacked the process, NFPA rules were changed to give its standards council the power to set aside convention floor decisions. The council also scrutinizes committees to assure balance among principal interest groups.

ASME (The American Society of Mechanical Engineers)

A nonprofit technical organization founded in 1880, the ASME promulgates over six hundred standards, the most famous of which is the Boiler and Pressure Vessel Code, a compilation of some eight thousand pages and the bible for industrial and ship boilers, central to much trade and industry. The code is celebrated enough to have a book written on its evolution, and is widely incorporated by reference in federal, state, and local governments. ASME is a "voluntary" association drawing upon industry and other interested parties, and like NFPA and other such conglomerates, vulnerable to disguised and hidden manipulation, such as the *Hydrolevel* incident, which resulted in a $9.5 million antitrust verdict against it.[7]

Notes

1. An Introduction to Standards: What They Do and Do Not Do

1. At least, that is the ideal of the "new harmonization." See chapter 5 for the reality. Of course, regulation of commerce "among the several states" in the United States must also be qualified.

2. "The Tunnel: Questions and Answers Most Raised," *(London) Times*, September 27, 1992, 5.

3. "Little Swiggle Makes Big Waves," *New York Times*, May 27, 1991, sec. 1, p. 3.

4. "European Community Gives Italian Condoms the Boot," *Minneapolis Star Tribune*, December 12, 1991, 12T.

5. See Dan R. Krislov, "Computers, Competition and the Revitalization of the U.S. Patent System," in Philip S. C. Lewis, *Law and Technology in the Pacific Community* (Boulder: Westview Press, 1994), 35–74; and "Computer 'Gangs' Stakeout Turf," *New York Times*, December 13, 1988 (business section), 33.

6. An excellent summary of work on these lines is to be found in John Earl Joseph's *Eloquence and Power: The Rise of Language Standards and Standard Languages* (London: Francis Pinter, 1987).

7. See Ernest Gellner, *Nations and Nationalism* (Ithaca: Cornell University Press, 1983), a succinct and brilliant book.

8. Robert Nozick, *Anarchy, State, and Utopia* (New York: Basic Books, 1974).

9. Joseph Nye, *Bound to Lead: The Changing Nature of American Power* (New York: Basic Books, 1990).

10. See below, chapter 2, for a fuller description of "simplification."

11. Alfred Kahn, "Cartels and Trade Associations," vol. 2, *International Encyclopedia of the Social Sciences* (New York: Crowell, 1968), 324.

12. Mancur Olson, *The Logic of Action* (Cambridge: Harvard University Press, 1965).

13. See Hobart Rowan, "Canada Bashing," *Washington Post*, March 12, 1992, A27.

14. See Stephen Breyer, *Regulation and Its Reform* (Cambridge: Harvard University Press), 104ff. Note, however, that Breyer believes that the distinction between design and performance standards is quickly blurred in practice.

15. "Yardsticks Almost Vanish as Science Seeks Precision," *New York Times*, August 22, 1993, 3.

16. Karl Mannheim, *Freedom, Power and Democratic Planning* (New York: Oxford University Press, 1950).

2. The Diverse Strands of Standardization

1. George Soule, "Standardization," *Encyclopedia of the Social Sciences* (New York: Macmillan, 1934) 5:379–82.

2. See Dickson Reck, ed., *National Standards in a Modern Economy* (New York: Harper, 1956) 12. Reck draws from F. C. Lane's *Venetian Ships and Shipbuilders of the Renaissance* (Baltimore: Johns Hopkins University Press, 1934).

3. See, for example, Raymond Cochrane, *Measures for Progress* (Washington: U.S. Department of Commerce, 1966), 84–86. See also Bruce Sinclair, *A Centennial History of the American Society of Mechanical Engineering* (New York: ASME, 1980), 40–53, on the drive for standardizing screw threads and pipe fittings, presented from the engineering perspective.

4. See Stephen Innes, *Creating the Commonwealth* (New York: Norton, 1995), esp. 222–23 (on guilds), and 233–35 (on patents).

5. Jeffrey Madrick, *The End of Affluence* (New York: Random House, 1995), esp. 39, 46–47, and 53. For careful and sober evaluation of the literature on which Madrick bases his arguments, see Paul David, *Technical Choice Innovation and Economic Growth* (Cambridge: Cambridge University Press, 1975), esp. 19–91 and 291–315.

6. Rosenberg's seminal work can be found in many volumes written over the years. Madrick relies heavily on *Technology and American Economic Growth* (New York: Harper and Row, 1972), esp. 43–47.

7. Madrick, *The End of Affluence,* esp. 72–75 and 102–04.

8. See, for example, Cochrane, *Measures for Progress,* 260–68.

9. David Mitrany, *A Working Peace System* (Chicago: Quadrangle Books, 1964); idem, *The Functional Theory of Politics* (London: M. Robertson, 1975).

10. A useful compilation of such organizing attempts is to be found in the *American Journal of International Law* 1, 2 (July and October 1907):808–29.

11. W. J. Feld and Robert S. Jordan, with L. Hurwitz, *International Organizations,* 2d ed. (New York: Praeger, 1988), 7.

12. Rupert Emerson, *From Empire to Nation* (Cambridge: Harvard University Press, 1960).

13. On the structural complexity of INGOs, see Feld et al., *International Organizations,* 21–26.

14. See table 2.1; and Gerald Mangone, *A Short History of International Organizations* (New York: McGraw Hill, 1954), appendix 3.

15. See below, chapter 5.

16. See Reck, *National Standards,* 14.

17. "Yardsticks Almost Vanish," 3.

18. See Douglas Williams, *The Specialized Agencies of the United Nations: The System in Crisis* (New York: St. Martin's, 1987), 4–8 and 260ff.

19. See Feld et al., *International Organizations,* esp. 24, for atypical developments; and Williams, *Specialized Agencies,* appendix C, 260ff.

20. See Thomas Weiss, "International Bureaucracy: The Myth and Reality," *International Affairs* 58 (1962):286; and Williams, *Specialized Agencies.*

21. See Williams, *Specialized Agencies.*

22. On the development of those agencies, see Victor S. Karabasz, "Simplification and Standardization in Europe," *Annals* 137 (1928):24.

23. Karabasz, "Standardization in Europe," 28–30.

24. See, for example, A. S. McAllister, "Certification Plan and Labelling System," *Annals* 137 (1928):240. For a sense of this, see Simon Collier, "Quality Control Standards," in Reck, *National Standards;* and Dale Hemenway, *Industry-Wide Volunteer Product Standards* (Cambridge: Ballinger, 1975).

25. W. Edwards Deming, *Out of the Crisis* (Cambridge: MIT Center for Advanced Engineering Study, 1986), 416.

26. See "U.S. Halts Recruitment of Cancer Patients," *New York Times,* March 30, 1994, sec. B, p. 1; "When Science Lies to the Public," *Los Angeles Times,* March 31, 1994 (editorial).

27. See, for example, K. D. Vernon, *Use of Management and Business Literature* (London: Butterworth, 1975), 153–83 and 295–320.

28. Lal C. Verman, *Standardization: A New Discipline* (Hampden, Conn.: Archon, 1973).

29. See, for example, L. Urwick, *The Making of Scientific Management* (rpt. London: Management Public Trust, 1995).

30. When Taylor served as president of the ASME, he applied "scientific management" to the conduct of the society, drastically increasing expenditures. See Sinclair, *A Centennial History of the American Society of Mechanical Engineering 1880–1980* (Toronto: Toronto University Press, 1980), 84–94, esp. 91.

31. A recent work by H. L. Schachter, *Frederick Taylor and the Public Administration Community* (Albany: State University of New York Press, 1989), argues that Taylor's actual teaching does not support the prevailing harsh judgments and that Taylor should be judged by his intentions not the application. Of course, this is an age-old plea: judge religion X or Marxism by its aspirations, not its faulty application. In the case of Taylorism, its usage suggests it was inherently flawed, since Taylor was inevitably hired and used only by management.

32. Frank Copley, *Frederick W. Taylor* (New York: Harper, 1923).

33. F. B. Gilbreth, *Primer of Scientific Management* (Easton, Penn.: Hive, 1973; originally published in 1914). This contains an effusive preface by Brandeis, who had continued contact with Taylor until the latter's death.

34. Deming's *Out of the Crisis* is his most lucid discussion.

35. See National Industrial Conference Board (NICB), *Rationalization of German Industry* (New York: NICB, 1931); and Robert A. Brady, *The Rationalization Movement in German Industry* (Berkeley: University of California Press, 1933).

36. NICB, *Rationalization,* 4–6.

37. This is the theme of Robert A. Brady's *Organization Automation and Society* (Berkeley: University of California Press, 1961).

38. Brady, *Rationalization.* The term had staying power in Eastern Europe, primarily through Soviet Taylorism, as is clear in Mark R. Beissinger, *Scientific Management, Socialist Discipline and Soviet Power* (Cambridge: Harvard University Press, 1988). See also Dorothy Douglas, *Transitional Economic System* (London: Routledge and Kegan Paul, 1959), esp. 150–65 and 338–40; David Granick's *Management of the Industrial Form in the USSR* (New York: Columbia University Press, 1954), 243, discusses a stratum of plant employees called "rationalizers."

39. Lyndall Urwick, *The Meaning of Rationalisation* (London: Nisbet and Co., 1929).

40. Idem, *The Golden Book of Management* (London: N. Neame, 1955).

41. Robert Brady, *Business as a System of Power* (New York: Columbia University Press, 1943), 812.

42. Brady, *Organization Automation and Society.*

43. See Cochrane, *Measures for Progress,* 229ff; and Sinclair, *Centennial History,* 10–14.

44. See Ellis Hawley, "Herbert Hoover, the Commerce Secretariat and the Vision of an Associative State," *Journal of American History* 61 (June 1974): 125.

45. Deming, *Out of the Crisis,* 297.

46. See William Barber's incisive *From New Era to the New Deal* (Cambridge: Cambridge University Press, 1985), esp. 10.

47. Ibid., 200n. 18.

48. S. Morrison and H. S. Commager, *Growth of the American Republic* (New York: Oxford University Press, 1950), 535–36.

49. This is nicely summarized in Cochrane's *Measures for Progress,* esp. 229–35 and 258–63.

50. See Barber, *From New Era,* 13–15; and Ellis Hawley, ed., *Herbert Hoover As Secretary of Commerce* (Iowa City: University of Iowa Press, 1971).

51. H. G. Wells, *New Worlds for Old* (Leipzig: Bernhard Tauchnitz, 1908), 231.

52. Sidney Webb, "Historic Basis of Socialism," *Fabian Essays in Socialism* (London: Fabian Society, 1889). Beatrice Webb's classic *My Apprenticeship* (London: Longmans, Green, 1950), 112–13, paints a poignant portrait of the general allure of "the cult of science" and faith in "machinery." Her diary at the time of writing indicates a growing sense of disillusion with both, only hinted at in the book. See Deborah Nord, *The Apprenticeship of Beatrice Webb* (Amherst: University of Massachusetts Press, 1985), 231–38.

53. George Bernard Shaw, "The Economic Basis of Socialism," in *Essays in Fabian Socialism* (London: Constable, 1932; originally published in 1889), 1–30. This essay represents his views just as well as many later and larger works.

54. H. G. Wells, *Russia in the Shadows* (New York: George Doran, 1921) stacks up well, especially in contrast to the Webbs and Shaw on Russia.

55. Idem, *The Wealth, Work and Happiness of Mankind* (Garden City: Doubleday, 1931), 309–14.

56. William Robson, *Socialism and the Standardized Life* (London: Fabian Society, 1924), Fabian Tract no. 219.

57. Robson, *The Standardized Life,* 8–9 and 14.

58. F. R. Leavis and Denys Thompson, *Culture and Environment: The Training of Critical Awareness* (London: Chatto and Windus, 1933).

59. See Joseph Nye, *Peace in Parts* (Boston: Little Brown, 1971), 74–75.

60. See ibid. for a good summary of the literature.

61. On the history of ISO, see Verman, *Standardization,* 154–57.

62. On the development of standards by ISO, see T. R. B. Sanders, *The Aims and Principles of Standardization* (Geneva: ISO, 1972), 66–70, esp. figure 7, p. 67.

63. See *ISO 9000,* 2d ed. (Geneva: ISO, 1992); and Maureen Breitenberg, *ISO 9000: Questions and Answers* (Gaithersburg, Md.: U.S. Department of Commerce, NIST, 1993).

3. The Many Faces of Standards

1. See James Q. Wilson, ed., *The Politics of Regulation* (New York: Basic Books, 1980). A number of the contributors (including Suzanne Weaver, Paul Quirk, Steven Kelman, and Alfred Marcus) have since published books on the agencies discussed.

2. Marver Bernstein, *Regulating Business by Independent Commission* (Princeton: Princeton University Press, 1955).

3. See Wilson, *Politics,* esp. 38–41, 73–74, 77, 91–96, 146–51, and 361ff.

4. See, for example, Kay Schlozman and John Tierney, *Organized Interests and American Democracy* (New York: Harper and Row, 1986), 276–79, and the literature cited therein.

5. Charles P. Kindleberger, "Standards as Public, Collective and Private Goods," *Kyklos* 36 (1983): 377.

6. Walter Adams and James W. Brock, "Integrated Monopoly and Market Power: System Selling Compatibility Standards and Market Control," *Quarterly Review of Economics and Business* 22, 4 (Winter 1982): 29–42.

7. Hearings before Subcommittee of House Governmental Operations Committee, June 16, 1994.

8. See "Creating Government That Works Better and Costs Less," Report of the National Performance Review, Executive Summary (Washington: GPO, 1993), 10.

9. On Alfred Kahn, see Douglas Anderson, "State Regulation of Utilities," in Wilson, *Politics,* 33–41; Bradley Behrman, "Civil Aeronautics Board," in ibid., 110–20; Thomas McCraw, *Prophets of Regulation* (Cambridge: Harvard University Press, 1984); and Kahn's own *Economics of Regulation* (New York: Wiley, 1970).

10. For a good summary of the evidence on deleterious overregulation of ethical drugs, see Quirk, "Food and Drug Administration," in Wilson, *Politics,* 214–32.

11. Cited in Subcommittee Hearings, June 16, 1974.

12. Stephen Breyer, *Breaking the Vicious Circle* (Cambridge: Harvard University Press, 1993).

13. See Eugene Bardach and Robert Kagin, *Going by the Book: The Problem of Regulatory Unreasonableness* (Philadelphia: Temple University Press, 1982); David Vogel, *National Styles of Regulation* (Ithaca: Cornell University Press, 1986). Gerald Rhodes, *Inspectorates in British Government Law Enforcement and Standards of Efficiency* (London: Allen and Unwin, 1981), presents a more complex but essentially similar view. See esp. 29ff, 53, and 173–76.

14. In a well-known study, Fritz Machlup concluded that the net advantage or cost of the patent system was indeterminable. It would appear that this also applies to the more complex issue of government standards. See Machlup, "An Economic Review of the Patent System" Study No. 15, Subcommittee on Patents, Trademarks and Copyright, Committee on the Judiciary, U.S. Senate 85th Cong 2d Sess (1958), esp. 79–80. See also Peckham, "Should the U.S. Patent Laws Be Abolished?" *Journal of Contemporary Law* 11 (1985):589, which comes to the same conclusion.

15. See Ian Maitland, "The Limits of Self-Regulation," *California Management Review* 27 (1985):132; and Kindleberger, "Standards as Public, Collective and Private Goods."

16. See, for example, Mark Green, ed., *The Monopoly Makers, Ralph Nader Study Group Report on Regulation and Competition* (New York: Grossman, 1973), for a characterization of meat regulations as "little more than a mask to deceive customers." See Arthur Kallet, "Food and Drugs for Customers" *Annals* 173 (1934):27. This issue generally reflects the consumer's point of view.

17. This is borne out by the fact that critics single out "exceptions," which are seldom identical from critic to critic.

18. Ross Cheit, *Setting Safety Standards* (Berkeley: University of California Press, 1990),

238–93; Robert Dixon, *Standards Development in the Private Sector: Thoughts on Interest Representation and Procedural Fairness* (Boston: National Fire Protection Association, 1978), 8–10.

19. See Cheit, *Setting Safety Standards,* 188ff, esp. n. 29; and *ASME v. Hydrolevel,* 102 S.Ct. 1935 (1982), majority opinion, nn. 13 and 15.

20. Given the dates, there may be a commonality between the memo Dixon used and the FTC proceedings and Hemenway's work discussed below, but I have not been able to trace any.

21. Dale Hemenway, *Industry-Wide Voluntary Product Standards.*

22. Robert Dixon, *Democratic Representation in Law and Politics* (New York: Oxford University Press, 1968).

23. See Dixon, *Standards,* esp. 22–29. He draws heavily on the literature on "functional representation," most popular in the 1930s.

24. See, for example, Stephen G. Glatzer's amicus brief in *ASME v. Hydrolevel,* which draws on his experience with another standards group as well as on testimony of ASME practices.

25. Paradoxically, the Court's message in *Allied Tube v. Indian Head Co.,* 486 US 495 (1988) can be paraphrased in the same way, though technically the case refused to apply the "government exception."

26. See, for example, Aubrey Silberston, *The Economic Consequences of International Standardization* (Geneva: ISO, 1967).

27. See "Some Regrets on the Decline of Brands," *New York Times,* July 18, 1993, sec. 10, p. 1.

28. See Harry Chase Brearly, *A Symbol of Safety* (Garden City: Doubleday Page, 1923). The original project dealt with solving the problem of automobile fires.

29. Author's interviews in Japan, summer 1993.

30. *Ran-Dav's County Kosher Inc. v. N.J.,* 608 A2d 1353 (1992).

31. See *New York Times,* "New Jersey Supreme Court Strikes Down Law," July 23, 1992, B4; and *Chicago Tribune,* "Separating Kosher Products in the Marketplace," April 12, 1992, p. 7.1.

32. "The European Community's Green Seals of Approval," *New York Times,* April 11, 1993, E5. See also "EU Stepping Up Efforts," *Christian Science Monitor,* March 25, 1994, 8.

33. The most useful material on the history of Consumers Research and Consumers Union is Samuel P. Kaidanosskey, *Consumer Standards,* TNEC Monograph no. 24 (Washington: GPO, 1941), 312ff.

34. Arthur Kallet and F. J. Schlink, *100,000,000 Guinea Pigs* (New York: Vanguard, 1932).

35. Mary Walton, *The Deming Management Method* (New York: Putnam, 1986), 35–39, 60–61.

36. For the critics, see Peter Huber, *Liability: The Legal Revolution and Its Consequences* (New York: Basic Books, 1988). For a more balanced account, see Peter Schuck, *Tort Law and the Public Interest* (New York: Norton, 1991), esp. part 2.

37. See "U.S. Court of Appeals Upholds Regulation," *New York Times,* December 7, 1982, I19; and "Agricultural Department Refuels Long-Standing Controversy," *New York Times,* September 3, 1982, A14.

38. Herbert Simon, *Administrative Behavior,* 3d ed. (New York: Free Press, 1945), chap. 3, "Rationality in Administrative Behavior."

4. Standards in American History

1. George Washington, *Annual Messages,* quoted in Gustavus A. Weber, *The Bureau of Standards: Its History, Activities, and Organization* (Baltimore: Johns Hopkins University Press, 1925), 7. I have drawn extensively from this monograph and from the NBS's official history, Cochrane's *Measures for Progress,* for the historical record.

2. Weber, *Bureau of Standards,* 8–12.

3. On Hassler, see Cochrane, *Measures for Progress,* 24–27; and Weber, *Bureau of Standards,* 14ff.

4. Cochrane, *Measures for Progress,* 31–34.

5. Ibid., 18–22 and 31.

6. See esp. Thomas W. McCraw, *Prophets of Regulation* (Cambridge: Harvard University Press, 1984).

7. See Wilson, *Politics,* 236–66 and 357ff.

8. Cochrane's *Measures for Progress* does an excellent job of describing departmental programs in various historical settings.

9. Ibid., 90ff.

10. *Ladies Home Journal* was one of the mammoth and highly successful Curtis-Bok family magazines; the bureau's efforts being featured in it was important enough to be recalled in Cochrane, *Measures for Progress,* 135–39.

11. *Waste in Industry* (New York: McGraw Hill, 1921).

12. Robert Brady, *Industrial Standardization* (New York: National Industrial Conference Board, 1929).

13. *Annals* 37 (May 1928): 231–39 and 247–53.

14. Robert Brady, *Business as a System of Power* (New York: Columbia University Press, 1943).

15. Stuart Chase and Frederick Schlink, *Your Money's Worth* (New York: Macmillan, 1927).

16. See Jesse Coles, *Standards and Labels for Consumers Goods* (New York: Ronald, 1949), 41. Coles's book was itself to join the canon of the consumer movement.

17. Chase and Schlink, *Your Money's Worth,* 203–05.

18. On the role of NRA's consumer committees and their accomplishments, see Coles, *Standards and Labels,* esp. 342–47.

19. See "Consumer Standards," *TNEC Reports,* Monograph 24 (Washington: GPO, 1941), prepared by Samuel Kaidanossky, 312ff.

20. Cochrane, *Measures for Progress,* 305.

21. See "Battery Additive AD-X2," Hearings before the Select Committee on Small Business, U.S. Senate 80th Cong (Washington: GPO, 1953); Samuel Lawrence, *The Battery Additive Controversy* (Tuscaloosa: University of Alabama Press, 1962); and Cochrane, *Measures for Progress,* 483ff.

22. See *Standards and Certification,* Federal Trade Commission's Proposed Rule and Staff Report, Bureau of Consumer Protection (December 1978); and the anticlimactic *Standards and Certification,* Final Staff Report, which had on the cover the epitaph to the whole debacle: "The Commission has neither reviewed nor adopted this report. The Commission's final determination will be made upon the rulemaking record as a whole." In fact, six years of effort produced little more than a thin argument that standard setting was power and could on occasion be

abused. The tight rules proposed in the preliminary report did not have to be rejected, since they were already withering away in the final report. For a typical reaction from the standards industry, see Wilbur Cross, *The Code: An Authorized History of the Boiler and Pressure Vessel Code* (New York: ASME, 1990), 211.

23. See William J. Barber, *From New Era to New Deal* (Cambridge: Cambridge University Press, 1985), 10.

24. See "National Bureau of Standards Authorization," Hearing before the Subcommittee on Science, Research and Technology of the House Committee on Science, Space and Technology, 100th Cong 2d Sess (March 15, 16, 17, 1988), 54ff, 146ff.

25. See "The Commerce Department May Be a Goner," *Business Week*, April 3, 1995, 65; "Going Out of Business," *Congressional Quarterly*, July 1, 1995, 1930; "GOP Finds Commerce Department is Hard to Uproot," *New York Times*, September 20, 1995, A1; "Shutting Down Commerce: Tougher Sell in the Senate," *Congressional Quarterly*, October 21, 1995, 2100.

26. "25 Nobelists Join to Save Institute," *New York Times*, July 26, 1995, A13.

27. "Profile of Dr. Avati Prabhakar," *New York Times*, August 1, 1993, sec. 3, F8.

28. "NIST as a Means to Help," *Washington Post*, September 2, 1993.

5. The American "System" of Standards

1. Robert Toth, ed., *Standards Activities of Organizations in the United States* (Washington, D.C.: G.P.O., various years; latest 1991), 423; hereafter referred to as *Standards Directory* followed by year if other than 1991.

2. For the distinction between the "First New Deal" with corporatist overtones and the Brandeisian "Second New Deal," see A. M. Schlesinger Jr., *The Coming of the New Deal* (Boston: Houghton Mifflin, 1988).

3. *Standards Directory*, 7–8.

4. Ibid., 7.

5. Ibid., 89–90. Five members are appointed to the council by the secretary of commerce. "Virtually all of the lumber produced in the U.S. and Canada conforms to its standards" (89). See also Forest Products Laboratory, "History of Yard Lumber Size Standards" (Madison: 1964), mimeograph.

6. *Standards Directory*, 580.

7. See ibid., 16–18, 159–61, 460–61, and 512–13.

8. As the most publicly visible of standardizers, UL has been widely hailed and has often been permitted to praise itself. See, e.g., *Annals* (May 1928). In 1982, a critical article in *Mother Jones* on product testing noted that UL had "without question" been a major force in reducing hazards, but concluded the record was "checkered." Mark Dowie, "The Illusion of Safety," *Mother Jones* (July 1982), 35. Cheit reports that this mild criticism was viewed with alarm. One staff member at UL he interviewed called it "disastrous," citing its traditionally rave reviews. Cheit, *Setting Safety Standards*, 248–49n.

9. Cheit, *Setting Safety Standards*, 26.

10. "What the UL Seal of Approval Signifies," *New York Times*, March 23, 1991, 16; and Cheit, *Setting Safety Standards*, 240–48.

11. In *Allied Tube*, no one challenged Illinois's assertion of this claim. Rather, some two dozen states joined as amici and the U.S. and FTC in another amicus brief to argue that controlling private group excesses would not curtail this needed function, and that government

could not totally abandon crucial regulation to self-interested parties.

12. See Lawrence Friedman, *A History of American Law*, 2d ed. (New York: Simon and Schuster, 1985), 175.

13. The extent of that federal reach is illustrated by the Federal Safe Schoolyards Act of 1986, which forbids the sale of drugs within yards of a school. Prior to 1937, such a measure would not have been considered remotely defensible, and would have been seen as a clear invasion of state authority. It was invalidated in 1994 by a vote of five to four in what was regarded as a sea change in federal power.

14. *Parker v. Brown*, 317 US 34 (1943). See "Of Raisins and Mushrooms: Applying the *Parker* Anti-Trust Exemption," *Virginia Law Review* 58 (1972):1511 n.

15. See Lawrence Shepard, "Cartelization of the California-Arizona Orange Industry 1934–1981," *Journal of Law and Economics* 29 (1986): 83; and Thomas Lenard and Michael Mazor, "Harvest of Waste," *Regulation* (May–June 1985).

16. *Columbia, South Carolina v. Omni Outdoor Advertising* 449 US 365 (1991).

17. See *Lathrop v. Donohue* 367 US 820 (1961); and, for a thoughtful examination of the implications, Theodore Schneyer, "The Incoherence of the Unified Bar Concept," *American Bar Foundation Research Journal* (1983).

18. *California Retail Liquor Dealers Association v. Midcal Aluminum* 445 US 97 (1980).

19. *Federal Trade Commission v. Ticor Title Insurance Co.* 112 S.Ct. 216 (1992). A succinct summary is Timothy Muris's "Legality of Standardization Under the Anti-Trust Laws," *Standards and the Law* (New York: ANSI, 1984), 5–11.

20. *Eastern Railway President's Conference v. Noerr Motor Freight*, 365 US 141 (1961).

21. *Allied Tube and Conduit Corporation v. Indian Head, Inc.*, 486 US 492 (1988).

22. Ibid., 513.

23. Ibid., 510n. 13.

24. *ASME v. Hydrolevel*, 456 US 556 (1982).

25. See Cheit, *Setting Safety Standards*, 218. But also note his offhand conclusion that these decisions have curtailed that frankness somewhat.

26. To some judges, this tipped the scales against ASME.

27. *Radiant Burners, Inc. v. Peoples Gas Light and Coke Co., Inc.* 368 US 656 (1962). While this ended the anticompetition dispute, the battle over lawyers' fees persisted. See *Fitzgerald v. Freeman* 409F.2d 427 (1969), 428; *Fabrious v. Freeman* 468 f.2d 689 (1972).

28. See *ASME v. Hydrofoil*, majority opinion.

29. Cheit, *Setting Safety Standards*, esp. 188–92 and 204–07.

30. See Robert Dixon, *Standards Development in the Private Sector: Thoughts on Interest Representation and Procedural Fairness* (Boston: National Fire Protection Association, 1978). Many of the NFPA and ASME modifications, especially the establishment of a review council exercising oversight, have now become standards. See *Regulations Governing ASTM Technical Communities* (July 1992), 14.

31. See Cross, *The Code*, 214–15.

6. Standards in the European Community: Building Blocks Toward Integration?

1. *Casis de Dijon* ECR 649, (1979). This was reinforced by a number of cases, most notably the even earlier *Procureur de Roi v. Dassonville* ECR 837 (1974), which permits "rea-

sonable" regulations for health and safety in the absence of Community legislation but otherwise requires free trade. See also C. D. Ehlermann, "The Internal Market Following the Single European Act," *Common Market Law Review* 24 (1987): 361; N. Forwood and M. Clough, "The Single European Act and Free Movement Legal Implications for the Provision for the Completion of the Internal Market," *Common Market Law Review* 23 (1986): 382; and Nicholas Green, Trevor Hartley, and John Usher, *The Legal Foundations of the Single European Market* (Oxford: Oxford University Press, 1991).

2. "Completing the Single Market," EEC Commission Document III./8/4 (1988), 3. See also its earlier statement of that position in Communication c. 256/2 (1980). For the earlier general situation, see Pieter J. Slot, *Technical and Administrative Obstacles to Trade in the EEC* (Leyden: Sijthoff, 1975).

3. Henry G. Schermers, "The Role of the European Court of Justice in the Free Movement of Goods," in T. Sandalow and E. Stein, eds., *Courts and Free Markets* (Oxford: Oxford University Press, 1982), 262.

4. On American hopes and fears, see "Europe 1992 and Its Effects on U.S. Science Technology and Competitiveness," Hearings, Committee on Science, Space and Technology, 101st Cong, 1st Sess, May 16, 1989; Report of the Subcommittee on International Economic Policy and Trade, May 1989, House Committee on Foreign Affairs, esp. 8 and 18–19; and "Competing in a Diverse World," *Washington Post,* December 12, 1991, A1.

5. "U. S. Lawyers Flock to Europe," *New York Times,* May 13, 1991, C1. The head of the Brussels office of Skaddon, Arps, Slate, Meagher and Flom described the influx of over twenty large firms in two years as "part of the 1992 madness."

6. See Gary C. Hufbauer, ed., *Europe 1992: An American Perspective* (Washington: Brookings Institution, 1990), for a discussion of efforts to allay fears by the EC, as well as a good statement of concerns. Especially valuable are his "overview" and pages 38–39.

7. Victoria Curzon Price, "Three Models of European Integration," in R. Dahrendorf et al., *Whose Europe? Competing Visions for 1992* (London: Institute of Economic Affairs, 1989), 27.

8. See Samuel Krislov, C. D. Ehlermann, and Joseph Weiler, "The Political Organs and the Decision-Making Process in the U.S. and the European Community," in Mauro Cappelletti et al., *Integration Through Law* (Berlin: DeGruyter, 1986), 2:81.

9. "European Bureaucrats," *Government Executive* (February 1989):21–24.

10. See S. A. B. Page, "The Revival of Protectionism and Its Consequence for Europe," *Journal of Common Market Studies* (1981):17–40. See also House of Lords, *Internal Market Barriers to Manufacturers,* 17th Report, 1981–1982 Session; and C. D. Cohen, *The Common Market Ten Years After* (London: Philip Allen, 1983).

11. See *Standardization and the Removal of Technical Barriers to Trade* (Brussels: EECS, 1991). A good summary of planning and analytic preludes to the Single Europe effort is Ernest Wistrich, *After 1992: the United States of Europe* (London: Routledge, 1991), esp. 2–8. The extravagant hopes once pinned on 1992 are exemplified in the subtitle and esp. 132–38.

12. For an example of national efforts limiting EC integration, see "Festooned With Red Tape," *Economist,* October 21, 1995, 54–55.

13. See Krislov et al., "Political Organs," 2:30–59.

14. See David Vogel, *Standards and Technical Barriers to Trade* (Brussels: Centre for Euro-

pean Policy Studies, 1990), 52–60; David Brooks, "Jam Sessions," *New Republic,* November 4, 1991, 57–59; and ". . . Towards a Single European Sausage," *Wall Street Journal,* October 26, 1993, B1.

15. See Vogel, *Standards and Technical Barriers,* esp. 9–11, for national politics and standards distortion.

16. *Reuwe-Zentrale Case,* ECR 181 (1976).

17. The Germans in turn developed more sophisticated products with a higher price tag to capture another market niche. See Cohen, *The Common Market,* 48. For aggregate data pointing to positive results from the expansion of the Common Market, see ibid., 45–46; and Jacques Pelkmans and Niall Bohan, "Removing Technical Barriers: Lessons from Europe for World Trade," Law and Society Association, June 1991, unpublished paper.

18. Vogel, *National Styles of Regulation.*

19. "It's 1993 and Europe Still Has Borders: Goods Move Freely, People Can't," *New York Times,* January 31, 1993, travel section, 6. This is reminiscent of a slogan used by a railroad tycoon in gaining control over the New York Central Railroad: "A hog can go cross-country without changing trains, but you can't."

20. Jacob Viner, *The Customs Union* (New York: Carnegie Endowment for Peace, 1950), esp. 50ff. This classic study summarized and eclipsed previous economic work on the unification effort and remains the starting point for analysis of economic unification in general. For stimulating and suggestive applications of the approach, especially to the Community, see Alexis Jacquemin and Andre Sapir, *The European Internal Market, Selected Readings* (Oxford: Oxford University Press, 1989).

21. See Michael Emerson et al., *The Economics of 1992* (Oxford: Oxford University Press, 1988), for the economic basis of the effort.

22. See report prepared by Leonard G. Kruger for the Subcommittee on International Trade, in *European Community: Issues Raised by 1992 Integration* (Washington: GPO, 1990), 43; and "EC Tackles Hidden Barriers," *Wall Street Journal,* January 5, 1992, A15.

23. See Pelkmans and Bohan, *Removing Technical Barriers,* 8. See also "European United On This: They Hate Technocrats," *Los Angeles Times,* October 2, 1993, A3.

24. See the valuable summaries *EC 1992: A Commerce Department Analysis of European Community Directives,* ed. Debra Miller (Washington: U.S. Department of Commerce, various dates). The testimony before the House Committee on science, space, and technology, May 16, 17, 1989, by Dr. Roy Ginsberg (*Europe 1992 and Its Effects* [Washington, D.C.: G.P.O., 1989], 38ff) is also succinct and helpful. For more popular evaluations, see "Europeans Say Buying Gets Easier," *New York Times,* December 22, 1992, A1; and "Across the EC the Barriers Slowly Fall," *Washington Post,* January 3, 1993, H1.

25. Commission of the European Communities, *The Community Internal Market,* 1993 report, pp. A, B, and 6.

26. Ibid., 6–11.

27. Ibid., 51–53.

28. "Common Standards for Enterprises" document of the Commission of the European Communities (CEC) LUC/EER (1988), 25.

29. See Price, "Three Models," 24–25.

30. There is substantial literature on the American-EEC analogy from a legal standpoint.

A good deal is summarized in Krislov et al., "Political Organs," 3–110. See Christian Meir-Schatz, "American Harmonization from a European Perspective," in R. M. Buxbaum et al., *European Business Law: Legal and Economic Analysis on Integration and Harmonization* (Berlin: DeGruyter, 1991); and Sandalow and Stein, *Courts and Markets.*

31. See "Internal Market of the EC Accomplished," *TUV Topics* (January 1993): 5; and U.S. Chamber of Commerce, *Europe 1992* (Washington, D.C., 1991), 22, and figure 5.1. For a useful chart of some typical regime directives, which also gives a sense of the pace of progress, see *TUV Topics* (February 1993): 3. See also "Business Struggles to Conform to Mountains of EC Standards," *Washington Post,* October 1992, 42.

32. *Financial Times,* July 27, 1993, 13. See also "Business Struggles."

33. For an example of how blunderbuss rule changes create unexpected situations, see "EC Rules Threaten Monk's Work," *Albany Times Union,* November 5, 1993, D10, reprinted from the *London Observer.* For the promise of future simplification, see CEC's *Annual Report* (Brussels: CEC, 1993), 93–95. See also "Little Wave Rocks Spain's Euroboat," *New York Times,* May 12, 1991, 3, on computers and compulsory tildes.

34. See Wistrich, *After 1992,* for a positive view of the creativity of the process.

35. CEC, *Annual Report* (1993), 40–45, esp. 45, and 57–59. Note also that litigation is already heavy in this area.

36. *TUV Topics* (July–August 1993): 7; and "The European Community's Green Seals of Approval," *New York Times,* April 11, 1993.

37. See "EC Racked by Fields of Fraud: Cheating the System is a Growing Problem in the European Community," *Los Angeles Times,* August 31, 1993, H1.

7. Standards and the Japanese Miracle: The Politics and Economics of Quality

1. See Peter Edelman, "Japanese Product Standards as Non-Tariff Barriers: When Regulatory Policy Becomes a Trade Issue," *Stanford Journal of International Law* 24 (Spring 1988): 389–446; and David Vogel, "Consumer Protection and Protectionisms in Japan," *Journal of Japanese Studies* 18 (Winter 1992):119.

2. *Report of the Japan-U.S. Economic Relations Group* (Tokyo, 981), 59. See also Setsuo Miyazawa, "Semi-conductor Computer Industry, Government and Lawyers in Japan," in Lewis, *Law and Technology,* 137ff.

3. On markings in Japan generally, see David Vogel, "Consumer Protection," *The JIS Yearbook* (Tokyo: Japanese Standards Association, various dates); *Outline of the JAS System* (Tokyo: JETRO, 1979); and *Industrial Standardization System in Japan* (JETRO, 1979). See also *Industrial Standardization in Japan* (Tokyo: JISC, 1991). This lists seventeen approved inspection bodies in Japan and seven abroad. Additionally, fourteen foreign bodies had limited approval authority.

4. OECD, *Consumer Policy In OECD Countries* (Paris: OECD, 1987), 219.

5. *U.S.-Japan Trade Study Report,* (Tokyo: Trade Commission, 1980). See also "Regulation Style," *New York Times,* September 9, 1991, C1.

6. Report of the Japan-U.S. Economic Relations Group, 1981, offprint.

7. "Trade and Investment in Japan: The Current Environment," prepared by A. T. Kearney, Report for the American Chamber of Commerce in Japan (1991).

8. MITI claims that the "type designation system" instituted by the Action Program of

1985 is the simplest in the world, particularly as to automobiles. See "Open to the World," August 1985, mimeograph.

9. See Frank Upham, *Law and Social Change in Postwar Japan* (Cambridge: Harvard University Press, 1987); and "Japan Debates Broader Power for Consumers," *New York Times*, March 7, 1993, A1.

10. Upham, *Law and Social Change*, 28–77. Events continue to unfold in this notorious scandal which affected, among others, the father-in-law of the crown prince. See "Mercury-poisoning Victims Win in Japanese Court," *Wall Street Journal*, November 29, 1993, A9.

11. "Japan Debates," *New York Times*, March 7, 1993, C2; and "Japanese Firms Brace for First Laws on Consumer Rights and Insurers Gain," *Wall Street Journal*, March 8, 1994, A12. See also H. Michael O'Brien, "Products Liability in Japan," *For the Defense*, February 1992, 14–19.

12. "Japan Debates"; and "Japan's Customers Turn Tough," *Wall Street Journal*, March 28, 1994, B7. See also "Myths Aside Japanese Do Look for Bargains," *New York Times*, February 29, 1993, sec. 4, p. E5.

13. "Full Court Pressure: Japanese Firms Learning How to Play Hardball in U.S. Courts of Law," *Minneapolis Star-Tribune*, April 25, 1992, 1D. As the article (originally in the *Los Angeles Times*) points out, Japanese are especially averse to litigation because of the potential consequences of U.S. discovery processes in revealing their firms' internal structure and patterns. Compare Miyazawa, "Lawyers in Japan"; and Dan R. Krislov, "Computers, Competition and the Revitalization of the U.S. Patent System," both in Lewis, *Law and Technology*, for participation of American and Japanese lawyers in the same industry.

14. On Hata, see "An Old Hand for a Fresh Start," *New York Times*, April 24, 1994, F15. On Japanese uniqueness, real and imagined, see "Japan's Radical Plan: Self-Service Gas," *New York Times*, July 14, 1994, D1; and Peter Dale, *The Myth of Japanese Uniqueness* (London: Croom Helm, 1986).

15. John Haley, *Authority Without Power* (Oxford: Oxford University Press, 1991); and "The Men Who Really Run Fortress Japan," *New York Times*, April 10, 1994, E1.

16. Hiroshi Ueda, *Japan Times*, March 26, 1992, 8.

17. Author's interviews with attorney from the industry in summer 1992 confirm this fact.

18. As late as 1982, the American Chamber of Commerce Committee on Barriers claimed *identical* foreign and Japanese products received different approval status (internal report, 1982). Mr. Robert Connally kindly gave me access to this and other nonconfidential but limited-circulation documents in his collection.

19. "Japan's Airlines Waive Limits," *Wall Street Journal*, November 23, 1992, A10.

20. See, e.g., "Japan's Customers Turn Tough," B7.

21. Philip Trezise, "Japan the Enemy?" *Brookings Review* (Winter 1989–1990): 312.

22. See e.g., "For a Japanese Keiretsu, It's a Family Affair," *Los Angeles Times*, June 21, 1993, D11; "Inside Japan Inc.," *Washington Post*, October 7, 1992, A1. But cf. "A Misguided Assault on Keiretsu," *New York Times*, March 22, 1992, A11; and "Japanese Firms Are Losing a Key Advantage," *Wall Street Journal*, March 29, 1993, A15, on the decline of internal and government financing.

23. See Edward Lincoln, *Japanese Unequal Trade* (Washington, D.C.: The Brookings Foundation, 1990); Trezise, "Japan the Enemy"; and Roger Benjamin et al., "The Fairness Debate in U.S.-Japan Economic Relations," (Santa Monica, Calif.: Rand, 1991).

24. See esp. Bela Balassa and Carol Balassa, "Industrial Protection in Developed Countries," *World Economy* (June 1984): 179–98; and Gary Saxonhouse, "The Micro and the Macro of Foreign Sales to Japan," in William Cline, ed., *Trade Policy for the 1980s* (Washington: Institute for International Economics, 1983).

25. Clyde V. Prestowitz Jr., *Trading Places* (New York: Basic Books, 1990); and Boone Pickens, "To Heck With Japanese Business," *Washington Post,* April 28, 1991, C1.

26. Fred Bergsten and William Cline, *The U.S.-Japan Economic Relationship* (Washington, D.C.: Institute for International Economy, 1985).

27. In *Trading Places,* Prestowitz cites successes he claims are the product of tough trading, and failures where Japanese polite words are accepted at face value. Cf. "Japan is Tough, but Xerox Prevails," *New York Times,* September 3, 1992, C1. See also "One American Victory Playing by Japanese Rules," *New York Times,* February 24, 1992, E3.

28. Author's interviews with U.S. Trade Representative, 1992.

29. This conclusion follows from interviews in 1992 and from a listing by MITI of 625 standards being drafted in 1992. Of 625 standards in progress only 7 were assigned for major drafting to MITI, and another 44 to identifiably consumerist nonprofits. Of the remaining hundreds of standards, the bulk were given to trade and manufacturers associations for major initial drafting. See MITI, *Standards Information* 84 (May 8, 1992). For a call for participation, see *News From MITI Standards Information* 85 (May 27, 1992), which relates to standards for home gas appliances.

8. Standards as Boundaries: The Abortive Efforts of Soviet Europe

1. This is not intended to minimize more basic problems, such as the denial of human rights or the establishment of Soviet colonialism. These are not, of course, the focus of this study, and are being dealt with by philosophers, historians, and social scientists in profusion, though the definitive epitaph has not yet been written.

2. For an attempt to apply this approach to nonmaterial standards, see Samuel Krislov, "Alternatives to Separation of Church and State in Countries Outside the United States," in James E. Wood Jr., ed., *Religion and the State* (Waco: Baylor University Press, 1985), 421–40.

3. Quoted in V. V. Boitsov, ed., *Standardization in the USSR,* (New Delhi: Oxonian Press, 1975), 7. This was the guidebook for Soviet standardizers, written to commemorate fifty years of Soviet standardization.

4. Ibid., esp. p. 7 n. 2

5. Ibid., 8.

6. Ibid., 8–10.

7. David Granick, *Management of the Industrial Firm in the USSR* (New York: Columbia University Press, 1954), 153.

8. Vladmir Sobell, *The Red Market: Industrial Co-operation and Specialization in COMECON* (Aldershot Hants: Gower, 1984), 5. Sobell gives only one illustration each for his types: EEC as an "ITS," COMECON as an IPS.

9. O. Bogomolov, "The International Market of the CMEA Countries," in T. Kiss, ed., *The Market of Socialist Economic Integration* (Budapest: Akademiai Kiado, 1973), 3. See also 58 and 43, where Bogomolov explains that this isolation was due to "pressures and threats of the imperialist states."

10. This is evident in the gratuitous insistence on not accepting UN-based trade for a decade and on not approving the proposed Standard International Trade Classification, adopted by the UN in 1958. When promulgated by COMECON, the Eastern version was only cosmetically different except in one area. It is therefore quite transparent that a political decision to disrupt East-West communication had been made.

11. Both the quotation and analysis are from Michael Kaser, *COMECON,* 2d ed. (Oxford: Oxford University Press, 1976), 52–54.

12. Sobell, *The Red Market,* 226 and 228.

13. See Kaser, *COMECON,* 166ff.

14. Derived from Sidney Dell, *Trade Blocs and Common Markets* (London: Constable, 1963), 238, based on *UN Monthly Bulletin of Statistics* (June 1960 and 1961); and Zygmunt Nagorski Jr., *The Psychology of East Trade* (New York: Mason and Lipscomb, 1974), 57–59, based on the *ECE Survey of Nations* (1984).

15. See Sobell, *The Red Market,* 225, which draws on COMECON data. Still, that meant that less than 6,000 standards out of 83,000 current in the system were even theoretically used throughout the bloc.

16. There was a boring homogeneity to many aspects of Soviet-style systems. While teaching in Poland during the transition period, I concluded that one of the deep problems of the Socialist regime was that it rewarded and promoted only one personality type—the ruthless apparatchik. Other types—visionaries, risk takers, warriors, poets, thinkers, researchers—either had to accept domination, even in what was in other societies *their* sphere, or be overtly or in their hearts in opposition.

17. Sobell, *The Red Market,* details the different allocations of responsibility.

18. Malcolm Hill and Richard McKay, *Soviet Product Quality* (London: Macmillan, 1988) 8–15ff; and Boitsov, *Standardization in the USSR,* 3–65.

19. Quoted in Hill and McKay, *Soviet Product Quality,* 187n. 10. See also table 11.4 on page 531 of M. J. Berry and Malcolm Hill's article in Richard Amman, ed. *The Technological Level of Soviet Industry* (New Haven: Yale University Press, 1977), which summarizes Soviet comments on areas of strength and weakness compared to those of the West.

20. Hill and McKay, *Soviet Product Quality,* esp. 36–37 and 49.

21. Ibid., 127.

22. See Zigurd L. Zile, "By Command Bribe and Cajolery: Soviet Law on Output Quality," in A. J. Schmidt, ed., *The Impact of Perestroika on Soviet Law* (Leiden: Kluwer, 1990), 259–78; and idem, "Product Quality and Liability in the USSR: An Exploratory Essay from a Consumer Perspective," in D. Barry et al., eds., *Law and the Gorbachev Era* (Leiden: Kluwer, 1988), 105–25. Berry and Hill, 532, note that production below the set standards was illegal. In some instances, dismissal or jail was prescribed

23. Before visiting Russia in the 1980s, I had gleaned from Hedrick Smith's *The Russians* that products were dated in the Soviet Union and consumers avoided those produced in the last days of the month when the drive to meet quotas were at a maximum. "Those days are gone," I was assured by the leader of our academic delegation. But on descending from a plane from Moscow to Kharkov, he reported with a chuckle that he had heard a passenger coming aboard say, "What a terrible plane. It must have been produced at the end of the *year!*"

24. Berry and Hill, *Law and the Gorbachev Era,* 539.

25. See William E. Butler, trans., *A Source Book on Socialist International Organizations* (Alpen Von de Rijn: Sijhtoff and Noordhoff, 1978), 82ff.

26. Ibid., 80–81.

9. The Evolution of Standards and the Processes of Formalization

1. This is essentially the argument of Lal C. Verman, *Standardization: A New Discipline* (Hampden, Conn.: Archon, 1973), and of Robert Toth, ed., *The Economics of Standardization* (Standards Engineering Society, 1984), esp. 8ff. Toth, however, is a "bottom line" engineer who suggests that profitability is a crucial element.

2. See "Automotive Lighting: Leaving the Dark Ages Behind," *New York Times,* April 11, 1993, F3.

3. See, for example, Walter Adams and James Brock, "Integrated Monopoly Market Power: System Compatibility Standards and Market Control," *Quarterly Review of Economics and Business* 11, 4 (Winter 1982): 29–42; and Peter Limgueco and Bruce McFarlane, eds., *Neo-Marxist Theories of Development* (New York: St. Martin's, 1983).

4. See David Vogel, "The Public Interest Movement and American Trade Policy," in Michael S. Creve and F. L. Smith Jr., eds., *Environmental Politics: Public Costs, Private Rewards* (New York: Praeger, 1992); C. Ford Runge, "Trade Protectionism and Environmental Regulations: The New Non-tariff Barriers," *Northwestern Journal of International Law and Business* (Spring 1989): 47–61; and Edelman, "Japanese Product Standards," 389–446.

5. See Fritz Machlup, "An Economic Review of the Patent System," Study No. 15, Subcommittee on Patents, Trademark and Copyright Committee on the Judiciary, U.S. Senate 85th Cong 2d Sess, 1958. See also the work of Jacob Schmokler, *Patents, Inventions and Economic Change* (Cambridge: Harvard University Press, 1972), which has generated considerable follow-up over the years and itself remains in print after over a quarter century.

6. Based on Irwin Feller et al., "Economic and Legal Aspects of the Benefit-Cost Relationships of Federal, State and Local Regulations Concerning the Production and Sale of Ground Beef," (State College, Pa.: Pennsylvania State University Center for the Study of Public Policy, 1977), and my experience as consultant on the project.

7. Stephen Breyer, *Regulation and Its Standard Reform,* 106–07.

8. See Alfred Marcus, "Environmental Protection Agency," in Wilson, *Politics;* idem, *Promise and Performance Choosing and Implementing an Environmental Policy* (New York: Greenwood, 1982); and R. Shep Melnick, *Regulation and the Courts: The Case of the Clean Air Act* (Washington: Brookings, 1983).

9. "The EPA Discovers the Worst Killer in the Air," *New York Times,* July 25, 1993, sec. 4, p. E2. Stephen Breyer's *Breaking the Vicious Circle* (Cambridge: Harvard University Press, 1993), documents many other distortions of effective policy by fiat decisions about technology. The Delaney Amendment is a well-known example.

10. See, for example, Peter Wathern, ed., *Environmental Impact Analysis* (New York: Routledge, Chapman Hall, 1990); and Stephen M. Kohn, *The Whistle Blowers Litigation Handbook* (New York: Wiley Law, 1991).

11. See "GAO Reviewing '73 Law," *New York Times,* June 30, 1975, 55, and April 28, 1976, 16.

12. See, for example, Murray Fesbach and Alfred Friendly Jr., *Ecocide in the USSR* (New York: Basic Books, 1993).

13. See Breyer, *Regulation and Its Reform,* 104–07; and Dale Hemenway, "Performance vs. Design Standards," prepared for the Office of Standards, Information, Analysis and Development, National Bureau of Standards NBS/GCR 80–287 (1980). Breyer argues the two meld in practice in most cases.

14. See e.g., "Taking the Measure of Metrics," *Washington Post,* September 1, 1992, A16.

15. See Robert Silverberg, *Light for the World: Edison and the Power Industry* (Princeton: Van Nostrand, 1967).

16. See, e.g., Barry Bluestone and Irving Bluestone, "Reviving American Industry," *Current* (May 1993).

17. Mancur Olson, *The Rise and Decline of Nations: Economic Growth, Stagflation and Social Rigidities* (New Haven: Yale University Press, 1982).

18. Alfred Marshall, *Principles of Economics,* 8th ed. (New York: Macmillan, 1948), 257.

19. See Edward Way, *The Just-In-Time Breakthrough* (New York: Wiley, 1988).

20. See "World Economies," *New York Times,* July 27, 1992, C2; "Japan Studies U.S. Workers," *New York Times,* February 8, 1992, B1; "In the Realm of Technology Japan Looms Ever Larger," *New York Times,* May 18, 1991, B5; and "Japanese Firm Productivity," *New York Times,* September 12, 1991, A21.

10. A World of Increasing Sameness?

1. See Mary Douglas and Aaron Wildavsky, *Risk and Culture* (Berkeley: University of California Press, 1982).

2. Gellner, *Nations and Nationalism;* and idem, "Scale and Nation," in his *Contemporary Thought and Politics* (London: Routledge and Kegan Paul, 1974), 141–58.

3. See Paul A. David, "Clio and the Economics of QWERTY," *American Economic Review* 75 (1985):332, a classic illustration of this point.

4. "The Tunnel: Questions and Answers Most Raised," *(London) Times,* September 27, 1992, 5.

5. Karl Deutsch, *Nationalism and Social Communication* (Cambridge: MIT Press, 1953).

6. Ferdinand Protzman, "To Track Unity in Europe," *New York Times,* Sunday, October 15, 1992, section V, p. 5.

7. "Festooned With Red Tape," 54–55.

8. For a good discussion of this condition, see David Mowery and Nathan Rosenberg, *Technology and the Pursuit of Economic Growth* (Cambridge: Cambridge University Press, 1989), 40–41.

9. See Liora Salter, *Mandated Science* (Boston: Kluwer, 1989).

10. See Jeffrey Madrick, *The End of Affluence* (New York: Random House, 1995), esp. 72–77, which is based upon Michael Fiore and Charles Sabell, *The Second Industrial Divide* (New York: Basic Books, 1984).

11. See Morris Teubal, *Innovation Performance, Learning and Government Policy* (Madison: University of Wisconsin Press, 1987), 84–96, esp. 87–90.

Appendix 2: A Profile of Standards Setters

1. *Standards Directory,* 92–94. In *Setting Safety Standards,* 97–99, Cheit describes the Board of Standard Review and provides information on the rate of approval by ANSI.

2. *Standards Directory,* 116–17; "The Work in the Field of Standardization of the Ameri-

can Society for Testing Materials," *Annals of the American Academy of Political and Social Science* (May 1928): 49–59; Cheit, *Setting Safety Standards,* 27.

3. See Cheit, *Setting Safety Standards,* 27–28; *Standards Directory,* 184–85, 224–25, 310–11, and 488–89.

4. *Brief Amicus Curiae,* State of Illinois, *Allied Tube and Conduit v. Indian Head,* 48 US 492 (1988).

5. *Standards Directory,* 392–393. The decision in *Allied Tube* and the briefs contain myriad details on the loose structure of NFPA, including its "town meeting" annual assembly. That structure has been sharply modified.

6. Cheit, *Setting Safety Standards,* 213.

7. On ASME, see *Standards Directory,* 125–26; Cross, *The Code.* ASME has many nuclear standards and boasts that over 120 have been adopted by the Department of Defense. *Hydrolevel* briefs are not particularly helpful on organizational aspects, since both sides focused on the manipulative conduct of the volunteer involved, but do provide a sense of the complexity of compiling, updating, and interpreting a major code. See *ASME v. Hydrolevel Corporation* 456 US 556 (1982).

Index

Adams, John Quincy, support for national standards by, 83–85

Advertising, opposition to, 46, 94

AD-X2 battery additive, controversy over, 97–98

Agencies: U.S., 55, 117–18, 123; for world trade, 228

Agriculture: and Japanese government, 164, 172–73; regulation of, 57–59; standards for, 117, 154

Airline industry: regulation of, 55, 59; standardization in, 92

Allied Tube and Conduit Corporation v. Indian Head, Inc., 127–28, 130, 248*n11*

Allison Commission, 86

All-Union Committee of Standardization, Soviet, 183, 188

American Engineering Standards Committee (AESC), 95–96

American exceptionalism, 3–4

American Gas Association (AGA): and antitrust suits, 130–31; laboratories of, 119–20

American Society for Testing Materials (ASTM): good reputation of, 65; industry influence over, 64; role of, 37; testing institute, 102

American Standards Association (ASA): formerly American Engineering Standards Committee, 95–96. *See also* ANSI

ANSI: and government, 114; and National Institute of Technology and Standards, 100–02; reputation of, 65, 116; roles of, 37, 132–33; standards used by, 119–20, 178

Antitrust suits, 124–32; and fear of setting standards, 104–05; and trade associations, 61–63

A&P, brand names of, 67–68

Approval, stamps of, 68–69

Arbitrazh, 190–91

ASME standards, and Defense Department, 258*n7*

ASME v. Hydrolevel Corporation, 129–32

Association of Railway Congresses, 34

Astin, Allen V., 98

Autarky, in Eastern bloc countries, 185, 188, 192–93, 196–97

Automobile industry: self-certification in, 76–77; state regulation of, 122

Bardach, Eugene, 59

Bilateralism, inefficiency of, 31–32

Bills of lading, European standardization of, 33

Bogomolov, G., 184

Brady, Robert, 41–42, 91–92, 95

Brand names, 65–68

Brennan, William, 128–29

Breyer, Justice, 59

Breyer, Stephen, 207

Brezhnev, Leonid, standardization under, 186

Britain: quality of products of, 189; standards of, 145, 152, 219

Building industry: and government standards, 114; standardization and flexibility in, 231; standards for, 101; standards set by, 107–08

Bureaucracies: and design standards, 212; in European Community, 140–44, 150–53; in industry, 68; in international standard setting, 35; in Japan, 18–19, 166–67, 169–71, 173–76

Business as a System of Power (Brady), 41, 92

California Retail Liquor Dealers Association v. Mid-Cal Aluminum, 126

Capital investment: preserved through restrictive model ofstandards, 205; and standardization, 14–15, 222–23; training workers as, 92

Cartels: European Coal and Steel Union as, 141; in German industry, 40–41

Casis de Dijon, 137–38, 248*n11*

CE symbol, 151; lawsuits over, 158; use of, 154, 159

Chase, Stuart, 44, 94–95

Cheit, Ross, 59, 62, 131; on Underwriters Laboratory, 120, 248*n8*

Chunnel, and railroad gauges, 5, 223

Clothing industry: labeling in, 70; standardization in, 215

Coast Survey, in standardization of tariffs, 85–86

Coca Cola, brand loyalty to, 67

Coinage. *See* Currency

Columbia v. Omni, and antitrust suits, 125

COMECON, 197, 255*n10;* and goals of Soviet industry, 183–84; and quality, 192–95; strengthening of, 186–87

Commerce: and antitrust suits, 124–32; Congress given powerover regulating, 84; standardization seen as interfering with, 86; and state and local governments, 120–24. *See also* Industry; Trade

Commerce Department, U.S., 117; National Bureau of Standards in, 93–94; reevaluation of government and science by, 96–97

Committee on Non-Governmental Organizations (CONGO), 31

Communism: and EEC, 139. *See also* Soviets

Competition: in harmonization process of standards, 144–45; in price, 172, 197. *See also* Protectionism

Components. *See* Modules/components

Computer industry, standard-setting in, 4, 6–7

259